Carnegie Public Library
Big Timber, Montana

RULES

Classic Myths
to
Read Aloud

Also by William F. Russell

The Gramma Game
The Parents' Handbook of Grammar and Usage
Classics to Read Aloud to Your Children
More Classics to Read Aloud to Your Children

WILLIAM F. RUSSELL, Ed.D.

Classic Myths
to
Read Aloud

Crown Publishers, Inc.
New York

Published by Crown Publishers, Inc., 201 East 50th Street, New York, New York 10022

CROWN is a trademark of Crown Publishers, Inc.
Manufactured in the United States of America
Library of Congress Cataloging-in-Publication Data

Russell, William F., 1945– *19,178*
   Classic myths to read aloud / by William F. Russell.
      p.   cm.
   Summary: Presents the essential Greek and Roman myths that form the basis of our cultural literary heritage.
   1. Mythology, Classical—Juvenile literature.   [1. Mythology, Classical.]   I. Title.
BL725.R87 1988
292'.13—dc19   88–16230
ISBN 0-517-57012-2   CIP
10 9 8 7 6 5 4

Contents

Reading Myths and the
Myths of Reading

The biggest mistake that parents and teachers make when helping children to read is that they *stop* reading aloud to them once the children have begun to read for themselves. In my previous collections of read-alouds for school-age children (*Classics to Read Aloud to Your Children* and *More Classics to Read Aloud to Your Children*), I discussed the findings from numerous research studies that show how and why continuing oral reading past the picture-book years improves both children's reading ability and their interest in reading. I also pointed out that when parents and teachers read good literature aloud—time-honored masterpieces to which the label "classic" can be properly applied—they allow children to become accustomed to the sound of Standard English Usage, a form of English that is not usually modeled by the rock stars, athletes, and television characters children see as heroes. Hearing well-crafted stories told in an artful language also causes a child's vocabulary and imagination to undergo an effortless enhancement.

Now I want to expand the argument in favor of reading classics aloud to include the likelihood that this practice may be our best hope for re-creating a "cultural literacy" among America's schoolchildren.

In his recent best-seller *Cultural Literacy*, Professor E.D.

Hirsch, Jr., laments the change in the public-school curriculum from being facts-centered to being skills-centered, and he confirms what many parents and teachers have suspected for some time: "More and more of our young people don't know things we used to assume they knew." Newspapers and magazines report almost daily, it seems, new studies that show how woefully inept American students are in geography, history, mathematics, and science compared with their counterparts in other industrialized countries and compared with American students of a generation ago.

This is a different crisis from the well-recognized loss of general literacy among our citizens. Yet our children's failure to know the factual information about their history or their culture or their planet is related to the decline in their ability to read and write, and for one simple reason: It is precisely these facts—these common and shared pieces of background information—that enable children to find meaning in what they read. The notion of "progressive" educators—that reading is merely a decoding skill that can be learned from any material, whether meaningful or not—fails to recognize that facts and skills are inseparable. Children are constantly trying to make some sense of their world, and when they are allowed to acquire a store of traditional information, when they are given meaningful reading materials that draw upon that store of shared knowledge, children (and adults, too) are able to create mental "hooks" on which they gather and attach new pieces of information. Not only is their world made more sensible and understandable by this process, but their motivation and intellectual self-confidence get a big boost as well. As Hirsch points out: "Our children need traditional background information early to make sense of significant reading materials, and thus gain further information that enables them to make further progress in reading and learning." In other words, the more you already know, the more you are able to learn.

Just as the great authors and their works have been gradually swept from the public-school curriculum during the last twenty years, so have the classic myths and legends. The ancient stories of gods and heroes that most of today's adults learned—not at home, but in the classroom—are no longer considered "proper" subject matter for elementary reading texts and are no longer "relevant" enough for inclusion in literature classes later on. The loss here is not just that our children are not allowed to be fascinated by the stories that have fascinated children for thousands of years, but that as our children grow to depend upon newspapers and novels and commentators instead of basal readers for their links with the larger world, they will not be able to understand the many allusions and references that are made to mythical characters and stories by writers and speakers who just assumed that knowledge of these myths was shared by all. The following story will illustrate what I mean.

Not long ago, I was riding a student bus that was taking me across a university campus to the school's Education Department. In front of me on that bus were two undergraduate women—sophomores or juniors, perhaps—who were having a most difficult time trying to figure out what a certain passage in their textbook meant by its reference to "the wooden horse of Troy." I could barely believe what I was hearing, but an even greater jolt was in store. The last words I heard them say before they, too, got off at the Education Building were "And who in the world is this guy Troy, anyway?"

I see two tragedies in this story. The first is that these students—who may have been bright, competent, and diligent in their studies—had never heard the story of Helen of Troy in all their years of schooling. The Trojan War, the sulking of Achilles, "beware of Greeks bearing gifts"—none of these would have any meaning to them, and so they would be as bewildered by any reference to, let's say, "the face that launched a thousand ships" as they were by their textbook's reference to the most famous ruse in history. The second tragedy is that, inasmuch as their bus stop and textbook were both associated with the Education Department, I assume that these students were studying to be teachers and are, by now, guiding the learning of somebody's children somewhere in the country.

The great myths, though, are valuable in their own right, not just because they provide the mental "hooks," or schemata, that enable us to gather and understand new material. These myths have survived through the centuries because they have had something important to say, and because people of widely disparate ages and cultures have found in these tales lessons and inspiration for their own lives. Your children will find that these stories require a more active use of their imagination than they are accustomed to providing, but although their creative powers may have been dulled by monster cartoons and by basal readers that feature such exciting tales as "Dick and Jane Go Shopping," these powers can be resuscitated by having to form a mental picture of someone extracting the teeth from a dragon, for example, or of the way the world would look to someone riding on the back of a flying horse.

Children will find their feelings stirred as well as their imaginations. Indeed, there is an abundance of sorrow and tragedy in these ancient stories, and you as the reader must take care that the selection you choose is appropriate for the current mood of your youthful listener. But just because a story is sad or includes a tragic scene does not mean that it is, therefore, inappropriate for all children at all times. Sad moments are part of a child's life, just as they are part of an adult's. Our children need to see and understand that they are not the only ones who feel the sting of sorrow or who suffer misfortunes. Indeed, there are countless tragedies and difficulties in a young life that can be soothed and understood better when they are shown to be similar to the hardships or the dilemmas that faced a mythical character whom the child has come to know and, perhaps, admire.

The names of these mythical characters will seem strange at first, for, with the exception of bold Jason and fair Helen, they are quite unlike the names of any boys or girls a child is likely to know. But, as you will discover in the sections titled "A Few Words More," some of these strange names lie at the very heart of many not-so-strange English words that are common to adults and children alike. You will also find that some gods and goddesses are called by two different names, this owing to their having been called one name by the early Greek myth-makers and, much later, another name by the Romans. The strangeness of the names and the dual identities of the gods tend to be more of a hindrance to adults than to children, so I suggest that you not belabor the problem or make it a repeated subject in your discussions. Just concentrate on making the pronunciations seem as comfortable and commonplace as possible, and rest assured that any identity crises will work themselves out in time.

The language I have used in telling these tales may seem somewhat old-fashioned, though I hope not archaic. For the most part, it is the language of the myths as I heard and read them when I was young, because I have based this collection on the venerable retellings found in Thomas Bulfinch's *The Age of Fable*, Hamilton Wright Mabie's *Myths That Every Child Should Know*, Gladys Davidson's *Wonder Tales from the Greek and Roman Myths*, and Alfred J. Church's classic versions of the *Iliad*, the *Odyssey*, and the *Aeneid*. I heartily recommend these sources to any parents or teachers who are looking for additional classic myths to use as read-alouds. The language and style of these early collections are much to be preferred, I think, to the modern and "up-to-date" retellings that have deities speaking in "hip" lingo, as though that were the only way to maintain a child's interest. (The corruption of these classic myths has, as we would expect, been aided by television, too. A mother wrote to me to say how appalled she was to find that her sons had watched an animated version of Ulysses' encounter with the Cyclops in which the Cyclops was not "a hideous giant with but one eye and that in the middle of his forehead, with the eyebrow below it," as Homer described the monster and as the story is told in *Classics to Read Aloud to Your Children*. No, in this supposedly "children's" version, the Cyclops is just a run-of-the-mill giant, but *with a patch over one eye!*)

The great myths can teach us many things, for in them we find history and geography and astronomy and word origins. But most of all we find the struggles of human beings, including all the passions and frailties that are to be found in humans today. We are connected to these ancient civilizations in Greece and Rome by some words in our language, to be sure, but we are even more directly connected to them by these myths, for it is in these tales that we see ourselves. Oh, we understand now why the seasons change and we know that lightning bolts aren't thrown by Zeus, but we still use ideas like "luck" and "UFOs" to help us explain what we can't otherwise understand. We struggle, just as the ancients did, to know where we fit on this planet and how we should conduct our lives, and we wonder on occasion, just as they did, whether our lives and actions are all part of some grand plan.

When earlier civilizations struggled with these problems, they wrote stories to help them see their world and their place in that world more clearly. The Greeks had a word for it, all right; to them, the word for "story" was *mythos*.

Using "A Few Words More"

At the end of each tale in the book, I have written a paragraph or two dealing with the origins of some of the words that appear in that tale. These paragraphs are *not* meant to be part of the read-aloud session itself.

I designed "A Few Words More" with you—the reader—in mind: I wanted these sections to be interesting, informative, illuminating, and occasionally fascinating—even startling. Startled: That's just how I feel when I learn something about a word that I've been using all my life, but hadn't known why or hadn't seen how it related to dozens of other words and ideas. All of a sudden, the clouds begin to part, a light bulb glows inside my brain, and I wonder how I could possibly have failed to see what was right in front of me all these years.

I hope that "A Few Words More" will help you experience this excitement on occasion—this wonderful feeling that somehow the world makes a little more sense than it did before—because if you do, then it is sure that you will want your listeners to feel it too. It will not happen for them, however, if you merely read my explanations aloud. Instead, you should read them to yourself when you are preparing and practicing the story. Then, after you have read the story aloud, try to weave the words and their histories into the discussion of the tale, or weave them into a later chat if the situation permits. Just remember two things: What is an absolutely stupefying piece of learning to you may not put so much as a glimmer in someone else's bulb, and this above all—timing is everything.

GREEK AND ROMAN GODS

Greek Name	Powers and Responsibilities	Roman Name
ZEUS	King of the gods; god of thunder and lightning	JUPITER OR JOVE
HERA	queen of the gods; goddess of marriage	JUNO
HADES OR PLUTO	king of the Underworld; ruler of the dead	PLUTO
POSEIDON	god of the sea	NEPTUNE
DEMETER	goddess of agriculture; goddess of fertility	CERES
ATHENA	goddess of wisdom; goddess of domestic arts	MINERVA
ARES	god of war and violence	MARS
HEPHAESTUS	god of fire and metalworking; blacksmith for the gods	VULCAN
PERSEPHONE	goddess of young grain; queen of the Underworld	PROSERPINA
APHRODITE	goddess of love and beauty	VENUS
EROS	god of love	CUPID
HERMES	messenger of the gods; god of herds, cunning, and travel	MERCURY
APOLLO	god of poetry, healing, prophecy; associated with the sun	APOLLO
HYPNOS	god of sleep	SOMNUS
ARTEMIS	goddess of the hunt and the moon	DIANA

Listening Level I

(Ages 5 and up)

The stories that I have included in this first section are not "childish" in any way, and so these myths are quite suitable for reading to children of any age. They provide an introduction into the ways that the Greeks and Romans perceived their gods, and they will allow your children to create these gods anew by picturing them in their own way, just as storytellers and listeners have done for thousands of years.

Yet there is much in these tales that remains unchanged, as it has through the centuries, and so these myths provide us with some of the makings of our common culture. Here are stories about humans who aspire to rise too high, or who are harmed by their own suspicions, or who seek such perfection that the real world can never satisfy them—all stories that are known throughout many lands and are called to mind by the mention of a mere word or phrase.

While the purpose of reading these myths aloud is to entertain and to enrich, far more than to educate, there are some quite natural learnings that will result from them just the same. The fact that there was a Greek civilization that flourished many centuries before there was a city called Rome is a lesson that can come as a natural part of explaining why the same gods are known by two different names in different myths.

The tales are arranged in a very general order, from the more simple to the more demanding. But even the very early stories should be read and practiced alone **BEFORE** reading them aloud to a child, not only because some of the pronunciations are challenging, but because so many ancient myths have tragic or unhappy endings. Such tales, therefore, do not make good bedtime stories, nor are they suitable for those times when a read-aloud can provide a much-needed cheering up. There are a few happy endings here, but pain and misfortune were a common lot for the ancients and required a supernatural explanation.

The Gift of Athena

About the story:
> *In Greek mythology, Zeus and his two brothers, Posei-
> don and Hades, divided up the universe among them-
> selves by casting lots. Poseidon became ruler of the
> oceans and the seas, Hades became ruler of the kingdom
> of the dead known as the Underworld, and Zeus became
> supreme god of all heaven and earth. Among Zeus's
> many children was gray-eyed Athena, who, it was said,
> was born in a very strange way: She leaped full-grown
> and in full battle dress out of Zeus's head! Athena was
> her father's favorite child, and she was possessed not
> only of great skill in warfare, but, as the following tale
> shows, of great wisdom as well.*

Approximate reading time: 6 minutes
Vocabulary and pronunciation guide:
> **Athena** [uth-EE-nuh]: the goddess of wisdom in Greek
> mythology; she is known as Minerva [mih-NERVE-
> uh] in Roman myths
> **Hades** [HAY-deez]
> **Zeus** [ZOOSE]: king of the gods in Greek mythology; he
> is called Jupiter or Jove in Roman myths
> **Poseidon** [po-SYE-dun]: god of the seas and rivers in
> Greek mythology; he is known as Neptune in Roman
> myths
> **Olympus** [oh-LIMM-pus]: the mountain on which the
> gods lived
> **deities** [DEE-it-eez]: gods; immortals
> **trident** [TRY-dent]: a three-pronged spear
> **chasm** [KAZ-um]: a deep opening in the earth's surface;
> a gorge

*L*ong, long ago, when this old world was a very young place, and when the few people there were had just begun to live together in groups for their own protection, the great gods selected the places for humans to build their cities. They looked down upon the earth, through the clouds that shrouded their home on the very peak of the high mountain called Olympus [oh-LIMM-pus], and they chose the sites they thought would provide everything mortals needed to live and to prosper.

Now, each god and goddess was eager to have a great city built in his or her honor, and so the prime locations—the very best places for the great cities to be built—came to cause much bickering and jealousy among the many deities [DEE-it-eez], for all wanted a great city built in their honor, a city whose people would worship that particular god or goddess above all others.

It happened that great Zeus [ZOOSE], the king and ruler of all the gods, had found a spot on earth that appeared to be absolutely ideal for the building of a noble city; indeed, he foresaw that the city that would be built there would someday become the noblest city on earth. Well, you can imagine that all the gods and goddesses wanted this city for their own, and you would be right. But the two who wanted it most of all were Athena [uth-EE-nuh], the goddess of wisdom, and Poseidon [po-SYE-dun], the god of the seas and rivers. Now, Athena was one of Zeus's daughters, and so you might expect that her father would honor her request, but Poseidon was great Zeus's brother, and Zeus did not want to disappoint him, either. Poseidon appealed to Zeus, saying that this location would provide the city with the greatest natural harbor in all the world and destine it to be a great seaport. Therefore, as god of the sea, it was only right that he, Poseidon, should be its chief god. But Athena argued just as earnestly that the greatness of this city would not lie in its commerce, but rather in the respect its people would someday have for art and learning. As goddess of wisdom, therefore, she should be its guardian.

Zeus, at last, decided upon a way to end this quarrel and to choose, fairly, between the two. He called for a great council to be held at the very site of the new city, and there, with all the gods and goddesses arrayed before him, Zeus spoke from his golden throne in a clear, commanding voice. "Listen," he said, "to the will of Zeus, who judges now between Poseidon and Athena. The city that is desired by each shall bear the name of that god who shall bring forth from the earth the better gift for the mortals who will dwell here. If Poseidon's gift be judged more useful, this city shall be called Poseidonia [po-sye-DOE-nee-uh], but if Athena's gift be deemed the better, the city shall forever after be known as Athens."

Upon hearing this, Poseidon arose in all his majesty, and he stuck his trident [TRY-dent] (that is, the long, three-pronged spear that he always carried)—he stuck this trident hard into the ground right where he stood. The earth shook violently all around until, at last, a great crack opened up in the surface. Out of this steaming chasm [KAZ-um] leaped a magnificent horse, his powerful white body fully arrayed in battle gear, a warhorse like none had ever seen before. "Behold my gift," said Poseidon, "and call the city after my name, for who can give these mortals a better present than the horse, which will ensure their protection from all their enemies."

But Athena looked steadfastly with her keen gray eyes at the assembled gods, and she stooped slowly down to touch the earth where she stood. She said nothing but continued to gaze calmly on that great council. Presently they all witnessed a small shoot growing from the ground where Athena had touched her hand. It grew swiftly and in minutes had sprouted thick and luscious boughs and leaves; higher and higher it rose until green fruit appeared on its clustering branches. "My gift is better, O Zeus, than that of Poseidon," she said. "The horse he has given shall bring war and strife and anguish to these mortals and their children, but my gift—the olive tree—is the sign of peace and plenty, of health and strength, and the pledge of happiness and freedom. Is it not more fitting, then, that the city to be founded here should be called after my name?"

Then the voices of the gods rose in the air as one: "The gift of Athena is better by far, for it is the token that this city shall be greater in peace than in war, and nobler in its freedom than in its power. Let the city be called Athens forevermore."

Hearing their appeal, Zeus then bowed his head as a sign of his judgment that the city should be named for Athena. The earth trembled as he rose from his golden throne to return to the halls of Olympus. Athena stood gazing over the land that her victory had given her, and she decided that it was here that she would make her home. "Here," she said, "my children will grow up in happiness, and they will come to understand that freedom is the greatest gift a people can receive. And when the torch of freedom has gone out in Athens, it will be passed on to other peoples in other lands throughout the world."

A Few Words More

For younger children, this myth can be a valuable introduction to the city of Athens and the country of Greece. On a map of the world (or, much better, on a globe), point out where Athens is in relation to your present location. Is your town, like Athens, named for a famous person?

For older children, this myth can be used to help them see that many of the words in our language are actually made up of words from other, far older languages. Here, for example, we see Poseidon (or Neptune) pictured as he always is, holding his three-pronged spear called a *trident*. *Trident* is actually a combination of a Latin prefix (used by the Romans) *tri-*, meaning "three," and the Latin root or stem *dent-*, meaning "tooth." The *trident*, then, is not just a spear, but one with "three teeth." What other words can you think of that begin with *tri-* and have "three" of something? (For example, *tricycle* means "three circles" or "three wheels" and *triangle*, "three angles.") What words do you know that are formed from *dent-* and have something to do with "teeth"? (How about *dentist* and *denture?*)

Icarus and Daedalus

About the story:
> *Daedalus was considered by the Greeks the most talented of all their artists, craftsmen, architects, and inventors. It was said that he had been taught by the goddess Athena, but however he came by his skill, it was certain that no other artisan could surpass his workmanship. It was Daedalus who was called upon to build the great labyrinth in Crete (see pages 112–117), but today he is known primarily as the man who discovered the secrets of flight. His name lives on in the Greek adjective* daidalos, *which means "cunningly made" or "skillfully worked."*

Approximate reading time: 7 minutes
Vocabulary and pronunciation guide:
> **Icarus** [ICK-are-us]
> **Daedalus** [DEAD-uh-luss]
> **Crete** [KREET]: the largest of the Greek islands
> **King Minos** [MY-nos]
> **Minotaur** [MY-nuh-tore]: a monster with the body of a man and the head of a bull
> **Labyrinth** [LAB-uh-rinth]: an intricate maze
> **Cupid** [CUE-pid]

Throughout all of Greece, Daedalus [DEAD-uh-lus] was known as the most skillful of men—a master craftsman, artist, architect, and inventor. Indeed, his fame had spread to the island of Crete [KREET], where King Minos [MY-nos] had pleaded for Daedalus to build him a cage or prison that could hold the terrible monster called the Minotaur [MY-nuh-tore]. This hideous beast devoured men, women, and children at his pleasure, and none in all the land could destroy or even control him.

Daedalus accepted this challenge and built for the king a large and fantastic maze he called the Labyrinth [LAB-uh-rinth], whose winding passageways were so cunningly tangled up and twisted around that, once inside, you could never find your way out again. And so the Minotaur was trapped within this ingenious device, and Daedalus was praised as a genius and given great honors by the king.

But King Minos was, after all, a tyrant—quick to anger at the slightest offense and cruel in his punishment of anyone who opposed him. And, before long, Daedalus fell out of the king's favor to such extent that Daedalus was imprisoned with his young son, Icarus [ICK-are-us], in a high tower. Although the two managed to escape from their cells, they could find no way to leave the island because King Minos had his guards keep strict watch all along the shore, permitting no ship to sail without the most careful search.

Daedalus, however, was determined to use his skill and cunning to find some way to make his escape. At last, after watching the sea gulls who soared far out of reach of Minos and his guards, Daedalus thought of a plan by which he could win freedom for Icarus and himself. "Though King Minos may block me off by land and sea," he said, "at least the sky still lies open. And that is the way we shall go."

Both father and son then set about gathering as many feathers as they could find, feathers that had been dropped by the gulls along the shore. Daedalus then placed these feathers in a row, beginning with the smallest, with a shorter one just below each longer one, and with such care and precision that you could almost believe that the feathers had once come from just such a row. Each succeeding row was fashioned in the same delicate way, the feathers secured into a framework with thread and wax. Each framework was then given a gentle curvature, and soon it was apparent that Daedalus, the master builder, had created a pair of wings, perfectly tailored to his own dimensions. When at last the work was done, Daedalus fastened the wings to his own shoulders, and after a few trial efforts, found that by waving his arms in a birdlike motion he could actually climb through the air! He held himself aloft, wavering this way and that, with the wind, against the wind, until at last, like a giant fledgling, he had taught himself to fly!

Settling to the ground once again, he immediately began to fashion another, smaller pair of wings for Icarus, and when the task was done, he taught his son what he had learned about their use.

The morning brought with it a perfect wind by which to make their escape. Daedalus called to his son and, as he fitted the wings to the boy's shoulders, he gave him his final instructions: "Icarus, remember always to maintain a moderate height, for if you fly too low, the fogs and vapors will weight down your feathers, and if you fly too high, the heat of the sun will surely melt them apart." The father's voice trembled and tears glistened in his eyes as he repeated his warning and then lifted himself aloft and flew ahead.

But for Icarus, his father's warnings simply went in one ear and out the other. Who could remember to be careful when he was about to fly for the first time? All that remained in his mind was the joy of escape and the thrill of performing what all children had dreamed about but none had ever before accomplished.

A few sweeps of his arms and Icarus felt his feet leave the earth; a few more and he was soaring behind his father, looking down on the shore and the ships and the astonished guards of King Minos. The shepherds and farmers who glimpsed them high above the treetops stopped their work and gazed in awe at what they thought must surely be gods—Apollo, perhaps, with Cupid [CUE-pid] following close behind.

At first there was terror mixed with the joy of Icarus and Daedalus, for the wide vacancy of the air dazed them, and every glance downward set their senses reeling. But gradually they began to master this power, and they became overjoyed with the ease and freedom of flight.

Icarus, though, grew more than just comfortable in the air— he grew bold. He stopped following his father and began to soar higher and higher toward the sky. He forgot everything that Daedalus had told him about staying on a middle course and not flying too close to the sun. He thought only about wanting to see what it was like to touch the sky and to play among the stars.

Poor Icarus! The nearer he flew to the blazing sun, the more its rays warmed the wax that held his feathers together. One by one they loosened and dropped away like so many snowflakes. Now, terrified, he fluttered his arms wildly, but there were not enough feathers left to hold him in the air. He cried out, "Father! Oh, Father! Save me or I shall surely die!" But Daedalus was by now too far away to hear these plaintive cries. And so Icarus fell like a leaf tossed down the wind, down and down, calling his father's name all the while, but there would be no help, and the boy drowned in the sea below.

When Daedalus saw that his son was no longer following him, he called out the boy's name in fear, but there was no reply. He sought high and low for the boy but found only some feathers afloat on the water, and he knew that Icarus lay in a watery grave. He flew on alone, bitterly cursing the skill that had allowed him to create this tragic invention, and when, at last, he arrived safely on land, he built a temple to Apollo and there hung up his wings as an offering to the god. And never again did he attempt to fly.

A Few Words More

Although Apollo was frequently called the "sun god" in Greek mythology, it was actually the god Helios [HEE-lee-ose] who had originally been given the power to direct the sun along its course. *Helios* was, after all, the Greek word that meant "sun," and so Helios became the "god of the sun." Today, the most widely known trace of this god's name in our language appears to have little connection with the sun at all.

Back in 1868, scientists analyzed the light from a solar eclipse and discovered a previously unknown element in the spectrum of this light. Because they believed that this unknown element existed only on the sun, they created a name for it out of the Greek word for "sun": *helium*. Almost thirty years later, helium was found to exist on earth, too, but its name will always remind us of its earliest discovery.

The Origin of the Seasons

About the story:

When Zeus overthrew his father, Cronus, and began to rule the universe, he and his two brothers cast lots in order to divide the vast territory among them. Hades became lord of the Underworld, where the souls of the dead reside; Poseidon took dominion over all the oceans and the seas; while Zeus himself became sovereign over heaven and earth. Among Zeus's three sisters was the noble-browed, broad-shouldered Demeter, who was given the considerable responsibility of being goddess of agriculture, fertility, and marriage. (The Romans called this goddess Ceres [pronounced SERIES], and it is from her name that we derive our word cereal.*)*

Approximate reading time: 12 minutes

Vocabulary and pronunciation guide:

Zeus [ZOOSE]

Cronus [CROW-nus]: father of Zeus; one of the early gods known as Titans; called Saturn by the Romans

Hades [HAY-deez]

Poseidon [po-SYE-dun]

Demeter [deh-ME-tur]

Persephone [purr-SEFF-uh-nee]

demeanor [dih-ME-nur]: a person's behavior or conduct; deportment

nymphs [NIMMFS]: beautiful female nature spirits; lesser divinities who inhabited the mountains, forests, meadows, and streams

reveled [REV-uld]: engaged in boisterous and festive merrymaking

chasm [KAZ-um]: a narrow gorge or deep crack in the earth's surface

Phoebus [FEE-bus] **Apollo:** god of the sun; *Phoebus* means "bright, golden like the sun" and characterizes everything about Apollo

Olympus [oh-LIMM-pus]: the mountain on which the gods made their home

Iris [EYE-riss]: the goddess of the rainbow

Hermes [HER-meez]: the messenger of the gods; called Mercury by the Romans

pomegranate [POMM-uh-gran-et]: a semitropical fruit similar in size to an orange but having a reddish, flavorful pulp and containing many small seeds

bade [BAD]: past tense of *bid*

D emeter [deh-ME-tur], the great earth mother, was goddess of the harvest and of all growing things. Tall and majestic was her appearance, and her hair was the color of ripe wheat. It was she who filled the earth with grain, for it was she who ripened the fruit and who saw to it that the grain grew tall and that the pastures were sweet and bountiful. In her honor white-robed women brought golden garlands of wheat as first fruits to the altar. Planting, reaping, threshing, winnowing—these she watched over and cared for, and hard-working farmers honored her with songs and feasts. All the laws that the farmer knew came from her: the time for plowing, what land would best bear crops, which was fit for grapes, and which was to be left for pasture. She was a goddess whom all called "the great mother" because of her generosity in giving to humankind the necessities of life.

Although Demeter found joy in her duties and in being served and honored by all the mortals on earth, still more did she love and cherish her only daughter, the beautiful Persephone [purr-SEFF-uh-nee]. Persephone was as young and fresh as the spring itself; her demeanor [dih-ME-nur] was always cheery, and when she was not helping her mother oversee the planting or the harvest, she frolicked about the countryside with her friends the nymphs [NIMMFS], dancing and singing and weaving garlands of wildflowers, while the valleys rang with their laughter and mirth.

Now it happened that these joyous sounds seeped down and down to the darkest regions of all—the gloomy and foreboding Underworld, the land of the dead, which was presided over by

Hades [HAY-deez], who was a brother of the great Zeus [ZOOSE]. Hades had long sought a mate who would live with him in his gloomy kingdom, but every maiden he asked had refused, and so he remained alone—bereft of all companionship save that of the dead souls who inhabited his dreary domain. But the sounds of joy and gaiety that issued now from the beautiful Persephone caused Hades to want her for his mate beyond all others. Indeed, so strong was his desire that he beseeched the mighty Zeus to grant him this favor and allow him to spirit the maiden away to live with him in his kingdom below. And Zeus, out of brotherly affection, and with no word of any kind to Demeter, did grant Hades' request and allowed a mother's greatest joy to be stolen from her, never to return.

That very day, while Persephone and her playmates danced and reveled [REV-uld] in a particularly bountiful meadow, a black cloud swept down upon them from the east, and so swiftly did it advance that no one could tell its cause or content. Only when it was too late did they see the hideous and terrifying figure of Hades and his ghostly chariot that was pulled by four coal-black and menacing steeds. In an instant the lord of the Underworld had grabbed the unsuspecting maiden, and clutching her tightly, he drove the horses to breakneck speed, for he feared that Demeter could pursue him while he remained on the surface of the earth. Soon the chariot came to a narrow fault in the land where, at Hades' command, a chasm [KAZ-um] opened before them, and they plunged headlong through the earth's crust and down and down as the opening closed behind them, sealing off the light of the sun and sealing Persephone's hopes of ever rejoicing with her friends or feeling the loving touch of her mother again.

Bitter was the grief of Demeter when she heard the news that her daughter had been mysteriously swept away, though no one could tell her where the maiden had been taken. Veiling herself with a dark cloud, she sped, swift as a wild bird, over land and ocean for nine days, searching everywhere and asking all she met if they had seen her daughter. She inquired of gods and mortals alike, but none could offer her any news or hope. Even the birds, who know what happens in the hills and the fields, knew only of Persephone's disappearance and nothing of her whereabouts. In abject despair, Demeter turned to

Phoebus [FEE-bus] Apollo, who sees all things on earth as he pulls the sun across the sky behind his golden chariot.

"Yes, I have seen your daughter," said the god at last. "Hades, with the consent of Zeus, has taken her as his queen, to dwell with him in the land of mist and gloom. She struggled, but her strength was no match for his, and at his command they were swallowed up by the earth to reside forever in the dark below."

When Demeter heard this, she fell into deep despair, for she knew that she could never rescue Persephone if Zeus himself had ordained that Hades should have his wish. She did not care anymore to plead her case in the palace on Olympus, nor did she care for anything but to spend her days alone, grieving over the loss of her only child. She took on the form of an old woman and wandered about the earth, seeing only its sorrows, finding no joy in anyone or in anyplace. To her, all was misery; all hope was lost.

Now it happened that during the months of her wandering, Demeter did not, indeed could not, attend to her duties as goddess of all growing things. And, without divine aid and blessing, the grasslands and pastures withered, the cattle died, the earth turned dry, and the birds feasted off the seed corn that would not sprout in the arid soil. The gods looked down and saw that a great famine had descended upon the land and that mortals had even begun to neglect their offerings and sacrifices, for they could no longer spare the gods what little they had for themselves.

Zeus heard the cries and lamentations rising from those who suffered on earth, and he heard the persistent entreaties from the gods asking that he end the famine and allow the mortals to resume their sacred offerings. And so he appointed the goddess Iris [EYE-riss] to descend to earth on a rainbow and tell Demeter to return to her duties and restore the crops and pastures to the earth. Dazzling Iris swept down from Olympus and found Demeter still in mourning, still in the garb of an old woman, still without care for her duties or for humankind. Iris offered her beautiful gifts and whatever powers among the gods she chose, but Demeter would not lift her head to listen. Still, Demeter was not blind to the strength of her position, for she realized that Zeus needed her powers, and that only through the powers of Zeus could she ever hope to see her daughter again. Her reply to Iris was both a threat and a bargain: She would neither set foot on Olympus nor let anything grow on earth unless and until Persephone was restored to her from the kingdom of the dead.

When Iris reported this proposition to Zeus, he knew what he must do, and so he sent Hermes [HER-meez] of the golden sandals to the dark reaches of the Underworld, there to tell Hades that Persephone must be set free to return to the light and to her mother on earth. The messenger found her, pale and sad, sitting beside Hades upon his throne. She had neither eaten nor drunk since she came to the land of the dead. But upon hearing the edict of almighty Zeus, she sprang up with joy, while the dark king became darker and gloomier than ever. Though he could not disobey the command of Zeus, Hades was crafty to the last, and he implored Persephone to eat and drink with him before they parted. Joyous as she was, she could not refuse his request, and although she was eager to begin her ascent, she took a pomegranate [POMM-uh-gran-et] from him to avoid further argument and delay. She did not eat the whole pomegranate; indeed, she ate only seven of its tiny seeds. But for some strange reason, even this satisfied Hades, and he bade [BAD] her farewell as Hermes took her with him up and up and finally into the light and the warm air.

When Demeter saw Hermes and her daughter, she gushed with a joy unknown, and Persephone embraced her mother with a passion unable to be put into words, and so the two caressed each other and sobbed their mutual love in complete happiness and understanding. Demeter was first to speak, saying, "Did you, my darling daughter, eat or drink anything at all during your stay in the Underworld?" And Persephone replied, "Nothing, Mother, until Hermes came for me, and then only seven seeds of a pomegranate."

"Alas, my daughter! Woe has befallen both of us again!" wailed Demeter, her grief now as intense as her joy had been just moments ago. For now the extent of Hades' deceit became clear as Demeter revealed the irreversible decree of the Fates: Whoever tastes of food in the kingdom of the dead shall be lost forever to the world above. Thus the Fates had decreed, and even Zeus was powerless to alter their law. Yet Persephone had not eaten the pomegranate, only seven small seeds thereof, and surely she could not be condemned for eternity by seven small seeds. This was the nature of Demeter's appeal to almighty Zeus, and its reason and fairness moved Zeus to compromise: Although he was powerless to change what the Fates had determined must be, he was able to interpret their decree. And so he ruled that because Persephone had eaten only the seeds of the pomegranate, she must only spend a month each year in the land of the dead for each of the forbidden seeds she had eaten. For seven months each year, therefore, she must dwell in the Underworld with Hades, as his queen, and the remaining five months she may spend with her mother on earth.

And so it is each year that for seven months Persephone is lost to Demeter, and for this time Demeter mourns, and trees shed their leaves, and cold comes over the earth, and the land lies still and dead. Persephone herself is pale and cold and sad, and she rules with Hades over the icy souls that inhabit the lifeless and bleak environs that know not laughter nor warmth nor hope. But after those seven months Persephone returns to the upper air, her mother is glad, and the earth rejoices. The crops spring up, bright, fresh, and green in the plowed land. Flowers unfold, birds sing, and young animals are born. Everywhere the heavens smile for joy or weep sudden showers of gladness upon the earth, and life abounds, bursting from every corner, renewing the world and all its people.

A Few Words More

Hermes, whom you saw in this myth as a messenger of the gods, was also the patron god of magic. The medieval practice of alchemy (which was the predecessor of chemistry and, in many ways, the predecessor of the science of medicine, too) was known as a *hermetic* art, for there appeared to be magic in what these alchemists could perform. The sealing of air into a bottle by heating and twisting the neck became known as putting a *hermetic seal*, or the seal of Hermes, on the bottle. Today, the words *hermetic* and *hermetical* are used to describe not only an airtight seal, but also the cloistering of someone or something away from outside influence.

An even more remarkable connection between everyday vocabulary and the mythical characters in this story stems from Iris, the goddess of the rainbow. One can easily see why the pigmented membrane of the eye would be called the *iris*, and how the brightly colored flower became known as an *iris*, too. But it is also worthwhile to realize that Iris is the root of the word *iridescent*, which means "producing a rainbowlike display of colors." Knowing the origin of *iridescent* helps you to overcome the two most frequent problems in spelling this word: Just like *Iris*, *iridescent* is spelled with only one *r*, and its third letter is an *i*.

Echo and Narcissus

About the story:

>*This is one of the many tales in which we see Jupiter's desire to stray occasionally away from his own home, and to consort both with mortals and nymphs on earth. His wife, Juno, is suspicious of this philandering, and she punishes those who encourage Jupiter in his wandering ways. Your children may think that the punishment in this story is misplaced or overly severe, but harsh and seemingly unjust punishments occur quite commonly in the ancient myths, as we shall see in other stories throughout this book.*

Approximate reading time: 11 minutes

Vocabulary and pronunciation guide:

>**Narcissus** [nar-SIS-us]
>
>**Jupiter:** king of the gods; the Roman name for the god that the Greeks called Zeus
>
>**nymphs** [NIMMFS]: spirits who looked like beautiful maidens but who were, in part, divine
>
>**Juno** [JEW-no]: queen of the gods and wife of Jupiter; the Roman name for the goddess that the Greeks called Hera
>
>**Olympus** [oh-LIMM-pus]: the mountain home of the gods
>
>**Nemesis** [NEMM-uh-sis]: the goddess of retribution and revenge

*I*n the days when the great gods and goddesses watched over the earth and cared for its people, there lived some lesser gods, too—more than mere mortals but without the magic powers of gods. Such were the nymphs [NIMMFS], those pretty young maidens who lived on earth—in the mountains or forests or rivers—but who were attendants to various gods and goddesses.

There was one dainty nymph named Echo, who was such a great chatterbox that she was seldom silent, and her love of talking was the cause of the sad misfortune that befell her.

Echo was one of the nymphs who served and attended to the needs of mighty Jupiter—king of all the gods on Olympus [oh-LIMM-pus]. When Jupiter came down to earth, as he did from time to time, the nymphs who served him would keep him company. Because they were partly divine themselves, they understood him and could entertain him in ways that mortals simply never could.

Now Jupiter was a great lover of beauty, and it was one of his favorite pleasures to talk with and be with these lovely nymphs whenever he could. But Jupiter's wife, Juno [JEW-no]—queen of Olympus—had a very jealous nature, and it made her exceedingly angry when her husband's roving fancy caused him to wander off to seek the entertainment of the dainty nymphs and the company of certain mortal maidens.

One day Jupiter set off for the valleys below Olympus to talk to his nymphs and to join in the merry games they loved to play, and as soon as Juno heard of this, she determined to go down into the valley herself, and to scold her truant husband if she found him enjoying the company of the nymphs, for she was very jealous of their youth and beauty. When she reached the entrance to the valley, however, she was met by Echo, who, guessing what the angry goddess had come for, and eager to save her lord Jupiter and her friends from any trouble, began talking to Juno—and talking, and talking—in order to give the other nymphs time to escape and hide themselves.

Echo held the queen in conversation for a long time, chattering like a magpie about everything that came into her mind. It was no great hardship for her to do this, since she dearly loved the sound of her own voice and was never at a loss for something to talk about. Juno tried to find an appropriate pause in which to break away, but Echo had so many interesting things to say and talked so incessantly that it was impossible to interrupt her. So, when at last the pretty chatterbox came to a stop for sheer lack of breath, and Juno seized the opportunity to rush past her, she found the valley deserted; all the nymphs had managed to escape by this time, and Jupiter had vanished, too.

Juno then realized how she had been tricked, and in her anger she determined to punish the dainty nymph who had detained her so long at the entrance to the valley. With her divine powers she caused the unfortunate Echo to lose, almost entirely, that one talent she used most: her ability to talk. The only words that Echo would be allowed to speak hereafter would be the very last words of the last sentences that she heard other people say—and then only in a faint, distant voice.

Poor, unfortunate Echo! Because of her concern for her friends, she had been punished so cruelly, and her sorrow was very great. It had always been such a delight to her to talk and to hear the sound of her own pretty voice. Now she could no longer chatter merrily to her friends, and she had to be contented merely to repeat, very faintly, the last two or three words of their sentences when they spoke to her. But her friends were very kind to her, and they would often call out a greeting to her from the hillside just so that Echo could gladly repeat the last words and be filled with joy at hearing the sound of her voice once more.

Now it happened that in this same valley there dwelt a beautiful youth named Narcissus [nar-SIS-us], who had such charm and such dazzling good looks that every maiden who saw him at once fell in love with him. But, sad to say, Narcissus himself had a cold heart and was quite incapable of feeling love for anyone, human or divine. He did everything in his power to escape his admirers, since he had no desire for their attentions and no love to give them in return.

One day Narcissus was wandering through the forest with some of his friends, when he stopped to pluck a wildflower and lost sight of his companions. He turned to take the path that he thought they had followed, and in doing so, he passed by a tree in which lovely Echo had been resting. The moment she beheld his marvelous beauty, she fell deeply in love with him and could not bear for him to be out of her sight. She followed him through the woods, longing to speak and tell him how she felt, but—thanks to Juno's wrath—she no longer had the power to do so. She did not dare make her presence known for fear that he would be angry or would quickly reject her because she could not speak, and so she just watched him, following closely but out of his sight.

They went on in this way for some time, Narcissus parting the branches in search of his friends and Echo stealing softly behind him, until the boy suddenly realized that he was lost, and he called out, "Is there anyone here?" Echo, stepping quickly behind a tree, answered, "Here!" for she could only repeat the final words of what was spoken in her presence. Well, you can imagine Narcissus' surprise, for he thought he was quite alone in this area of the woods. He looked all around, but he couldn't see anyone to whom the voice belonged. He cried out again, "Where are you? Come here!" whereupon Echo responded, "Here!"

This was bewildering. He could see no one, and yet every cry of his was answered by a voice that seemed quite close by. He went on calling and questioning, and each time Echo answered with his last words. She did not dare to show herself, but she could not help answering.

At long last she decided to take a chance, thinking that he just might be understanding and loving, and he might not be angry with her for secretly following his steps. She came out from behind the tree and ran to meet him. She twined her dainty arms around his neck, trying to express with her actions the love she could not put into words.

Alas! Echo's hopes were rudely dashed, for Narcissus hated to have anyone show him even the slightest affection. He pushed the lovely nymph aside with a rough hand, and he fled at once into the deepest part of the woods.

Poor Echo! His harsh glares and unkind actions had broken her heart. She hid herself in the woods and mourned and grieved, thinking of the beautiful youth whom she loved so much, but who had treated her so rudely. She wept day and night and wouldn't touch any food. Before long she grew pale and thin and began to waste away to a shadow, as people say, until at last her body vanished altogether, and nothing remained but her voice, which can still be heard today among the hills and valleys, answering every call.

As for the cold-hearted Narcissus, he, too, came to a sad and lonely end. One of the many maidens whom he had so harshly scorned prayed to the gods that Narcissus be punished for tormenting people so, and that prayer was answered. It fell to the goddess Nemesis [NEMM-uh-sis], who was the goddess of retribution and punishment, to determine his fate: "May he who will not love others love only himself," she decreed.

It happened that one day, after tracking some game through the forest for many hours, Narcissus came to a shady spot surrounding a clear, deep pool, from which he could quench his thirst. As he stooped down to drink from it, he was overcome with surprise and delight at the image that appeared on the smooth surface of the water. It was a face, but such a lovely face that he could not take his eyes from it. The longer he looked, the more beautiful the face did seem, and at length he had fallen passionately in love with the image in the pool. Yes, Narcissus had fallen in love with his own reflection!

He spoke to the beautiful image, and its lips parted as though they were answering him, but no sound could he hear. He smiled, and the face in the pool smiled back. When he beckoned the image to come to him, the image beckoned, too. But when he tried to touch it, the lovely face became rippled and blurred and disappeared from view.

Poor Narcissus! Although he finally realized that it was his own face that was reflected in the pool, it was a face of such marvelous beauty that he could not tear himself away from the spot. So deep was this passion for his own fair looks, and so strong the power of his love, that he could not resist it. He lost all desire for food or for sleep, and night and day he lay upon the grass, gazing at his own image reflected in the water. And so, over time, Narcissus the beautiful—like the dainty Echo whom he had scorned—gradually wasted away, his body growing thinner and thinner until he died.

When the fair youth had breathed his last, the gods, in pity for his sad fate, transformed his body into a beautiful, sweet-scented flower with a bright golden center and soft, white petals, which nodded to its reflection in the pool. And to this day that lovely flower, called the narcissus, is found by quiet pools, gazing at its image in the water.

A Few Words More

It should now be clear how this myth helped to add the word *echo* and the name of the flower *narcissus* to the vocabulary of modern English. There is, in addition, the word *narcissism*, which has lost much of its psycho-analytic identity, and has taken on the common meaning of "an excessive admiration for oneself."

Another character in this story, the goddess Nemesis, also is the source of the English word that is spelled and pronounced just like the goddess's name. A person's *nemesis* is a rival or an opponent who torments that person and occasionally brings about his or her defeat. Nemesis was the goddess of retribution, and it was her task to maintain a balance between good and evil in the universe. Although she would reward the just as well as punish transgressors, it is only this sense of vengeance that is still associated with her name. While the notion of retribution has been lost in this most common meaning, the word *nemesis* still carries with it the sense of an outside force who seeks vengeance, just as Nemesis did.

Damon and Pythias

About the story:

This tale comes from an anecdote that was told by the Roman orator Cicero to show that the tyrant Dionysius did not know the meaning of true friendship. Originally, one of the heroes was named Phintias, but his name was changed to Pythias through a blunder by a scribe who was copying the manuscript. Inaccurate or not, it is the names Damon and Pythias that today are inseparable symbols of the ideal friendship.

Approximate reading time: 7 minutes
Vocabulary and pronunciation guide:
    Damon [DAY-mun]
    Pythias [PITH-ee-us]
    Dionysius [die-oh-NISH-us]
    Sicily [SIS-uh-lee]: the large island that lies just off the "toe" of the boot-shaped Italian peninsula

Damon [DAY-mun] and Pythias [PITH-ee-us] were two noble young men who lived on the island of Sicily [SIS-uh-lee] in a city called Syracuse. They were such close companions and were so devoted to each other that all the people of the city admired them as the highest examples of true friendship. Each trusted the other so completely that nobody could ever have persuaded one that the other had been unfaithful or dishonest, even if that had been the case.

Now it happened that Syracuse was, at that time, ruled by a famous tyrant named Dionysius [die-oh-NISH-us], who had gained the throne for himself through treachery, and who from then on flaunted his power by behaving cruelly to his own subjects and to all strangers and enemies who were so unfortunate as to fall into his clutches. This tyrant, Dionysius, was so unjustly cruel that once, when he awoke from a restless sleep during which he dreamt that a certain man in the town had attempted to kill him, he immediately had that man put to death.

It happened that Pythias had, quite unjustly, been accused by Dionysius of trying to overthrow him, and for this supposed crime of treason Pythias was sentenced by the king to die. Try as he might, Pythias could not prove his innocence to the king's satisfaction, and so, all hope now lost, the noble youth asked only for a few days' freedom so that he could settle his business affairs and see to it that his relatives would be cared for after he was executed. Dionysius, the hardhearted tyrant, however, would not believe Pythias's promise to return and would not allow him to leave unless he left behind him a hostage, someone who would be put to death in his place if he should fail to return within the stated time.

Pythias immediately thought of his friend Damon, and he unhesitatingly sent for him in this hour of dire necessity, never thinking for a moment that his trusty companion would refuse his request. Nor did he, for Damon hastened straightaway to the palace—much to the amazement of King Dionysius—and gladly offered to be held hostage for his friend, in spite of the dangerous condition that had been attached to this favor. Therefore, Pythias was permitted to settle his earthly affairs before departing to the Land of the Shades, while Damon remained behind in the dungeon, the captive of the tyrant Dionysius.

After Pythias had been released, Dionysius asked Damon if he did not feel afraid, for Pythias might very well take advantage of the opportunity he had been given and simply not return at all, and then he, Damon, would be executed in his place. But Damon replied at once with a willing smile: "There is no need for me to feel afraid, O King, since I have perfect faith in the word of my true friend, and I know that he will certainly return before the appointed time—unless, of course, he dies or is held captive by some evil force. Even so, even should the noble Pythias be captured and held against his will, it would be an honor for me to die in his place."

Such devotion and perfect faith as this was unheard of to the friendless tyrant; still, though he could not help admiring the true nobility of his captive, he nevertheless determined that

Damon should certainly be put to death should Pythias not return by the appointed time.

And, as the Fates would have it, by a strange turn of events, Pythias *was* detained far longer in his task than he had imagined. Though he never for a single minute intended to evade the sentence of death to which he had been so unjustly committed, Pythias met with several accidents and unavoidable delays. Now his time was running out and he had yet to overcome the many impediments that had been placed in his path. At last he succeeded in clearing away all the hindrances, and he sped back the many miles to the palace of the king, his heart almost bursting with grief and fear that he might arrive too late.

Meanwhile, when the last day of the allotted time arrived, Dionysius commanded that the place of execution should be readied at once, since he was still ruthlessly determined that if one of his victims escaped him, the other should not. And so, entering the chamber in which Damon was confined, he began to utter words of sarcastic pity for the "foolish faith," as he termed it, that the young man of Syracuse had in his friend.

In reply, however, Damon merely smiled, since, in spite of the fact that the eleventh hour had already arrived, he still believed that his lifelong companion would not fail him. Even when, a short time later, he was actually led out to the site of his execution, his serenity remained the same.

Great excitement stirred the crowd that had gathered to witness the execution, for all the people had heard of the bargain that had been struck between the two friends. There was much sobbing and cries of sympathy were heard all around as the captive was brought out, though he himself somehow retained complete composure even at this moment of darkest danger.

Presently the excitement grew more intense still as a swift runner could be seen approaching the palace courtyard at an astonishing speed, and wild shrieks of relief and joy went up as Pythias, breathless and exhausted, rushed headlong through the crowd and flung himself into the arms of his beloved friend, sobbing with relief that he had, by the grace of the gods, arrived in time to save Damon's life.

This final exhibition of devoted love and faithfulness was more than even the stony heart of Dionysius, the tyrant, could resist. As the throng of spectators melted into tears at the companions' embrace, the king approached the pair and declared that Pythias was hereby pardoned and his death sentence canceled. In addition, he begged the pair to allow him to become their friend, to try to be as much a friend to them both as they had shown each other to be.

Thus did the two friends of Syracuse, by the faithful love they bore to each other, conquer the hard heart of a tyrant king, and in the annals of true friendship there are no more honored names than those of Damon and Pythias—for no person can do more than be willing to lay down his life for the sake of his friend.

A Few Words More

Damon and Pythias were the closest of *companions*, a word that comes to us from the ancient idea that the sharing of food is the basis for friendship. The combination of the Latin words *cum*, meaning "with," and *panis*, meaning "bread," gives us the sense that a *companion* is someone who eats bread with us. Similarly, when we invite friends over for an evening, perhaps to share our food, we say that they are our *company*. The word *accompany* attaches the Latin prefix for "to" onto *cum* and *panis*; originally this word meant "to go along with someone and share bread together."

The Battle of Marathon

About the story:

> *This story about the Battle of Marathon is not actually a myth, for the battle itself is a matter of historical record; indeed, it is considered to be one of the most famous battles ever fought. But it has an aura of myth about it, for, as you will read in "A Few Words More," the Greeks believed that they had been aided in their fight by one of the gods. Then, too, the story has certainly been embellished by countless retellings over time; the mythlike ending in which a runner dashes from Marathon to Athens with the news of victory was not recorded until six centuries after the battle took place.*

Approximate reading time: 11 minutes

Vocabulary and pronunciation guide:

> **covetous** [CUV-uh-tuss]: greedy; desiring someone else's possessions
> **Darius** [DARE-ee-us]
> **Plataeans** [platt-EE-ans]
> **Miltiades** [mill-TYE-uh-deez]
> **Phidippides** [fie-DIP-ih-deez]
> **Acropolis** [uh-CROP-oh-liss]: the walled fortress built at the highest part of Athens; literally, "highest city"
> **Nike** [NYE-key]

*I*magine if you can what life was like in Greece twenty-five hundred years ago. The nation of Greece itself did not exist; the various city-states—such as Athens, Sparta, Ithaca, and the rest—all had their own armies and customs and territories. But one of these cities, Athens, was special in many ways.

Athens was the oldest of the cities, having been founded

when Athena, the goddess of wisdom, chose the olive tree as her gift to the mortals who would dwell there. Since that time, Athens had flourished in every endeavor: It was home to the greatest sculptors in the world, the best architects, the finest poets and playwrights and musicians; its people had a high regard for learning, and they honored the mathematicians and philosophers who called this city home. But greater than all these artistic and scholarly achievements was the fact that Athens had given birth to the concept of freedom. Nowhere in all the world, except in Athens, did people believe that they had the right to decide for themselves how to run their lives. In every land, since humans began to live in groups, people had just accepted the notion that a king, a queen, or some other powerful ruler had the right to determine how everyone else should live. But it was only in Athens that people had freedom and so could choose to govern themselves. In Athens, then, and only in Athens, each farmer or shepherd or worker was a citizen and could take part in the doings of government; every citizen was equal before the law. This idea of a free people acting together had never been thought of before, much less tried as a form of government.

You can imagine, then, how dearly the people of Athens valued their freedom, and how they feared losing their freedom more than losing their lives. The very thought of being enslaved by some tyrant was the most hideous torture in their minds. You can imagine, too, that the powerful tyrants who ruled the rest of the world looked upon this lovely city with a covetous [CUV-uh-tuss] eye, for the beauties and the riches that freedom had brought to Athens were prizes that many kings found hard to resist.

One of these kings, Darius [DARE-ee-us] of Persia, decided that the time had come for Athens to fall under his rule. And what could stand in his way? The vast Persian Empire had created an army that was feared all over the Mediterranean world; its troops had conquered cities and countries throughout Asia and Africa; the very mention of the "Persians" sent terror into all who dared to oppose them. And the Athenians? Well, they had no army to speak of; they were poets and scholars and farmers for the most part. But they were also free people, who would fight to the death to keep their freedom, and so they prepared to defend their city—every able citizen became a soldier in the defense of the Athenian way of life.

Still, the Athenians could gather a force of, perhaps, ten thousand men, and these would certainly be no match for the fifty thousand well-trained troops that the Persians were sending against them. And so the Athenians sent messengers to all the kingdoms in the land, asking for support. But each messenger returned with the same news: No leader would send his warriors to aid such a hopeless cause. The reputation of the Persians caused all to cower in fear for their own lands and their own people. All, that is, except the Plataens [platt-EE-ans], who sent their entire army—one thousand soldiers—to help their Athenian neighbors. Grateful as the Athenians were for this help, they knew that things looked bleak for them indeed.

Still, they had not yet heard from the Spartans; if only the Spartans would join them, victory might still be theirs. The men of Sparta, you see, were famous throughout the world for their fierceness in battle. The Spartans were not poets or writers or scholars as were the Athenians; they were fighters, through and through. Among the things that Spartan boys learned at an early age was how to endure pain without flinching; they were taught that the worst fate that can happen to a warrior is not death, but surrender. When a young Spartan left home for the field of battle, his mother would hand him his shield and say, "Come back with this, or upon this." Oh, yes, if the Spartans would send just a few thousand men, there would still be hope.

But this was not to be. The Spartans, you see, worshiped one god above all the others, and that god was Pan. Pan was a boisterous and merry god who had both human features and the horns and hooves of a goat; he was the shepherds' god and ruled over the forests, the mountains, and all wild places. It just so happened that the Spartans were in the midst of a holy celebration in honor of Pan, and they were not permitted to fight in any way until the next full moon brought an end to these holy days, for by doing so they would dishonor their god and he would punish them for such disobedience. The Spartans did, however, pray to Pan to help the Athenians, and their chief priest reported that Pan had heard their prayers and would answer them by sending down a disease to afflict the Persian army.

The Athenians received this news with great dismay. They had hoped for a few thousand Spartan warriors, but all they received was the promise of some disease instead. There would be no help other than what the Plataeans had sent, for by now the Persians' ships had landed in the bay at Marathon, just twenty miles or so to the northeast, and their soldiers were already preparing to march on Athens.

The Athenian generals decided that they must somehow prevent the Persians from attacking the city itself, and so they chose to engage the Persian army on the plains that spread out from the bay at Marathon. The Persians amassed their troops with practiced precision in columns and rows along a line fronting the bay, each rank of spearmen protecting tiers of expert archers and cavalry. The vastly outnumbered Athenian army looked out upon this terrifying war machine from their positions about a mile away, and they prepared for what would surely be their last battle.

But an Athenian general named Miltiades [mill-TYE-uh-deez] had devised a plan, and this is what it was: He stretched his soldiers out in a line the same length as that of the Persian line, but with so few soldiers, of course, the line could be nowhere near as deep as the ranks of the Persians. Miltiades put most of his troops at the ends of his battle line, and therefore had very few in the middle. He wanted the Persians to break through the middle of his line and to be cut off when the more powerful forces at the ends eventually closed together. When the battle began, Miltiades ordered his troops to charge on a dead run right at the Persian line, the first time this maneuver had ever been used in warfare. Not only had the Persian soldiers never been charged before (and so they feared they were facing an army of madmen), but this headlong rush also made it difficult for the Persian bowmen to hit their targets, and so allowed the Athenians to concentrate their forces in hand-to-hand combat.

It was not long after the Athenian charge that the Persians fell into Miltiades' trap. They broke through the center quite easily and rushed forth like floodwaters blasting through the weak spot in a dam. But the strengthened flanks of the Athenian army proved superior to their Persian counterparts, and they gradually began to close together behind the original Persian battle line. Now the Persians could see that they were cut off from their ships and were in danger of being surrounded. They broke their ranks and ran about as if in a rage; it was each man for himself and the Persian officers could not bring them back to order. Because they were now fighting as so many individuals instead of as a well-drilled and disciplined army, these Persian soldiers became rather easy targets for the Athenians, who remained in their units and under the control of their generals.

By the afternoon, the Athenians had captured and burned seven of the Persian ships in the bay, and any Persian soldiers who could had climbed aboard the others and sailed away. The plains of Marathon were strewn with bodies, but the final count showed the Persian dead to number about 6,400, while the Athenians had lost a total of 192 brave men. A great victory had been won, for freedom had been preserved in the city where it was born and among the people who revered it.

The rest of the citizens of Athens awaited news from the battleground, hoping for the best but fearing that their army would be routed and that they would be either killed or captured and placed in bondage. The day wore on, and still there was no word from Marathon. Then a runner appeared on the horizon. It was Phidippides [fie-DIP-ih-deez], the greatest runner in all of Athens, who had been sent from the battlefield. He had, in fact, run the entire distance—more than twenty miles—and as the people looked over the city walls, they could see that he was nearly exhausted from his mission. Was he dashing in such haste to tell them to flee, for the Persians would soon be sacking their beautiful city? They waited, almost trembling in fear of what his message might be. Phidippides reached the steps of the Acropolis [uh-CROP-oh-liss] and continued to run up to the city gate. There he fell at the feet of the gathered crowd, and then, his life almost drained away by his run, he uttered one last dying word: "*Nike!*" [NYE-key]— the Greek word meaning "Victory!"

A Few Words More

The modern marathon run covers a precise distance: 26 miles, 385 yards. Whether Phidippides actually made the run from the battlefield to Athens is not known, but the distance would have depended upon several factors, which could have altered the length of the route by five miles or more. In fact, the longest race that was included in the ancient Greek Olympics covered a distance of approximately three miles. The modern distance for the marathon run was not established until the 1908 Olympic Games in London.

One very common English word, however, does trace its origin to the battle of Marathon. You will recall that the Spartans told the Athenians that Pan had promised to send down a disease that would afflict the Persian army and cause their defeat. Well, when the Athenian soldiers saw the highly trained, experienced Persian troops break their ranks and scatter about in complete disarray, they were certain that this must have been caused by the disease that Pan had promised. Indeed, the *-ikos* ("disease") of Pan was known as *pan-ikos*, and that is why we call a sudden, overpowering terror *panic*.

Europa and Cadmus

About the story:

> *The story of Europa's abduction (as well as the story of how her name became applied to the continent of Europe) is quite different in its Greek version from the later Roman telling of this tale. Both stories, however, lead into the legend of Cadmus and the founding of the great city of Thebes, the city that would become the setting for the tragic story of Oedipus (pages 141–150).*

Approximate reading time: 13 minutes
Vocabulary and pronunciation guide:

> **Europa** [you-ROW-pa]
> **Thebes** [THEEBZ]: an ancient city in Greece
> **Oedipus** [ED-uh-pus]
> **Agenor** [uh-JEE-nor]
> **Phoenicia** [fuh-NEE-sha]: an ancient country at the eastern end of the Mediterranean, in the area where Syria and Lebanon are today
> **Phoenix** [FEE-nicks]
> **Cilix** [SILL-icks]
> **Crete** [KREET]: a large island south of Greece
> **doleful:** mournful; melancholy
> **Minerva** [mih-NERVE-uh]: the Roman goddess of wisdom; the Greeks called her Athena
> **Delphi** [DELL-fie]: an ancient town in central Greece
> **oracle** [OR-uh-cull]: a temple where a priest or priestess would issue prophecies and answers to questions
> **brindled** [BRINN-dulled]: having dark streaks or spots, usually on a tawny or gray background
> **gnashing** [NASH-ing]: grinding or striking the teeth together in anger
> **Harmonia** [harr-MOE-nee-uh]

King Agenor [uh-JEE-nor], who ruled over the land of Phoenicia [fuh-NEE-sha], was a happy king, for he had been blessed with four wonderful children: three handsome sons named Cadmus, Phoenix [FEE-nicks], and Cilix [SILL-icks], and one very beautiful daughter named Europa [you-ROW-pa]. Now the king loved all his children as much as any father ever had, but, in truth, lovely Europa was his favorite. He was so proud of her beauty and so afraid that someone might steal her away because she was so beautiful, that he never allowed the little princess to play outside the palace gates unless her brothers were there to protect her. And he was always relieved when his four children returned safely from their day of play and wandering.

The three boys were all willing to take on the responsibility of protecting their fair sister, for they were quite proud of her beauty, too. But Cadmus, who was the eldest of the princes, loved her most of all, and it was he that the king held chiefly responsible for her care and safety.

As Europa grew, so did her beauty, but still she retained a childlike innocence and charm, and still she enjoyed frolicking in the open fields and pastures just as she had when she was a little girl. Now it happened that on one of her springtime ventures into the flowery fields beyond the palace walls, Europa and her brothers (oh, yes, it was still their duty to guard and protect her) became so taken up in their play that they quite forgot how danger can lurk even in the most peaceful and happy places. The young princes began to make colorful wreaths out of the bright flowers, and they decorated their fair sister with these and with long trails of blossoms that made her appear like a goddess. In a short time, Europa was nearly smothered with flowers, and with a merry laugh she told her brothers to go off and chase butterflies so that she could rest in peace for a while. And this the boys did, running after the colorful butterflies that flitted here and there while Europa lay down among the long grasses and lazily played with the garlands of sweet-scented flowers that she wore.

Now Jupiter, the mighty god of the heavens and the king of all the gods on Mount Olympus, had watched the princess Europa grow to become the beautiful maiden that she was, and Jupiter had long awaited an opportunity to carry her away and possess her as one of his many handmaidens. Here, at last, he saw that his chance had come, for as he looked down from Olympus he could see that the princess was unprotected—her brothers being all engaged in chasing butterflies at the other end of the meadow. So the great Jupiter—who was not always noble and good, but was sometimes unkind and greedy in his desires—came down to earth and changed himself into a beautiful white bull, and he drew near to the spot where the fair princess lay.

Europa had almost fallen asleep, when she heard a rustling in the grass behind her and the trampling of some creature approaching. Springing to her feet, she was greatly alarmed at the sight of this strange white bull so close to her. But she did not cry out, for the beautiful animal, with its tender-looking brown eyes, appeared to be so gentle and so harmless that Europa's fears quickly vanished, and she began to pat the bull's glossy white coat and stroke the curly hair on its forehead. A feeling of admiration for the animal swept over her, and she looked upon the gentle beast as a friend. She took off some of the wreaths and chains of flowers she wore and hung them over his shining horns and around his neck.

Then the beast began to frolic with the young princess, and he knelt down on his knees before her, as though inviting her to take a ride upon his back. Europa's playful spirit surfaced as she began to think that it would be great fun, indeed, to gallop across the field on the back of this new pet and astonish her brothers, who were still amusing themselves at the other end of the meadow.

At last, when the kneeling bull stared up at Europa with a look of pleading in his large brown eyes, she could no longer resist the temptation, and with a merry laugh she seated herself lightly upon the back of the creature, playfully using the chain of flowers she had flung around his neck as reins. In an instant, the white bull arose and began to trot across the meadow.

Her three brothers were amazed and greatly alarmed when they saw Europa approaching them, mounted upon such a strange beast, but when she gaily waved her hand and called out a happy greeting to them as she passed by, they were somewhat relieved. Still, Cadmus felt that something was amiss, and so he ran in haste after his sister, all the while wishing that he had never left her alone. When Cadmus closed in upon the pair, the white bull suddenly began to gallop away swiftly toward the shore, and now Cadmus was terrified, for he knew that his sister was in great peril. He followed the bull in frantic haste, but it sped across the sandy shore and plunged into the sea, swimming swiftly through the waves.

In vain did poor Europa, now fully aware of her danger, cry out to her brothers for help. The white bull, bellowing with triumph, swam steadily over the crested billows, and Europa was compelled to cling tightly to his horns to prevent herself from falling into the sea and being drowned. In a short time, they both vanished from the sight of the despairing Cadmus, never to return.

The cunning Jupiter had succeeded in carrying off the beautiful Princess Europa to be his handmaiden and companion, and he landed her safely on the distant island of Crete [KREET], where he showered her with love and with treasures so that Europa lived in happiness and splendor for the rest of her life.

Such a happy outcome was not the lot of the three princes who had been left behind on the shore, full of grief at the loss of their sister. When they finally found the courage to return home and tell the story of what had happened and why Europa was not with them, their royal parents were plunged into the deepest woe. King Agenor was filled not only with grief, but with wrath against his sons for having left their fair sister unprotected in the meadow. In particular, he blamed Cadmus for the tragedy, because he was the eldest and was most responsible for the welfare of his brothers and his sister. In his anger and rage, Agenor threw the young prince out of his home, saying, "Leave here, you who have destroyed my happiness, and never come into my sight again unless you bring with you my beloved daughter, whom I have now lost because of your carelessness!"

And so Prince Cadmus was driven from the palace of his father, and grieving sorely for the loss of his beautiful sister whom he loved so well, the doleful youth wandered forth, not knowing what to do or which way to turn.

For many years Cadmus roamed from country to country in

search of his sister, but nowhere did he learn any clues to her whereabouts, and since he could not return to his father's palace without her, he realized that he was fated to be an exile for the rest of his life.

At last, however, the good goddess Minerva [mih-NERVE-uh] took pity upon him and directed his steps toward the city of Delphi [DELL-fie], so that he could learn his future from the oracle [OR-uh-cull] at Apollo's temple there. When Cadmus entered the temple to pray for guidance in his now hopeless search, the voice of the oracle replied clearly: "Seek no more for the sister you have lost, O Cadmus, for she is happy where she is and will remain there forever."

"But what, then, shall I do, O great Apollo?" Cadmus asked, still kneeling in prayer. "My home and my parents are lost to me now, and I know not where to go."

And the mysterious voice replied: "Go forth, Cadmus, and follow the first brindled [BRINN-dulled] cow you come upon. In the place where that cow lies down, there you shall build a great city, and you shall win great renown as its king."

This message, as you would expect, greatly cheered Cadmus, although he was somewhat mystified by what it commanded him to do. He set out once again upon his wanderings and, before long, he did indeed see a brindled cow walking lazily along the hillside before him, and he followed the cow just as he had been instructed to do. For several days and nights that brindled cow kept plodding along, never stopping to lie down, and Cadmus kept plodding along behind. Such a strange sight did not go unnoticed by the idlers and adventurers along the way who were curious to see what would happen, and Cadmus soon had many young men join him to follow wherever the brindled cow would lead.

At last, after a weary journey, the cow could go no farther, and it lay down in a lonely place to rest. "Here, on this spot," thought Cadmus, "I will establish a great city just as Apollo decreed, and those who have followed me shall help me build it." But his followers had gone off to a neighboring spring to slake their thirst, and Cadmus waited for them to come back. He waited and he waited, but still they did not return, and so Cadmus took up his trusty sword and went off to the spring to discover the cause of their delay.

It was soon apparent what fate had befallen them, for Cadmus found a large cave behind the well, and in that cave lived a ferocious dragon who had eaten all the young men as they drank the water from the well. Now Cadmus had no desire to meet a similar fate, and so when the monster rushed toward him, gnashing [NASH-ing] its terrible teeth and shaking the earth with its huge scaly body, Cadmus struck out with his sword and dealt the dragon a series of deadly blows about its neck and head. The monster gave out one last tired roar, and then rolled on its side and ceased to move.

While Cadmus stood there contemplating his lifeless foe, he was more than a bit concerned about how he was to go about building a great city, since all his followers had now been slain. Just then he heard Minerva's voice speaking to him again. "Take out the dragon's teeth," the voice said, "and plant them in the ground." This Cadmus proceeded to do, and when he had finished planting all the teeth in a pasture not far away, he stood back in amazement, for the teeth began to sprout and push up through the ground! But no green and leafy sprouts were these, for as the clods of earth began to move, Cadmus could see the points of spears appear above the surface. Next there were helmets, with their nodding plumes, poking through the soil, and then shoulders and breasts and limbs of men with weapons. In time, there stood before Cadmus a whole harvest of armed warriors, all pledging their lives to him and calling him their king!

With these soldiers to assist him, Cadmus built a city, which he called Thebes [THEEBZ], and as the years went on it grew to become a metropolis, and Cadmus and the people of Thebes gained great renown and glory. In spite of his fame, Cadmus still grieved for his lost sister Europa, and in order to comfort him, the gods sent down from Olympus a maiden named Harmonia [harr-MOE-nee-uh] to be his bride. Harmonia was the daughter of Mars, the god of war, and Venus, the goddess of love and beauty. She brought to Cadmus such a peacefulness that he forgot his grief, and together they lived in happiness for the rest of their lives.

A Few Words More

The goddess Harmonia took her name from a Greek word that meant "a means of coming together or joining" (from *harmos*, which meant "a joint"). It is from her name that we derive such words as *harmony, harmonize, harmonious,* and even *harmonica,* all of which carry the sense of joining or combining elements together to produce a pleasing or agreeable result.

Another important root that can be found in this tale lies in the word *metropolis,* which the city of Thebes grew to become. This modern word combines the Greek word for "mother" *(meter)* and the Greek word for "city" *(polis)* to describe the "mother city," that is, the largest and most important city in the area. The idea of "city" lies at the heart of many words. A *citizen,* for example, was originally a person who lived in a city and participated in its affairs, and the Greeks called such a person *polites.* Today we have several common words that owe their origin to *polis* and *polites,* most notably *politics, politician, political, policy, police,* and *cosmopolitan,* which means literally "a citizen of the world *(cosmos)."*

The Sword of Damocles

About the story:

In this story, as in the tale of Damon and Pythias, the tyrant Dionysius does not appear to be terribly cruel. But it is good to remember that history shows him to be a ruthless killer and a traitor who would sacrifice anyone or anything in order to increase his power. Some care should be taken, too, not to confuse Dionysius [die-oh-NISH-us], the tyrant of Syracuse, with Dionysus [die-oh-NYE-sus], the Greek god of wine.

Approximate reading time: 8 minutes

Vocabulary and pronunciation guide:

> **Damocles** [DAM-oh-kleez]
> **Damon** [DAY-mun]
> **Pythias** [PITH-ee-us]
> **Sicily** [SIS-uh-lee]: the large island that lies just off the "toe" of the boot-shaped Italian peninsula
> **courtiers** [COURT-ee-erz]: attendants at the court or palace of the king

D ionysius [die-oh-NISH-us], the tyrant of Syracuse and the cruel king of the island of Sicily—the same harsh ruler who tested the friendship of Damon [DAY-mun] and Pythias [PITH-ee-us]—lived every day of his reign in fear for his life. The cruel way he treated his subjects and the terror he inspired in the citizens of neighboring lands made him a very hated man, and many would have slain him—and gladly—if they had ever had the chance.

Dionysius, however, was well aware that he was hated, and so he employed many guards to protect him. Then, too, there were many members of his court—advisers, minor officials, and nobles—who owed their positions to the king, and so did not want any harm to come to him. These courtiers [COURT-ee-erz], themselves, lived in fear—fear that the king would, for whatever reason, become displeased with them and take away their privileges or their positions or their land—or even their lives. And so they flattered him whenever possible, telling him how great and how wise a king he was, and how beloved he was by all his subjects.

Among the most foolish of all these flatterers was a courtier named Damocles [DAM-oh-kleez], who laughed whenever the king laughed, who repeated every opinion held by the king, and who always talked about how wonderful it must be to live the carefree and happy life of a monarch. "Surely there can be no greater happiness in the world," he said, "than to live a life of such power and respect as does the mighty Dionysius!"

Now if Dionysius had been a weak or vain king, he might have been pleased by such empty flattery, but he was not deceived, and he knew that these compliments amounted only to the praise of a fool. Therefore he resolved to teach this fawning courtier a lesson he would never forget and, at the same time, to provide some entertainment for the king's own grim sense of humor.

One day, after Damocles had made yet another remark about how wondrous it would be to sit upon the throne, Dionysius said to him: "Since you are so constantly praising the delights of being a king, I will give you a taste of the happiness that you find so alluring. Tomorrow I am giving a banquet that will be attended by many fine lords and princes, and I want you, friend Damocles, to sit upon the throne in my place throughout the feast. In this way, you will know firsthand the delights of being a king. But know this—that it is my belief that at the end of the evening you will be more than eager to give up your exalted seat and become a plain subject once again."

But Damocles declared more excessively than ever that, on the contrary, he would never want to leave the throne and that he would be grief-stricken to have to give up the happiness that would be his while he was king. And so he awaited the next day in the greatest excitement, vainly boasting to his companions of the wonderful honor that Dionysius was about to bestow upon him—permitting him, of all people, to reign as king for a few hours.

On the following day, when the time for the banquet arrived

and all the noble guests had assembled in the great hall of the palace, Damocles, who had been clothed in splendid royal robes for this occasion, was called by the king to ascend the throne. A golden crown was then placed upon his head, while all the guests were commanded to give to Damocles the same respect and honor that they would have given to Dionysius himself.

Although the heavy gold crown made his head ache after a while, and although it was rather inconvenient to have to wait to eat until the royal tasters had sampled every dish (to make certain the food had not been poisoned), Damocles still enjoyed his kingly position and found the flattery and praise his guests directed to him to be extremely pleasant. Yes, he could live in this style very comfortably, thank you.

Then, and quite suddenly too, he received a terrible shock, and would have instantly dashed from his seat of honor had not Dionysius sternly commanded him to remain where he was. The shock that had frightened him so had come about in this way: As he tossed his head back in pure enjoyment and looked up as if to thank the gods for granting his every wish, he beheld in horror a sharp, double-edged sword suspended above him, its point barely a foot from the center of his head and its hilt attached to the ceiling beam only by a single, long, slender hair! He realized at once that if that slender hair should break—as it seemed very likely to do—he would be instantly killed! The terror of this thought caused him to cry out to Dionysius, begging to be allowed to take a more humble seat among the guests, but the tyrant refused.

"Stay where you are," the king replied with a cruel smile, greatly enjoying the discomfort of his flattering attendant. "It is true that the naked sword suspended above you may fall at any moment; but, on the other hand, it may not. Nevertheless, I intend for you to sit throughout this banquet with death hanging over your head, so that you may learn how kings and others of high positions must, in truth, live in constant fear for their lives, for they never know, in spite of their seeming glory, when evil will befall them. It takes a brave heart, indeed, to smile and to appear happy under such circumstances, does it not, good Damocles?"

Appearing brave was something that Damocles was powerless to do, for he was a coward at heart, and he became so paralyzed with fear that he could not eat another morsel of food. He sat absolutely motionless, looking up—as if in a trance—at the point of the sword that was hanging by that slender thread just above his skull, every moment expecting the thread to break and the sword to cleave him in two.

After several hours, the banquet came to an end, the evening's guest of honor (as well as the evening's entertainment) still transfixed, still staring at the sword over his head. Then Damocles was allowed to come down from the throne; his temporary crown was removed, and his royal robes were taken from him. Never was a man more eager to give up the trappings of high office than was poor Damocles, who had learned well the lesson that boundless wealth or kingly power does not necessarily bring happiness. Though high position has its honor and glory, it also has its dangers. Those who would rise above their fellows cannot fear the heights to which they aspire, nor can they be tempted to believe what foolish flatterers would say about them.

A Few Words More

Today, the "sword of Damocles" symbolizes the insecurity—the sense of impending doom—that hangs over anyone who is in the public eye or in a position of power. Shakespeare had this same idea in mind when he wrote, "Uneasy lies the head that wears a crown."

It is good to recall, however, that the holding of public office was thought by the ancient Greeks—the founders of democracy—to be part of what it meant to be a citizen. Many people, therefore, wanted to hold public office, and those who did not were called "private persons," or in Greek, *idiotes*. When the Romans acquired the word (and changed its form to *idiota*), the term began to apply to those who were unfit to hold office, until today it has become strictly a term of abuse: *idiot*.

Pegasus, the Wingèd Horse

About the story:

There are many versions of the famous story that fol-lows, some of which tell a different tale about how the young hero came to ride the great wingèd horse, and some continue the hero's adventures into battles with enemy soldiers and even battles against the warlike women called Amazons. But it is the fantasy of riding a great flying horse up into the skies, and of slaying a terrible monster from this lofty height, that makes the image of Pegasus one of the most enduring in all of classic literature.

Approximate reading time: 12 minutes

Vocabulary and pronunciation guide:

Pegasus [PEG-uh-sus]

Bellerophon [bell-AIR-oh-fahn]

Proetus [pro-EE-tus]

Anteia [an-TYE-uh]

Lycia [LISH-uh]

Iobates [ih-OBB-uh-teez]

Chimaera [kih-MEER-uh]

Minerva [mih-NERVE-uh]: the Roman goddess of wisdom; the Greeks called this goddess Athena

wingèd [WING-id]: having wings (a poetic pronunciation commonly used in mythology)

Medusa [meh-DEW-suh]: a snaky-haired monster who was slain by Perseus (see pages 133–140)

Perseus [PER-syoos]

alabaster [AL-uh-bass-tur]: a dense, white gypsum, used in the making of plaster

There once was a young man named Bellerophon [bell--AIR-oh-fahn], a handsome and virtuous prince who was the son of the king of Corinth. Now, a very unfortunate circumstance occurred, and Bellerophon—by sheer accident—killed his own brother. The people of Corinth were outraged, for they did not know that the killing was completely accidental, and they demanded that Bellerophon be put to death for his crime. Well, the king could not bring himself to arrest his good and noble son, and so he sent the boy to a land far away, where he might take refuge until the anger of the people subsided.

Bellerophon was sent to a land called Argos, where its king, Proetus [pro-EE-tus], received him kindly and sympathized in the misfortune that had befallen him. Here the young prince might have lived in peace for many years had it not been for Proetus's wife, Anteia [an-TYE-uh], the queen of Argos. The queen, you see, was a creature of vanity, for she thought of herself as being extremely beautiful, and she encouraged those around her to praise and flatter her at every occasion. She thought she could attract any man she chose in the kingdom to be her lover, and many there were who complied with her wishes. And so, when the tall and fair Bellerophon first came to her court, she quickly selected him to be the next of her many lovers, and she did everything in her power to attain his affections.

Bellerophon, however, was too upright and honorable to yield to such a temptation, and, not wishing to anger King Proetus, who had shown him such kindness, he repulsed the advances of the queen and steadfastly refused even to be alone with her. This conduct so enraged Anteia that she resolved to punish this lad who had been so bold as to reject her, and therefore she falsely accused him to her husband of the crime she had tried to entice him to commit, but which he had so successfully resisted.

King Proetus was now in a dilemma, for he knew Bellerophon to be a noble youth, and yet Anteia claimed that the prince's actions were anything but noble. The king believed that his wife would not tell him a lie, yet if what she said was true, he would be forced to severely punish the young prince, and doing harm to someone who is a guest in your home violates the laws of hospitality and is frowned upon by the gods. What was he to do?

After giving the situation much thought, Proetus devised a solution that seemed to be the answer to his prayers. He would send Bellerophon to the kingdom of Lycia [LISH-uh], where Proetus's father-in-law, Iobates [ih-OBB-uh-teez], ruled as king. He would give Bellerophon some documents, which, he would say, would introduce the prince and make him welcome in the kingdom of Lycia. But actually, the documents would tell King Iobates to have whoever carried them killed, for the bearer had committed a terrible crime against Queen Anteia. With this plan, Proetus would neither have to refuse his queen nor kill his guest; it was perfect. Quickly, the king drew up the deadly instructions in a letter to Iobates, and he folded the letter twice to seal it from prying eyes. This he gave to Bellerophon, telling him that the letter would be a favorable introduction to his new host, and then he sent the prince off to Lycia, and to his doom.

Now, when Bellerophon arrived at last in Lycia, he went immediately to the palace of King Iobates, and he handed the king the letter that had been given him by Proetus. Iobates read the letter slowly, his eyes from time to time glancing up at the smiling youth who stood in front of him, a youth who appeared to be so innocent and noble, but who had apparently committed a great evil in Corinth. And now it was Iobates who was under a great dilemma, for he knew that it was his duty to punish Bellerophon, as he had been instructed to do in the letter, but doing so would violate the laws of hospitality and would call down upon him the wrath of the gods. So this king, too, devised a plan that would solve his predicament.

It so happened that there was, at that time, a terrible monster called the Chimaera [kih-MERE-uh] who was loose in the kingdom of Lycia. The Chimaera was a strange monster, indeed, for it had the head of a lion, the body of a goat, and the tail of a serpent. From its mouth there issued hot gases and long tongues of flame that would scorch a fiery path for the beast to follow and would incinerate anyone who happened to be in his way. Iobates told Bellerophon about how his kingdom had been plagued for many years by this terrible Chimaera and how the beast had scorched all the fields so that nothing would grow. And he lamented the fact that there was no one who was brave enough or strong enough to rid Lycia of this monster, but if there were, such a hero would have the undying love of all the people in the kingdom.

Just as Iobates had hoped, the rash Bellerophon jumped at the opportunity to be a hero in this new land, and he promised the king that he, himself, would kill the Chimaera or die in the attempt. "So be it!" said the king, who had, in this way, condemned the prince to death, as he had been instructed in the letter, without having to carry out the sentence by his own hands. Surely the boy would stand no chance against the fire-breathing Chimaera, and Iobates smugly congratulated himself on devising such an ideal way out of his dilemma.

Bellerophon left the palace and embarked upon his quest, though the magnitude of his challenge was just now becoming apparent to him. How could he possibly defeat such a monster? Why had he leaped into such an adventure without thinking? What was he to do? The more he thought about his situation, the bleaker it appeared. Finally, at his wits' end, he prayed to the goddess Minerva [mih-NERVE-uh] for help and for wisdom, and Minerva, who knew well that he had been wrongfully accused of a crime he had never committed, heard his prayer, and she decided to send him help in the form of Pegasus [PEG-uh-sus], the famous wingèd [WING-id] horse.

Now, it was said that Pegasus had sprung from the blood of Medusa [meh-DEW-suh], when the great hero Perseus [PER-syoos] cut off her head. But however this magnificent horse came to be, it was certain that he was quite unlike any horse that had ever been seen before or since. Pegasus was as white as alabaster [AL-uh-bass-tur], and his muscular frame and noble head would have given him the appearance of a god even without the one feature that distinguished him most. For at his sides were two giant wings, which were covered with the whitest of shining feathers, and with these wings Pegasus could soar up into the sky in an instant, and he could fly from land to land as quickly as a human might run from his own cottage to that of his neighbor.

Pegasus was cared for by Minerva, who had tamed him so that he would accept a rider on his back. But only a rider of fearless courage would attempt to sit on this steed, for not only was Pegasus the swiftest and most powerful of horses, but the dizzying heights to which he rose would send chills through anyone who had spent his life anchored to the ground. Yet, when Minerva brought her wingèd horse to Bellerophon, the prince promptly and without any fear sprang upon the back of the great steed, who immediately unfolded his great wings and mounted into the air with Bellerophon astride, clinging to the horse's mane.

By exercising great caution and patience, the courageous Bellerophon succeeded in making Pegasus obey his will, and he practiced many aerial maneuvers with the horse, and even a few reckless stunts as well. It was not long, though, before Bellerophon remembered that he had a serious mission to complete, and he directed Pegasus to soar over the plains of Lycia until they located the fiery Chimaera. They hovered just above the terrible beast, who shot forth streams of flames that reached almost up to them, but never touched horse or rider.

The monster ground his lion's teeth together, and he lashed his serpent's tail wildly about, but there was nothing he could do to the pair who tormented him from above. Then did Bellerophon take from his back the bow he had brought, and he fitted it with one of the arrows from his quiver. Guiding Pegasus into a position just above the monster's head, the prince pulled back the string with all his might and let the shaft fly. Straight down it went and embedded itself in the Chimaera's neck, causing the fiend to cry out a most horrible scream of pain. Again and again Bellerophon sent arrows from aloft into the body of the beast, until, at last, the long-feared Chimaera fell to the ground in a lifeless, smoldering mass.

Now the people of Lycia rejoiced and praised the name of Bellerophon in every corner of the land. And when King Iobates heard that the prince he had sent to his doom had not died after all, but had, instead, rid Lycia of the terrible monster that had ravaged the land for so long, the king could not help feeling grateful to the brave young Bellerophon. Nor did he believe anymore that a youth who was surely favored in the eyes of the gods could be guilty of the crime that he was alleged to have committed. And so Iobates not only ceased to seek the death of Bellerophon, but, as a reward for his heroism, bestowed upon him in marriage his own daughter, together with a portion of his kingdom.

Here in Lycia, young Bellerophon might have dwelt long in peace and prosperity, but a forbidden ambition seized him one day, and he left his home to ride once again on the back of Pegasus. While this he had done on many occasions since ridding the land of the Chimaera, now it was his aim to ride the mighty horse up into the heavens, and there to join the gods. Such ambitions are not for mortal men, and when Jupiter looked down and saw Bellerophon approaching his domain, he hurled down a thunderbolt that struck the prince full-square and toppled him off his wingèd steed. Down and down he fell until he crashed to the earth and crippled himself so badly that he shunned the eyes of men from that time on. Bellerophon spent the rest of his days alone, wandering aimlessly through many lands, suffering many pains, until he died a homeless vagrant.

Pegasus, though, was permitted to continue his upward flight until he reached the heavens, where he was given a place among the constellations, and where he can be seen even today.

A Few Words More

The Chimaera was a fantastic creature, don't you think? I mean that it was a creature of fantasy. The picture of a fire-breathing monster made up of parts of a lion, a goat, and a serpent is a fantastic one, to be sure, and it is this sense of fantasy that has come down to us in the word *chimera* [kih-MEER-uh], which means "a foolish or impossible fancy." Today, we might label a scheme or plan as being *chimerical* [kih-MARE-ih-cull] if we want others to see it as "impossible, impractical, or illusory."

It is interesting to see that King Proetus wrote out his instructions in a letter, and then folded it twice to indicate that its message was of a private nature. The Greek word for "a paper folded twice" was *diploma,* and we can see the prefix *di,* meaning "twice or double,' at the beginning of the word. A *diploma* came to mean "an important document" in Latin, and the people who would carry such documents came to be called *diplomats.*

Baucis and Philemon

About the story:

Little is known about the elderly couple Baucis and Philemon, for they remain unidentified except for their names and the town in which they lived. But their story serves to point out how strongly the Greeks and the Romans felt about their responsibilities to those who came to their door in need. The laws of hospitality were absolute, and we find throughout the myths that whenever guests were ill treated or strangers turned away, the gods were both swift and severe in meting out punishment to the offenders.

Approximate reading time: 10 minutes

Vocabulary and pronunciation guide:

Baucis [BOUGH-sis]

Philemon [fih-LEE-mun]

Phrygia [FRIJ-ee-uh]: an ancient kingdom that lay east of Greece, in what is now west-central Turkey

ambrosia [am-BRO-zhuh] **and nectar:** the food and the drink of the gods

hospitably [hos-PIT-uh-blee]: behaving in a generous way toward guests

hearth [HARTH]: a fireplace, often at floor level and used for cooking

inhospitable [in-hos-PIT-uh-bull]: unfriendly; not offering comfort or shelter

Land of Shades: the land of the dead

*L*ong ago, in an ancient land called Phrygia [FRIJ-ee-uh], there was a town whose people had grown to be wicked and selfish and mean of spirit. Whenever strangers came to this town, instead of welcoming them with kind words and offering them a place to rest, the people treated them cruelly and turned them away from their doors, sometimes even pelting them with rocks and sticks.

The gods were angered to hear so many tales of such cruel treatment of strangers, for hospitality was a virtue that mortals were expected to show their guests, and so mighty Jupiter took it upon himself to see whether the stories he had heard about this town were, in fact, true. He took with him his son Mercury, and, disguised as weary travelers, both made their way to the village gate. For the next several hours, even as a storm began to soak their long cloaks, they knocked on many doors seeking only rest and shelter, but at each house they were rudely turned away and scorned and called all manner of names.

At last they reached a very humble cottage on the outskirts of town; it was very small and very ordinary, with a thatched roof and precious little property within the posts of its fence. In it dwelt an old couple, Baucis [BOUGH-sis] and her husband, Philemon [fih-LEE-mun], who were very, very poor, but who were also very contented and happy. Their cottage was separated from the rest of the village, just as they were, for in spite of their poverty, they never turned any stranger from their door nor failed to offer anyone in need what little they had for themselves. They had married while in their youth, and they had grown old together in that very cottage. Throughout their lives they retained their steadfast love and admiration for each other, such that neither was a master or a servant in their home—they were equally masters and servants together.

It was on this humble doorstep that Jupiter and Mercury appeared asking for shelter from the storm. Philemon, not recognizing their true identities but seeing only that they were soaked and in need, ushered them in, saying, "Friends, our cottage is small and our food is simple, but we will be honored if you will share them with us."

The strangers gladly accepted and, ducking their heads to pass beneath the low doorway, were soon seated by the warm fireside; their wet cloaks were hung up to dry, and Baucis hurried to make ready a simple supper. She propped up the one short table leg with a piece of slate so that the top would be stable for their guests; she wiped the tabletop with fresh mint; and she set out a small bowl of olives—the fruit that the goddess Athena had given to the earth. Soon the strangers seated themselves at the table, and the old couple filled plates for them. There was only bread and milk, with sweet honey and a few grapes from their garden, but the guests seemed to enjoy their meal as much as if it had been ambrosia [am-BRO-zhuh] and nectar.

As their guests ate, Baucis and Philemon marked their appearance. The elder and taller stranger had handsome features and an air of majesty about him, while the graceful youth, though also very dignified, seemed strange in several details. For one thing, he had little wings on his sandals and on his cap, and he was so light and quick in his movements that he scarcely seemed to touch the ground as he walked. Also, the staff he carried with him had little wings on it, as well as a pair of serpents twisted around it. The old couple had never seen such strange people before, but they were far too polite to make any remarks or to stare or to inquire about these peculiarities.

But there was still another oddity, and this caused the couple to become quite curious. The guests kept filling and refilling their glasses with the sweet milk from the pitcher, and Baucis became worried because she knew that the pitcher would soon be empty and there was no more milk in the house. You can imagine her surprise when, looking into the pitcher, she saw that it was still full to the brim, and that every time the strangers emptied it, it refilled itself! Everything the strangers touched they made more beautiful and rich. The little grapes in the dish grew larger and juicier than any ever seen in that land before, and the bread and honey tasted more delicious than the richest foods at a royal feast.

When they saw these wonders, Baucis and Philemon realized that their guests were not simple travelers, but they were too polite to question them about these miracles. At last, the guests arose from the table saying that they had eaten enough and would now like a place in which to sleep, for they had come a great distance that day and were very weary. The old couple hospitably [hos-PIT-uh-blee] gave up their own sleeping chamber (which was the only bedroom in the cottage) and laid themselves down upon the hard floor to sleep in front of the hearth [HARTH].

Next morning, the kind old couple rose early in order to prepare another meal for their visitors, but Jupiter and Mercury declared that they would, instead, be starting out early on their journey. It was then that Jupiter revealed his identity and that of his companion to the startled couple, and when they heard that mighty Jupiter and swift Mercury had been their guests for the night, old Baucis and Philemon fell to their knees in fear before the gods.

Jupiter, however, commanded them to rise, saying, "You have nothing to fear from me, good Baucis and Philemon. My son and I came here as weary travelers, and you treated us well; therefore, we will do well by you. The purpose of our visit was to see whether the people of this village were really as inhospitable [in-hos-PIT-uh-bull] and evil as we had been told, and we have found that what we had heard is true. Walk with us awhile up this hillside and see how I have punished them for their cruelty to strangers."

When the four arrived near the top of the hill and looked back down into the valley, Baucis and Philemon were astonished to see that what used to be their village was now a deep lake, Jupiter having caused a thunderstorm to cover all the houses and to drown all the people.

"Do not weep for them," Jupiter said, "for they do not deserve your pity. You alone of all the villagers have been saved, and in place of your humble cottage I have built a wonderful temple of gold with beautiful gardens and many pleasant rooms. Now tell me, kind couple, what you desire most, and I will see that it will be yours."

"But we have our love for each other, and we're already perfectly happy," Philemon replied, "so what more could we want?"

"Think long and hard," Jupiter insisted; and when the good couple had discussed the matter together, they came to the mighty Jupiter with this request: "Though we are happy," they said, "yet we are old and must expect someday to be parted from each other. Is it too much to ask, gracious lord, that we be allowed to be guardians of your beautiful temple, and when it comes our time to leave this world for the Land of Shades, that we may die in the same hour, still full of love as we have ever been, and depart this life together?"

Jupiter was quick to reply. "It shall be just as you ask," he said. "You shall dwell together for many more happy years, and your hearts shall always remain young and full of love; and when death shall come at last—as come it must—you shall depart together to the Land of Shades." Then Jupiter and Mercury were gone—vanishing all of a sudden in a vivid flash of lightning, followed by a loud peal of thunder.

So Baucis and Philemon grew very, very old, serving Jupiter all the while by welcoming every weary wayfarer and by feeding every poor beggar who came past that way. And so full of love were they for each other that in the eyes of Philemon Baucis was still as beautiful as she was in her youth, and in the eyes of Baucis Philemon was still as handsome as when he had first wooed her so many years ago.

And then, at last, sitting side by side at the temple door at sunset, they passed from this mortal world at the same time, and Mercury, the messenger of the gods, conducted their gentle spirits to the Land of Shades. In their place, on either side of the temple door, rose an oak tree and a linden, their branches intertwined as though they were whispering loving secrets to each other. The people of the area still point out the place where the trees stand, side by side, forever entwined, and they call them Baucis and Philemon.

A Few Words More

Ambrosia was the food of the gods, while *nectar* was the divine drink. In Greek, the words meant "immortal," and both ambrosia and nectar had the power to make those who partook of them immune to death. Today, *ambrosia* describes any food that is so delicious that even the gods would enjoy it. *Nectar* describes any sweet and delectable drink, as well as the sugary fluid that bees extract from flowers to make honey. The smooth-skinned peach called the *nectarine* is so named because its juice tasted as sweet and as pleasant as the "nectar" of the gods.

The Spinning Contest

About the story:

Although the gods were immortal and more powerful than humans could even imagine, still they had some traits that you might not think too godlike. They were, for instance, extremely jealous of their superiority over all mortals, and any mortals who were presumptuous enough to compare themselves in any way to gods were committing the sin known as **hubris** *[HUE-briss]. There are many tales, in both the Greek and the Roman myths, that involve a god having to teach humility to a human, and, as in the story that follows, often the lesson is a hard one.*

Approximate reading time: 9 minutes

Vocabulary and pronunciation guide:

Aegean Sea [uh-JEE-an]: the northern arm of the Mediterranean Sea, which lies between Greece and Turkey

Arachne [uh-RACK-nee]

nymphs [NIMMFS]: beautiful female nature spirits, lesser divinities who inhabited the mountains, forests, meadows, and streams

Athena [uth-EE-nuh]: Greek goddess of wisdom and goddess of the household arts

There was once an ancient city that lay across the Aegean [uh-JEE-an] Sea from Greece, and in that city dwelt a certain maiden, Arachne [uh-RACK-nee] by name. Though her parents had been very poor, Arachne brought wealth and comfort to their little cottage through her great skill in weaving and embroidering. Such beautiful things did she fashion with her wool, and so graceful did she look as she worked with her spindle, that lords and ladies came from every part of the land to see her at her work and to purchase the products of her loom.

So, because of Arachne's skill in creating these most intricate and delicate fabrics, prosperity took the place of poverty in Arachne's home, and her parents blessed their daughter, and all of them lived very happily. Now this cheery state could have continued had not the maiden fallen victim to her own pride and listened too earnestly to the praises that were showered upon her for her skill with the loom and needle. Even the nymphs [NIMMFS] themselves would leave their play in the woodlands and the waters to come and admire her as she performed at her loom. Her work was so beautiful, not only when finished, but also beautiful to watch in the doing, that the nymphs would say on occasion that "Surely the goddess Athena [uth-EE-nuh] herself must have taught you, for only she alone, in all the world, has more mastery and skill than you." But Arachne was so proud and so vain that she would not acknowledge her debt to anyone, even to the goddess who was the protector of all handicrafts and household arts, and by whose grace alone one had any skill in them. "I learned not from Athena," she replied. "Indeed, Athena could learn much about weaving from me. If she thinks her work is a match for mine," Arachne boasted, "let her come here and put it to the test."

The nymphs and all others who were within earshot shivered when they heard this, for there was no human fault that displeased the gods more than the arrogance of overbearing pride, and mortals who dared to compare themselves with deities always paid a heavy price for their vanity.

It so happened that mighty Athena heard Arachne's bold words, and she was so astonished that she decided to visit this mortal maiden to see what she meant by her boast. Athena disguised herself as an old, gray-haired woman, and leaning on her cane as though too feeble to walk erect, she came into the little room where Arachne was spinning. She joined the circle of admirers who watched Arachne spindle with unbelievable speed and dexterity, and she heard the maiden boast again of having skills that were no match even for the gods.

"My dear," Athena said at last, laying her hand on Arachne's shoulder, "listen to the advice of an old woman who has had much experience in life. Challenge any mortal you wish, but do not compare yourself with the gods. Ask pardon for the foolish words you have just spoken. Athena is merciful, and I promise that she will forgive your wild boast."

Arachne stopped her spinning and looked at the old woman with anger. "Keep your foolish advice for your granddaughters and handmaidens," she snarled. "I stand by what I said, and Athena knows full well its truth, else why is she afraid to come here and accept my challenge?"

"She has come!" cried the old woman, dropping her disguise and revealing her tall, majestic form in all her godlike splendor, including her helmet of brightest gold. The nymphs and by-standers at once fell upon the ground in fear and reverence, but Arachne, foolish Arachne, held her head high and did not show the least fear or awe. On the contrary, she repeated her boastful challenge to Athena, saying, "In the end, you will be asking for my forgiveness, and all shall see who is the teacher and who the pupil."

No more words were spoken, nor did they need be. The contest began as the mortal maid and the immortal goddess each took her place in front of an empty loom, working in silence. Both began weaving with great speed, their skillful hands moving swiftly in the excitement of the competition.

Athena used wools of many contrasting colors, and her loom began to shimmer like a marvelous rainbow. In the center of her web, she wove the story of her great contest with Poseidon over which god should be given the city of Athens, and into each of the four corners she wove pictures showing how mortals who had dared to compete with the gods had been punished. These were meant to be a final warning to her rival to give up the contest before it was too late.

But Arachne worked on at her loom, the color glowing in her cheeks and her breath coming fast with excitement. And such beauty as had never been seen before began to grow in the pictures that appeared under her skillful fingers! You could almost see the birds fly and hear the lapping of the waves on the shore, and the clouds seemed to float through woven air! The stories that she pictured were all chosen to show that even the gods could sometimes make mistakes—disrespectful stories, to be sure, but all woven so miraculously that Athena herself had to stop for a moment to admire the handiwork.

The goddess was forced to admit that Arachne had won the

contest, but this only increased her wrath at the girl's insolence. When Arachne saw the look of anger in Athena's face,
she suddenly realized how foolish and wrong she had been,
but it was too late for repentance now. Athena seized the girl's
beautiful web and tore it to shreds. Then she touched Arachne
with the shuttle three times on the head, saying, "Since you
were so vain about your weaving, you shall live on a thread
and continue to weave forever."

In an instant, Arachne began to shrink; her face disappeared,
and her fingers were changed into little black legs, and before
long she had been utterly transformed into a spider! There she
stayed, hanging on a thread, forever spinning and weaving,
and so have all spiders ever since been punished for Arachne's
pride and for her foolish disrespect for the gods.

A Few Words More

This story is typical of the way that ancient peoples created myths to explain the mysteries that their world
held for them. They did not know, for instance, how
things as strange as spiders ever came to be, and so they
"explained" this wonder—at least to their own satisfaction—by creating a story that not only showed divine
intervention, but also accounted for what they could
see with their own eyes, namely, the intricate way in
which spiders "weave" their webs. *Arachne*, the Greek
word for "spider," is today seen in the scientific word
arachnid [uh-RACK-nidd], which describes the biolog-
ical class to which spiders belong. Technically, you see,
spiders are not insects or even bugs; they are *arachnids*.

Orpheus and Eurydice

About the story:

> *Orpheus sailed with Jason on his quest for the Golden Fleece (see pages 118–130), but his primary claim to mythic fame was that he was one of the very few mortals ever to journey to the Lower World and return to the light of earth. He was favored because of his talent to produce magical musical sounds, and those who could bring joy to life by the power of their sweet music were honored by the ancient Greeks and Romans. The power of music to excite as well as soothe, and the position of importance held by those who can create such effects, has endured down through the centuries to the crooners of the past and the rock stars of today.*

Approximate reading time: 9 minutes

Vocabulary and pronunciation guide:

> **Orpheus** [OR-fee-us]
> **Eurydice** [you-RID-uh-see]
> **lyre** [LYE-er]: an ancient stringed instrument, somewhat like a guitar without a neck
> **Calliope** [kuh-LYE-uh-pee]: one of the nine Muses, she watched over the production and performance of epic poetry
> **gnashing** [NASH-ing]: grinding the teeth together
> **Styx** [STICKS]
> **Charon** [CARE-on]
> **Cerberus** [SIR-burr-us]
> **Hades** [HAY-deez]
> **Persephone** [purr-SEFF-uh-nee]

*L*ong ago, when the earth was very young, there were only two kinds of musical instruments: the pipes, which were invented by the god Pan and made musical tones when a person blew into them, and the lyre [LYE-er], which was a stringed instrument, rather like a small harp. It is said that the lyre was invented by Mercury while he was still just a baby. He fastened a few strings of various lengths across the hollow of a tortoise shell, and he entertained himself by plucking the strings and listening to the pretty sounds that would come out of the shell. These pretty sounds were soon heard by the great and glorious god Apollo, who bought the instrument, and, being the god of music as well as the god of the sun, Apollo soon mastered all its artistic possibilities and composed many songs, each of which was more beautiful than any music that had been heard before.

Now the first mortal to play upon the lyre was a poet named Orpheus [OR-fee-us], whose mother, a Muse called Calliope, [kuh-LYE-uh-pee], was also the goddess of epic poetry. Orpheus used the artistic talents given him by his mother to compose sweet melodies, which he played upon his lyre so beautifully that all nature seemed to draw near and listen. The buds on spring flowers would open to the sound of his singing and playing; the fiercest wild beasts became tame and gentle and would follow Orpheus about like lambs; storms would cease to toss the seas; and even the evil thoughts that were in the minds of the mortals who heard him play would be transformed to thoughts of love and kindness.

When this master singer and musician returned from helping Jason and the Argonauts on their quest for the Golden Fleece, he wooed and wed a beautiful maiden named Eurydice [you-RID-uh-see], whom he loved so deeply that he could scarcely bear to have her out of his sight. And all could see that Eurydice was in love with him, too, as she would sit in the sunshine listening to Orpheus's beautiful music, while the beasts came round to hear the soothing sounds, and the trees bowed down their heads to hear him play.

These two dwelt in perfect sweetness and bliss until, as the Fates sometimes decree, the heights of their happiness became matched by the depths of their woe. For one day, as Eurydice walked in the woods alone, she happened to step on a serpent that had been hidden by the long grass; its fangs pierced her dainty foot, and its venom oozed into her body and mixed with her blood. She cried out to Orpheus, though he was far away at the time and so did not know that his beloved bride was dying.

She slowly laid her head down on the soft grass and, before long, she died.

When this tragic news reached Orpheus, his grief was terrible to see. He took up his golden lyre but did not play a note, nor did he open his lips to sing. The animals that used to listen to him wondered why Orpheus sat all alone on the green bank where Eurydice used to sit with him, and why it was that he never made any more beautiful music. Day after day he sat there, and his cheeks were often wet with tears. Finally, he could bear his loneliness no longer, and he decided to go to the Lower World, the land of the dead, to find his bride and to bring her back.

For many long days, with his lyre in hand, Orpheus persisted on his gloomy journey, down and down from the mouth of a distant cave into the blackness of the earth. At last he came to the black waters of the river Styx [STICKS], which marks the border of the land of the dead. But he could not cross it alone, and the ferryman, Charon [CARE-on], refused to take him in his boat. Orpheus was, after all, still alive, and only the souls of the dead were allowed beyond the river's edge. But Orpheus began to strum his lyre and to sing so sweetly that the boatman melted with tears and agreed not only to take him across, but to do so without the payment of a coin, which he usually charged for his efforts.

After some travel along shadowy paths shrouded in mist, Orpheus arrived at an imposing iron gateway that was guarded by a monstrous dog like no dog ever seen on earth, for this beast had three large heads, each with fiery eyes and gnashing [NASH-ing] teeth. The dog—who was called Cerberus [SIR-burr-us]—roared terribly as Orpheus approached, and rose up ready to pounce on the unfortunate mortal and tear him to pieces. But again, Orpheus began to pluck the strings of his lyre, and the melodious sounds that came forth instantly soothed the beast, and Cerberus became as gentle as a house pet. Even the iron gate sprang open to allow Orpheus to continue on his journey.

Finally Orpheus arrived at the gloomy palace of Hades [HAY-deez], lord of the Underworld, king of the land of the dead (a land that, itself, is often called Hades). He made his way to the great hall, and there, on the throne, were King Hades and his youthful queen, Persephone [purr-SEFF-uh-nee]. Hades bellowed out in a terrible voice, "Who are you, and how dare you to come here? Don't you know that only the dead are permitted here? For your insolence I will chain you in a dungeon here until you are one of us!" Orpheus said nothing, but once more put his fingers to the lyre and began to sing more sweetly and gently than ever. And as he sang, the face of the king began to look almost glad, and his anger passed so thoroughly that, when the song ended, Hades proclaimed: "Your music has made me feel happy—a feeling I have never had before. Ask of me what you will and I shall grant your wish."

"O King," replied Orpheus, "give me back my dear Eurydice, and let her go from this gloomy place to live with me on the bright earth again." King Hades thought awhile and said, "I will give you what you ask, but under one condition: When you leave this land for earth, you will lead and your wife will follow; but you must never look back at her until she has reached the surface, else she will be lost to you forever, and not even your sweetest songs will allow you to see her again."

So Orpheus promised the king that he would go up to earth without stopping to look behind and see whether Eurydice was coming after him. And this he did, passing back through the great iron gateway (for Cerberus knew that the king had permitted Orpheus to leave), across the river Styx, and then climbing higher and higher through the gloomy passages until he came near the land of the living, and he saw just a little streak of light above him, made by the glorious sun. He had almost reached the surface when a sudden fear struck him that Eurydice might have stumbled or fallen victim to one of the dangers that lay along the way. Before he could think of what he was doing, he turned his head quickly to see whether she was still following. But alas! he caught only a glimpse of her, as, with her arms stretched toward him and her lips speaking a last farewell, Eurydice was seized by hundreds of unseen hands that reached out from the dreary walls and snatched her back down into the Land of the Shades, to dwell in the Underworld forever.

Orpheus sat down at the mouth of the cave, weeping over his loss, mourning his beloved Eurydice. There he stayed day after day, without eating or sleeping, and his cheeks became paler and his body weaker, till at last he knew that he must be dying. And Orpheus was not sorry, for although he loved the bright earth, with all its flowers and grass and sunny streams, he knew that he could not be with Eurydice again until he had left it. So at last he laid his head upon the earth, and fell asleep and died.

Though all of nature mourned and grieved over the death of this sweet singer, Orpheus, himself, was of happy heart as his soul made its way toward the land of the dead. This time Charon gladly ferried him across the Styx, and the ferocious Cerberus wagged his tail in a friendly greeting. Soon he saw Eurydice, waiting to welcome him, and he rushed forward to meet his dear wife and put his arms about her, happy in the thought that they would never again be parted.

A Few Words More

The lyre played by Orpheus in this myth is the source for the English word *lyrics*, which are words or verses that could be accompanied by a lyre. A *lyricist* [LEER-uh-sist] is one who writes the words for a piece of music.

The goddess Calliope was Orpheus's mother, and her name came from a Greek word meaning "beautiful voice." Today, you may hear a steam organ made from a set of shrill whistles playing at a circus; this instrument is called a *calliope*, but few would see any similarity in the "beauty" of its sound.

The Story of Io

About the story:

> *The portrait of Juno in Roman mythology, just like that of her counterpart, Hera [HAIR-uh], in Greek mythology, is one of an extremely jealous goddess who knows about her husband's philandering ways and does everything she can to discourage him. Jupiter, the king of all the gods (whom the Greeks called Zeus), fears his wife's wrath, but he still sneaks away to earth on occasion to frolic with nymphs and mortal maidens. The story of Io is just one of several tales that deal with these entanglements and divine deceptions.*

Approximate reading time: 9 minutes
Vocabulary and pronunciation guide:

> **Io** [EYE-oh]
> **nymph** [NIMMF]: a young and beautiful female spirit
> **Juno** [JEW-no]
> **Inachus** [IN-uh-cuss]
> **Isis** [EYE-sis]

*I*n a certain part of Greece, there was a beautiful grove, bordered on all sides by denser woods. Through it there flowed a restless river, dashing over rocks and scattering its spray, like fine mist, over all the trees on its banks.

The god of the river, Inachus [IN-uh-cuss], had one child, a girl named Io [EYE-oh], and there was nothing she liked better than to wander in the grove by the side of her father's stream.

One day, when mighty Jupiter had come down to earth to wander through this pleasant grove himself, he met Io there and began to talk with her. Now Io was a beautiful and graceful nymph [NIMFF], and Jupiter thought her so lovely that he came again and again to the grove and spent many pleasant hours wandering with her along the banks of the stream. Io did not know who Jupiter was, for he always came disguised as a shepherd lad, but she found him to be a pleasant companion, and it must be said that she was as much attracted to him as he was to her.

This friendship was not without its complications, however, for Jupiter's wife, Juno [JEW-no], was a very jealous queen, and in truth it must be said that Jupiter's interest in the young beauties of earth gave her much cause for concern. Juno, you see, could not bear to have Jupiter care for any woman other than herself.

One day, when her husband had been away from home for many hours, Juno suddenly made up her mind to go down to earth and see the maiden that was occupying so much of Jupiter's time and attention. Her heart was filled with bitter feelings, and as she entered the grove, her frown was so dark that it seemed almost to hide the sunlight.

Jupiter was in the midst of a long embrace with his dear Io when, with a mystical power that only gods have, he felt Juno's wrath before she even came into the grove. Fearing that she would surely do some harm to his companion, he quickly changed Io into a young cow—a sleek white heifer. When Juno came to the side of the river, all that she saw was her husband in his own true form and the white heifer nibbling the grass at his side.

Now Juno knew that the animal was really Io, for she was wise to her husband's tricks, but she pretended that all was as it appeared to be. She went up beside the animal and stroked its glossy neck, and then, turning to Jupiter, she said, "Even though this is but a lowly heifer, it gives me much pleasure. Will you give it to me, my husband, as a present, for surely a cow cannot mean much to the great Jupiter, and I do wish it for my own."

Well, what could Jupiter do? If he refused his wife such an insignificant gift, she would surely guess what had happened, and so he had to say yes, although it was much against his will.

As Juno led Io away, she said to herself, "Now that I have you, I will take good care to see that you never go near my husband again." So she gave the cow to one of her servants, Argus, for him to watch over. And there was no better watchman than Argus, for he had a hundred eyes, and no matter how tired he became, he never closed more than half of his hundred eyes at any one time. So there were always at least fifty sharp eyes watching every move that Io made, day and night. Never for a moment was Io left unguarded. At night she was tied to a tree, but during the day she could wander about as she pleased, still, though, under the keen gaze of Argus.

The poor girl did not quite know what had happened to her. One minute she was a pretty maiden, and the next she had become a cow. Instead of the food to which she was accustomed, she had to eat leaves and grass. She slept on the cold, hard ground instead of in her cozy bed, and she drank not from a cup, but right out of the running brooks. When she tried to stretch forth her arms to ask Argus for pity, she found, to her surprise, that she had no arms; and instead of the plaintive words she meant to speak, she heard only a strange lowing sound come out of her own lips.

This frightened her terribly, but when she went to the banks of the river where she had so often walked with Jupiter before, she was even more terrified to see her own image reflected in the water—horns and all! The water nymphs who used to be her friends did not recognize her, and even her father, the river god, only patted her neck and plucked some fresh grass to feed her. Oh, how sad could it be—not to have her own father know her!

She could not speak to him, but with her hoof she inscribed her story in the sandy riverbank. When he read the sad tale, her father wept aloud, and, throwing his arms about his daughter's neck, he poured out his grief in tears. Meanwhile, Argus faithfully kept watch, and he saw all that had passed between father and daughter. He now thought it time to separate them, so he led the heifer away to a distant pasture and seated himself on the top of a hill, from which he could see all that happened in the pasture below.

Now mighty Jupiter had not forgotten Io, and he knew well that it was only because of his attentions (and the jealousy of his wife) that the girl was being punished, so he wished to help her if he possibly could. And he called his messenger, Mercury, to come to him, and he ordered Mercury to use all his cunning in finding a way to kill the hundred-eyed beast who watched over the girl.

Mercury flew swiftly to earth, and there he put on the disguise of a shepherd boy and pretended to be gathering stray sheep that crossed his path. When he came near the hill where Argus sat watching, he began to play sweet melodies on a pipe of hollow reeds that he carried with him. When Argus heard the sounds of the pipe, he was pleased, and he called out to Mercury, "Come here, stranger, and share this shady spot with me. Your sheep can feed in the rich pasture, and you can rest your weary feet."

Mercury then seated himself on the hillside and tried to put Argus to sleep by talking on and on in a wearying tone, stopping only to play some restful music on his pipe. This went on for a long time, but the watchman would never close more than half his hundred eyes. Still Mercury persisted, relating a long and tragic story about how the pipe of reeds came into being, and telling it in a soft and sleepy manner. When the tale was finished, Mercury saw, to his delight, that Argus was sound asleep—every eye was closed. Mercury quickly unsheathed the short sword he carried with him, and with one swift stroke he cut off the head with its hundred starry eyes, and there it lay beside the watchman's body.

Mercury quickly returned to Olympus, but before Jupiter could make his way to earth to change Io back to her true form, Queen Juno happened by the pasture and saw the tragedy that had befallen her watchman. Oh, she did grieve so over Argus's lifeless form, for he had been her favorite, and to honor him she removed his eyes and set them in the tail of her favorite bird, the peacock, where you may see them shining in splendor to this day. But the queen blamed poor Io for all this trouble, and, to punish her, sent a large gadfly to torment her, night and day, biting and stinging the poor girl, until Io was beside herself in pain.

She wandered from one country to another trying in vain to rid herself of the gadfly. At last she came to the land of Egypt where, tired and weary from her long travels, she lay down by the side of the river Nile and tried with her groans and pitiful cries to ask the gods to relieve her suffering.

Jupiter could no longer bear to see her tormented so, and he begged Juno to take pity on Io, and he promised never again to speak to the maiden, if only the queen would set her free. Juno herself was moved with pity, and so decided to restore Io to her own shape. The people of the land found her by the side of the river Nile, and they thought her so beautiful and good that they made her their queen.

And there she lived happily for many years, and when at last she died, the people carved a great statue of their queen and placed it in a magnificent temple. They called the statue Isis [EYE-sis], and for hundreds of years, the people of Egypt came and laid flowers and other gifts at the feet of the statue of Isis, to show how much they loved their beautiful queen.

A Few Words More

The verb that the Romans would have used to relate how Io traced or *inscribed* her story in the sand was *scribo*, which meant "to write," and from which we get many modern words that all deal with writing; for example, *scribble, scribe, describe, prescribe, scripture,* and many others as well. The Greeks, on the other hand, used the word *graphein*, which appears today in many common English words, such as *photography* ("to write with light"), *geography* ("to write about the earth"), *telegraph* ("to write from afar"). A "lead pencil" is a misnomer because pencils do not contain lead; they write with *graphite*.

But lead has a curious history of its own. Lead was very important to the Romans because it was such a soft metal and could be formed and bent easily into goblets, pitchers, even pipes. It is the Latin word for lead, *plumbum*, that gives us our word *plumber*, and especially the strange and silent *b* in its spelling. (This is also the source of the symbol for lead, *Pb*, in the table of elements.) To see whether a wall, for example, is *plumb*, that is, "vertical, straight up and down," we use a lead weight at the end of a line, which is called a *plumb line* or a *plumb bob*. And if this lead weight were dropped into a pond, it would *plummet* straight to the bottom.

One last oddity: Although there is no lead in a "lead pencil," the graphite that is there has another name— *plumbago*.

Halcyone's Dream

About the story:

> *Although this seems to be a tragic story, filled with the human despair that comes from the death of a loved one, it is resolved in the end, as many classic myths are, by a mystical act of kindness. The Roman poet Ovid is the primary source for this story, and so we get the colorful descriptions, such as that of the shipwreck, that are common in his works; his stories also, of course, make use of the Roman names for the gods.*

Approximate reading time: 8 minutes

Vocabulary and pronunciation guide:

> **Halcyone** [HAL-see-on]
>
> **Ceyx** [SEE-icks]
>
> **oracle** [OR-uh-cull]: a temple where priest or priestess would issue prophecies and answers to questions
>
> **spar:** a long, heavy pole used to support the ropes and sails on a ship
>
> **Juno** [JEW-no]: Roman name for the queen of the gods; the Greeks called this goddess Hera
>
> **Iris** [EYE-ris]: goddess of the rainbow
>
> **Somnus** [SAHM-nus]: the Roman god of sleep

*T*his is the sad story of a king and queen named Ceyx [SEE-icks] and Halcyone [HAL-see-on], who loved each other very dearly—so dearly, in fact, that they could not bear to be apart.

Ceyx and Halcyone lived together happily for many years, and in all that time, they had never been separated but briefly, for they treasured each other's company more than that of others. Now it happened that the king was forced to make a long journey to a distant country in order to consult an oracle [OR-uh-cull]. He grieved much at the thought of leaving Halcyone for so long a time, and she tried to make him give up the idea of going away so far. But at last, when she found that he was bent on going, she begged him to take her with him. Ceyx would not think of subjecting Halcyone to such a dangerous voyage, and, although it grieved him to leave her, he felt that he must go, promising to return to her just as soon as he could.

The ship was fitted out for the voyage, and all too soon came the day of departure. Hand in hand, husband and wife went down to the place where the vessel was moored. There they parted, with many kisses and many words of tenderness. Through her tears, Halycone pretended to laugh, and would talk only of the time when the ship would turn its prow homeward.

She stood on the shore, waving her hand, until the ship passed out of sight and only the water, with the dazzling sunlight on it, met her tearful gaze and heard her muffled sobs. Then she went back to her palace.

Meanwhile, the vessel bearing Ceyx and his sailors sped swiftly along before the wind; the sails flapped merrily, while the happy-hearted crew sang as they worked. Ceyx was thinking all the while of his dear wife, and praying that no harm might befall her while he was away.

For a time, all went well, but on the fifth day, toward evening, dark clouds gathered in the sky, and a fierce gale arose. Soon the quiet waves had changed into great white-capped mountains of water that dashed and beat relentlessly against the frail vessel's sides.

Night came on, and the storm grew in fury. The moon and the stars were hidden in dense blackness, broken now and then by a blinding flash of lightning. The roaring of the waves and the rumbling of the thunder filled the air, so that the sailors could no longer hear the orders that Ceyx shouted to them.

Soon the sails flapped helplessly on the broken masts, and the water came pouring into the ship from all sides. At last there came a crash, followed by groans and cries, and the next instant the boat and all the crew sank beneath the raging waters.

Ceyx alone clung to a broken spar that supported his weight, and so escaped death for a time. As he drifted along, now rising on the top of a high wave, now sinking into the foaming depths below, he seemed to see before him, on the water, the face of his beloved wife, Halcyone.

At last a large, green wave rose before him, and he had time only to cry, in sad farewell, "Halcyone! Halcyone!" before he sank beneath the wall of water.

Meanwhile, Halcyone impatiently awaited her husband's return. Every morning she went to the temple of Juno [JEW-no] and prayed that her husband's life might be spared, and that he might soon come back from his voyage and be in her arms once again. At last, Juno could no longer bear to hear these prayers for the safety of a man who was already dead. She called her messenger, Iris [EYE-ris], and ordered her to go to the home of the god of sleep, Somnus [SAHM-nus], and ask him to send Halcyone a dream that would reveal to her that Ceyx was dead.

Iris, in her rainbow-colored robe, flew swiftly through the air, till she came to the dark cavern of Somnus, the god of sleep. Into this cavern no ray of sunlight ever pierced; a dull, heavy darkness surrounded it night and day. No singing of birds or barking of dogs disturbed the perfect quiet of the dark king's home. In front of the musty doors there grew strange plants—poppies and other herbs that send mortals to sleep. In the center of the cavern, on a great couch of black ebony, lay Somnus, wrapped in slumber.

When the beautiful Iris had entered this dark cave, it shone with a splendor of light and color such as had never before been known within the place. Awakened by the brightness, Somnus drowsily raised his head, and Iris spoke: "God of sleep, thou gentlest of gods, who brings rest and peace to the weary heart and mind, I come from great Juno, who asks thee to send to Halcyone a vision in the form of Ceyx, to tell her of the shipwreck, so that she will no longer pray for what can never be." So saying, Iris flew back out of the darkness into the bright, sunlit day.

Now, what Juno commanded, no lesser god could refuse, and so Somnus took on the form of Ceyx, and made a visit that very night to Halcyone. With swift, noiseless wings he sped through the air till he came to the palace of the queen. He entered and stood by the side of her bed, wearing the form of her dear husband, his hair wet and dripping, his garments covered with seaweed and shells.

In a sad voice he told the story of the shipwreck, and he ended with these words: "Weep no more for me, dear one, for I can never come back to my beloved Halcyone."

Halcyone awoke with a cry. The vision had been so real that she looked for wet footprints on the floor; but shadows leave no signs, and the room was empty and undisturbed.

She was so troubled by her dream that she could no longer sleep. She arose and dressed, and, as the gray light of morning broke, she hastened down to the shore, to visit again the spot where she and her husband had exchanged their last farewell.

She had been standing there for some time, when she saw, far out at sea, something white tossed about by the waves. Nearer and nearer to the shore it came, and with a beating heart, scarcely knowing why, Halcyone watched its approach.

Soon she could see that it was the body of dead Ceyx—covered in seaweed and shells, just as she had seen it in her dream the night before. She fell to her knees and cried, "O my beloved, my dream was all too true!" She could not bear to think of her lonely life without Ceyx, and she felt that she would rather be with him, even in the land of the dead, than live in the bright world without him. So she sprang into the sea and swam to the body of the dead Ceyx, and then she dived deep down into the cold, dark waters below.

But she was not drowned, for instead of sinking into the waves she found herself somehow flying above them, and her body was covered with feathers! The gods, you see, had so pitied her that they changed her into a white kingfisher bird. She flew to the body of her husband, but it was gone, for Ceyx, too, had been changed into a bird just like herself. And here they stayed, riding the waves together or soaring on currents of warm air side by side, for their love had remained unchanged.

A Few Words More

For many years it was believed that the kingfisher spent its entire life floating on the sea or soaring over it, and that this species even made its nest and laid its eggs on the surface of the water itself. Therefore, it was thought that the period of calm seas and still air that always seemed to occur during the week before and the week after the winter solstice was provided specifically so that the eggs of the kingfisher could hatch unbroken. The Greek word meaning "kingfisher" was *halcyon*, and the myth of Halcyone and Ceyx developed as a way to explain this fourteen days of calm.

Today we know that the kingfisher actually lays its eggs in a hole near the shore, but the phrase *halcyon days* endures as a way to express those times in which everything was peaceful and calm, as in "memories of the halcyon days before the war."

Somnus, too, lives on today, primarily in the word *insomnia*, which uses the prefix *in-*, meaning "without," and the name of the Roman god of sleep, to describe a condition in which a person is "without sleep"—that is, "unable to fall asleep." A person suffering from prolonged sleeplessness is called an *insomniac*.

Phaëton and the Chariot of the Sun

About the story:

> *Both the Greeks and the Romans worshiped the god
> Apollo and assigned to him more duties, perhaps, than
> those of any other deity. Apollo was the god of music, of
> prophecy, of archery, of medicine, and the protector of
> communities as well as the protector of shepherds' flocks.
> In addition, because Apollo was sometimes called the god
> of the sun by the Greeks, and the Romans always saw him
> as the sun god, he was often portrayed as being a shining,
> golden figure, and that is why he frequently bore the name
> Phoebus [FEE-bus], which means "bright" or "brilliant."
> The sun's route across the sky each day was, to the
> ancients, the journey of Phoebus Apollo in his chariot,
> and his sister Diana (whom the Greeks called Artemis)
> was responsible for the journey of the moon.*

Approximate reading time: 13 minutes

Vocabulary and pronunciation guide:

> **Phaëton** [FAY-eh-ton]
> **Artemis** [ART-ih-miss]
> **nymph** [NIMMF]: a beautiful female nature spirit
> **Clymene** [KLIMM-eh-nee]
> **wingèd** [WING-id]: having wings; a pronunciation
>   commonly used in poetry and mythology
> **Fortuna** [for-TOO-nah]: Roman goddess of chance
> **Neptune:** Roman god of the sea
> **Jove:** another name for the Roman god Jupiter

In the sunny plains of Greece there once dwelt a fair nymph
[NIMMF] named Clymene [KLIMM-eh-nee], who had
been loved by the sun god Apollo and who bore him a
golden-haired boy named Phaëton [FAY-eh-ton]. Early every
morning, when the sun first appeared above the horizon,

Clymene would point it out to her boy and would tell him that his father, Apollo, was setting out in his golden chariot on his daily drive across the heavens. Clymene so often entertained her child with stories of his father's beauty and power that, as Phaëton grew, he became quite conceited about his parentage, and he acquired the habit of boasting loudly about how he was the son of great Apollo himself.

Phaëton's schoolmates, after a time, grew weary of his bragging and his arrogance, and at last they challenged him to give them some proof that he was, indeed, Apollo's son, and they laughed at him when all he could offer was to say, "My mother has told me that this is so."

With their ridicule and mockery still ringing in his ears, Phaëton hastened to his mother and said, "If I am truly of heavenly birth, I beg you, Mother, give me some proof of it, so I can establish my claim to honor." And Clymene answered him saying, "I swear to you that you are Apollo's child, but if you must have more proof than this, then you must go to your father's house in the east, where he begins his journey each day, and ask him if you are truly his son." And this is what Phaëton chose to do.

For many days and weeks he traveled to the east, first through his own country, then crossing Ethiopia and India, until he could go east no more, for he had come to the place where the sun rises in the morning. Here the palace of Apollo stood on a hill, its lofty columns glittering with gold and precious stones; the ceilings were made of polished ivory, and the doors of shining silver. Everything about the palace flashed and glowed and sparkled, and Phaëton had to turn his head and shield his eyes as he made his way toward the throne room.

He stopped some distance from the throne itself, for the brilliance of the light that flashed from it was more than he could bear. Gradually his eyes began to see through the dazzling radiance, and he beheld a golden throne studded with diamonds and emeralds, and on that throne sat glorious Apollo, dressed in a purple robe and surrounded by his many attendants.

"What is the reason for your coming here, Phaëton?" Apollo asked the boy. "Do not fear to speak your mind, for you are my son, and I have a father's pride in seeing how like a man you have become."

And Phaëton replied. "O light of the universe, Apollo, my

father, if you permit me to call you Father, then give me some proof, I beg you, by which I may be known as your true son and remove this doubt from my mind."

Then Apollo took off his sparkling crown of light and asked the boy to come nearer. He embraced his son, saying, "You are worthy to be called my son, and Clymene has told you the truth about your birth. And so that you may have no doubt at all, ask whatever favor you wish, and I will see that it is granted unto you."

He had scarcely spoken when the boy asked for his father's chariot and the right to drive his wingèd [WING-id] horses for one day. Then his father regretted his promise. Shaking his shining head three or four times, he said, "I have spoken in haste; this is the one request that I must deny, and I ask you to withdraw it. You, my son, are of mortal flesh, and what you seek to do cannot even be accomplished by the gods them selves. None but myself may drive the flaming car of day; not even great Jupiter, with all his power and might, can undertake this treacherous journey."

But seeing that Phaëton was resolute in his desire, Apollo described to him the task that he sought to undertake. "The first part of the path is steep, and the horses can make their way up it only with great difficulty, even though it is morning and they are fresh. In mid-heaven the road is very high, and it often brings fear to me to look down on the sea and lands from there, and my heart trembles with terror. The last part of the road descends abruptly and requires most careful driving. The sea gods that wait to receive me often tremble in fear that I may fall headlong and crash into their waters."

Still Phaëton was not moved to change his request, and Apollo, knowing that he could not go back on a promise once made, continued, saying, "Do you dream, my son, that there are wonderful cities in the heavens, full of beautiful things? On the contrary, the road is through the midst of frightful monsters. You pass by the horns of the Bull, in front of the Archer, and near the Lion's jaws, and where the Scorpion stretches its arms in one direction and the Crab in another. Nor will you find it easy to guide these horses, with their breasts full of fire that they breathe forth from their mouths and nostrils. I can scarcely govern them myself, when they are unruly and resist the reins. Beware, my son, lest I be the donor of a fatal gift—

recall your request while you still may. Look around the world and choose whatever you will from the treasures of the earth or the sea, and I will grant it to you at once. But do not ask me to provide the means of your own destruction. If it is proof you want that you are sprung from my blood, what better proof is there than my fears for you? If you could look into my heart, there you would see a father's anxiety for his own child."

Apollo finished his warnings, but his son rejected them all and demanded that his father be true to his word and grant the request he had already made. There was no time for further en-treaties, for Aurora, the goddess of the dawn, was now flinging open her purple gates, and her halls in the east were filling with a rosy glow. The stars were beginning to flee from the sky, and Apollo knew that he could delay no longer. He led Pha-ëton to the place where the chariot was kept, and the boy was stunned by its brilliance, for it was made of solid gold with many sparkling diamonds strewn about its surface. Then the attendants led in the four fire-breathing horses and harnessed up their clinking bridles.

Now Apollo spread a sacred ointment all about his son's face, which made him capable of enduring the brightness of the flame, and he set on his head his shining crown, sighing deeply as he said, "Obey, at least, these warnings, my son: Spare the whip and keep tight hold on the reins. Keep away from both the deep southern and far northern parts of the heavens, and stay in the middle zone. And so that the sky and the earth may receive equal heat, do not go too high, lest you burn up the roof of heaven, nor too low, or you will set the earth afire. The middle course is safest and best, and you will see the clear tracks of my wheels to guide you. The rest I en-trust to the goddess Fortuna [for-TOO-nah], and I pray that she may take better care of you than you take of yourself."

The agile youth sprang into the chariot, stood erect, and grasped the reins with delight, pouring out thanks to his reluc-tant parent. Then the great steeds sprang forth and rose up-ward through the clouds, outrunning the morning breezes. They could feel that their load was unusually light this morning (for young Phaëton weighed much less than his mighty father), and the horses tossed the cart about as though it were empty. They began to rush headlong, and soon the chariot had left the well-trodden path. Phaëton was now terrified with panic, for he did not know how to manage the reins that had been entrusted to him, nor did he know the right course to follow.

The boy looked down upon the lands that were spread out far, far below him, and he grew pale and his knees shook with sudden fear. Oh, how he wished he had never set foot in his father's chariot, and how he regretted learning of his birth and being granted what he begged for. He was powerless to do anything but hold on for his life, for he was being carried along just like a sailing ship that is driven before a gale.

But what was he to do? Much of the sky was left behind him, but more still lay ahead. He turned his eyes in terror from one direction to the next as all about him rose up the monstrous forms that were scattered over the surface of heaven. The Scorpion reached out at Phaëton with his two great claws, and the reins fell from the frightened boy's hands. The horses, now feeling the reins loose on their backs, dashed unrestrained into unknown regions of the sky, in among the stars, hurling the chariot over pathless places, now up in high heaven, now down almost to the surface of the earth. The clouds began to smoke, and the mountaintops were engulfed in flames from the fireball that passed so near above them; the fields all over the earth were parched with the heat, and the plants withered, and all the harvests were ablaze! Great cities perished, their once mighty walls and happy people now left in ashes! Phaëton looked down and saw that the whole world was on fire, and all because he had not heeded his father's warnings.

Now the rivers began to shrink from their banks, and large seas shriveled so that, where water was before, now there was only a dry plain. The fishes sought out the lowest depths of the oceans, and dolphins no longer frolicked above the waves. Mighty Neptune himself three times tried to rise above the surface to see what was wearing away his waters, and three times he was driven back by the heat.

Then it was that great Jupiter looked down from Olympus and saw that, unless he acted at once, all the world would be consumed in utter destruction. But now there were no clouds for him to spread over the wide earth, as he had done before when the crops needed to be screened from the sun, nor were there any cooling rains for him to send down. And so he took up a great lightning bolt in his hand, and he aimed it at the boy in the chariot. Now he hurled the bolt with all his might, and his aim was true, for it struck Phaëton with full force and sent him tumbling from the cart. The boy's long hair was set ablaze, and it burned brightly as he fell headlong toward the earth, like a shooting star that streaks the heavens with its brightness.

The horses and the riderless carriage now sped upward toward the west and soon disappeared from view, and the earth was cooled in the balm of darkness. But Phaëton's life was ended by the lightning bolt and his fall to earth. His scorched body was laid to rest in a far-off land, and an inscription was carved on his tomb:

Driver of Apollo's chariot, Phaëton,
Struck by Jove's thunder, rests beneath this stone.
He could not rule his father's car of fire,
Yet was it much, so nobly to aspire.

A Few Words More

Apollo warned his son about the monstrous animals that lay along the road through the heavens. The Scorpion, the Bull, the Lion, and the rest were all major constellations in the sky and were parts of the ancient circular calendar we now know as the zodiac. The basis for this term is the Greek word zoon, which meant "animals" and which found its way into the name of the first great public collection of wild animals, the Zoological [ZOH-uh-LAHJ-ih-cull] Gardens in London. People quickly began shortening the name of this park to "the Zoological," and finally just to "the zoo."

In this tale we also see Apollo trusting his son's fate to the goddess Fortuna, the Roman goddess of chance, even though raw chance or fate could produce disastrous outcomes as well as fortunate ones. Although the modern word fortune can mean simply "one's destiny" or "that which happens by chance," implying neither a good nor bad outcome, it can also imply a prosperous or favorable condition, as does the word fortunate. Adults may want to keep in mind, however, that there is another word that comes from this goddess's name, and its meaning is much more in keeping with her powers and duties. The adjective *fortuitous* [for-TOO-it-us] is often mistakenly used as a synonym for *fortunate,* but *fortuitous* does not imply a favorable outcome; instead, it describes an event that occurs strictly by chance or luck, sometimes good luck and sometimes bad.

Cupid and Psyche

About the story:

The tragic events that befall the lovely Psyche stem from her persistent curiosity. Encouraged by her jealous sisters, she is not content with the pleasurable life she has been given, and she is driven to know for a fact the one thing that she has been told she must accept on faith alone. Because of this, Psyche is rather like Pandora, a maiden whose curiosity loosed all the evils into the world, after they had been imprisoned in a box. You can find this classic myth of "Pandora's Box" in **More Classics to Read Aloud to Your Children.**

Approximate reading time: 20 minutes

Vocabulary and pronunciation guide:

Psyche [SYE-key]

oracle [OR-uh-cull]: a temple where a priest or priestess would issue prophecies and answers to questions

distraught [dis-TRAWT]: deeply worried; agitated; bewildered

Zephyr [ZEFF-er]: the West Wind

Juno [JEW-no]: queen of the gods; wife of Jupiter

Hercules [HER-cue-leez]

gnashing [NASH-ing]: grinding the teeth, usually in anger

Proserpine [PRAH-sir-pine]: the Roman equivalent of Persephone, goddess of the Underworld

Hades [HAY-deez]: the land of the dead; the Underworld; in Roman myth, this land was ruled by King Pluto and Queen Proserpine

ambrosia [am-BRO-zhuh] **and nectar:** the food and drink of the gods

There was a time, long, long ago, that Cupid himself lost his immortal heart to an earthly maiden, and this is how it came to pass.

There was a certain king who had three lovely daughters. The older two married princes of wealth and fame, but the youngest, who was named Psyche [SYE-key], was so radiantly beautiful, so strikingly attractive, that it seemed no man could be worthy of her. People used to gather in the streets just to see her pass by; they sang hymns in her praise, and some strangers even mistook her for Venus, the goddess of beauty herself.

Now, this praise for the beauty of a mortal maiden, in time, reached the ears of Venus, high on Mount Olympus, and it angered the goddess so much that she vowed to punish her earthly rival. One day, she called her son, whose name was Cupid, and told him to sharpen his arrows for a very special mission. Cupid, you see, was a more dangerous archer than even mighty Apollo, for, although Apollo's arrows could drain one's life blood in an instant, a wound from Cupid's arrows would cause one to fall deeply in love, and that could mean a lifetime of joy, or it could also mean a lifetime of sorrow and grief if that love was not returned or shared.

"Avenge your mother," Venus commanded. "Wound this mortal maid, Psyche, and make her fall in love with some poor and unmannered man who will treat her cruelly and be a torment to her throughout all her days."

Cupid gathered and readied his weapons and then, making himself invisible, flew down to earth and found Psyche asleep in her bedchamber. Cupid carefully touched her heart with the tip of his golden arrow of love, which caused Psyche to awaken suddenly with a start. She opened her beautiful eyes and looked right at Cupid, who forgot momentarily that he was invisible and was so taken by the incomparable beauty of this mortal maid that he accidentally wounded himself with that same arrow. Ignoring the hurt he had inflicted upon himself, he quickly prepared a healing potion that would undo the effect of his arrows, and he poured this soothing vapor over her golden locks. Back to her dream the princess went, unaffected by any thoughts of love. Cupid, now strangely not so light of heart, returned to the heavens, but he did not say a word of the events that had actually taken place that night.

Venus waited several days and watched Psyche's every move from high above, but, much to her dismay, she saw no sign whatsoever of Psyche's love for any mortal, rich or poor, and so she decided to send down her own spell upon this unsuspecting princess. From that time on, lovely as Psyche was, not a suitor came to ask for her hand; not a man in the kingdom, high born or low, tried to woo her, or win her smile, or attract the slightest response from her.

This sudden lack of interest in obtaining Psyche's favor made her parents quite concerned, for they so dearly wanted Psyche to marry a noble prince and to live a happy life. Now they wondered if she would ever marry at all. Thinking that her lonely situation might be the result of some offense that she had unwittingly given to the gods—some affront that had angered them into changing her fate—they took their daughter to the oracle [OR-uh-cull] of Apollo, and they asked the oracle to give them advice and counsel.

After some time, a voice from inside the temple spoke to them: "The princess Psyche shall never wed a mortal man. She must be given to him who waits for her on the top of yonder mountain, one against whom both gods and men are powerless." Hearing this, her poor parents were distraught [dis-TRAWT], and they gave themselves up to grief as they pictured the fate that was in store for their beloved princess. Surely there must be a hideous monster awaiting her on the mountain, and she must now be delivered unto him. Only Psyche herself remained undismayed, saying, "We have angered Venus in some way, and now I must atone for that sin so that you and our kingdom will be allowed to prosper once more. It is the will of the gods, and so we must obey."

At last, her parents consented and preparations were made for Psyche to be delivered to, and wed to, whoever or whatever awaited her on the mountain. The royal maid took her place in the procession that wound its way up the steep slope, and, when they reached the very top, they left her there—alone.

Full of courage, but in secret fear, she watched her people proceed down the mountain path, weeping for her fate, too sad to look back. Only when they were out of sight, then did she weep, and her tears ran like raindrops down her cheeks.

But now a sudden breeze drew near and dried her tears and

caressed her hair, seeming to murmur comfort to her. It was Zephyr [ZEFF-er], the gentle West Wind, who had come to befriend her. He lifted her up in his arms, and he carried her up and over the crest of the fateful mountain and into a valley below. There he left her, resting on a bank of lush grass, and there she fell asleep.

When she awoke it was near sunset. She looked about her for some sign of the monster's approach, but she heard and saw nothing unusual . . . nothing, that is, until she peered through a clump of nearby bushes and saw, much to her amazement, the most magnificent castle her eyes had ever beheld! Its golden pillars supported a high, arching roof; its walls of purest silver and walkways inlaid with precious gems reflected the light of the setting sun. There was no lock or chain on the great doorway, and there was no guard to stop her from entering, which she did. As she gazed in awe at the splashing fountains and the marbled hallways, a sweet and comforting voice spoke to her, saying: "Do not fear, gentle princess, for all that you see is yours. Many servants await your every wish. Lie down now and rest; your bath is being prepared, and a feast will follow."

And, indeed, for the next several days, Psyche's smallest requests were immediately answered. She was waited upon by unseen spirits and sung to by invisible choirs; and every night she heard the soothing voice of the man to whom she had been given, although she never beheld his form. Only after sunset would he come to her, and his voice, the beautiful voice of a god, would inspire her to trust her strange destiny and to believe in his absolute love for her. Often she begged him to stay with her through the day, so that she might see his face, but this he would not grant.

"Never doubt me, dearest Psyche," he would say. "Perhaps you would fear me if you saw my form, and your love is all I ask. There is a reason that I must remain hidden for now. Trust me, and believe."

Surely, thought Psyche, this spirit, whom the oracle had called her husband, was no monster. But what was he? And why must he remain unseen? These questions haunted the princess even as she partook of all the pleasures of her new surroundings. And she thought of her dear parents, who were, no doubt, mourning her loss at the hands of some cruel beast.

And she missed the company of her two sisters, who were suffering the life of mere mortals while she lived as a goddess. One night she told her husband of these regrets, and begged that her sisters at least might come to visit her. He sighed but did not refuse.

"Zephyr shall bring them here," said he. And on the following morning, swift as a bird, the West Wind came over the crest of the high mountain and down into the enchanted valley, bearing her two sisters.

They greeted Psyche with joy and amazement, hardly knowing how they had come to be where they were. But when she led them through her palace and showed them all the treasures that were hers, envy and bitterness arose in the hearts of the sisters. They asked a thousand questions, hoping to find some flaw in her good fortune, and when Psyche finally had to confess that she had never seen her husband, they laughed at her steadfast faith, saying, "Have you forgotten what the oracle decreed, that you would be given to a creature that overcomes both gods and men? Are you so deceived by this show of kindliness that you are blind to his evil intent? Be warned, dear sister: Your husband is some sort of dragon who feeds you well for the present so that he may feast upon you someday soon! Trust not his words, but see for yourself. Some night when the monster is asleep, light a lamp and take with you a sharp dagger; then you can put him to death, and all his riches will be yours—and ours."

After the sisters had gone, Psyche brooded over what they had said, not seeing their evil intent. Little by little, suspicion ate at her, like a moth, until one night, in shame and fear, she hid a lamp and dagger in her bedchamber. Toward midnight, when her husband was fast asleep, up she rose, hardly daring to breathe, and coming softly to his side, she uncovered the lamp in order to see the monster's face.

But there before her, in the light of the lamp, the youngest of the gods lay sleeping; it was Cupid himself, the most beautiful, the most irresistible of all the immortals. His hair shone golden as the sun, his face was radiant as springtime, and from his shoulders sprang two wings showing all the colors of the rainbow.

Poor Psyche was overcome with fear, love, and guilt. Her hands trembled as she turned to quench her lamp, but as she did so, some of its burning oil fell upon the shoulder of fair Cupid, awakening him with a start. He opened his eyes to see his bride and the dark suspicion in her heart.

"O doubting Psyche," he said, "is this how you repay my love? After having disobeyed my mother's command and taken you for my wife, I had so hoped that your faith would be as constant as my love. But I see that you find your sisters' advice preferable to mine, and so I must leave you forever. Love can never dwell where there is suspicion." And so saying, he seized his bow and quiver, unfurled his wings, and flew away out the open window.

Psyche tried to follow him and explain to him and apologize for the doubts she had had, but she could not fly and so tumbled to the ground in a daze. When her senses returned, she stared about her and saw that she was alone; the palace and gardens had vanished, and the valley was beautiful no longer. From that moment, she began to wander day and night, throughout many lands, seeking her beloved Cupid and a chance to make amends for her faithlessness.

Meanwhile, Cupid lay in his mother's chamber, wounded not only by the burning oil, but more seriously by his own arrow of love, which had pierced his heart when he first beheld the loveliness of Psyche. Venus grew exceedingly angry with her son for having fallen in love with this unworthy mortal maid, but she was still more angry with the maid herself for causing Cupid to be so sick at heart. And Venus would have destroyed poor Psyche on the spot, had not great Juno [JEW-no] stopped her and declared her judgment that the pair had committed no evil; they had merely fallen in love and were now suffering as lovers often do. Hearing this, Venus returned to care for her son, but she harbored still a deep resentment for the princess Psyche.

After wandering long and far without success, Psyche decided to seek the forgiveness of Venus and submit to whatever punishment or penance Venus might demand. She presented herself at the goddess's temple and asked to be allowed to serve in any way she could. As Psyche knelt, sobbing, at the entrance, the beautiful Venus herself appeared, but wearing a most angry look.

"Have you come to see your husband, whom you so cruelly wounded and whose love you so heartlessly cast aside?" the goddess asked. "Well, we shall see whether through your cleverness and hard work you can earn the right to take your apology to him."

So saying, she led Psyche to a large storehouse filled with great quantities of wheat, barley, beans, and many other seeds and grains as well, all mingled together into one immense heap. "Separate these—grain by grain and seed by seed," Venus commanded, "so that each kind is in a pile of its own. And see to it that you are finished by nightfall." Then Venus departed, and Psyche sank to her knees in tears, knowing that such a task would be impossible even for the mighty Hercules [HER-cue-leez]. What Psyche didn't know, however, was that Cupid was watching over her—still as ardently in love with her as ever. From the corner of her eye she began to see a moving black thread that seemed to emerge and crawl from a crevice in the storehouse wall. Bending nearer to investigate, she saw that it was a great army of ants in columns that had come to her aid. The industrious little creatures worked so rapidly and so diligently that, even before the last light streaked the evening sky, all the grains and seeds were separated and the impossible task was completed.

When Venus saw that the storehouse had been completely transformed just as she had requested, she knew that Psyche must have had some divine help, and she became even more determined to make the mortal princess suffer for the way she had treated Cupid. On the next morning, she ordered Psyche to gather some wool from each of the ferocious rams with golden fleece that grazed in a nearby grove—not just some of the golden wool, mind you, but some from each ram, else Psyche must return to her family at once and forever. Well, poor Psyche couldn't even cross the mighty river that bordered the grove, much less did she know how she would overcome the sharp horns and gnashing [NASH-ing] teeth that awaited her on the other side, and once again she wept in despair. But Cupid persuaded the river god to help her in her quest, and soon she was carried across the treacherous waters and instructed to pick the golden wool not from the rams themselves, but from the bushes and briars that had touched the coats of all the rams as they passed by.

Once again, Venus became enraged when Psyche returned, her arms full of the shining fleece. "I know very well that it is not by your own doing that you have succeeded in these tasks," the goddess fumed. "But whoever is aiding you against me will be of no help to you this time. Here, take this box and make your way into the Underworld; there you are to find Proserpine [PRAH-sir-pine] and say to her, 'My mistress Venus asks that you send a little of your beauty to her, for she has lost some of her own in caring for her injured son.' Now, Psyche, let us see if your wits are the match for this challenge."

Psyche was certain now that her destruction was near, for she knew well that mortals did not venture into Hades [HAY-deez] and return to earth alive. And so it was in utter despair that she climbed a high cliff and prepared to kill herself by jumping from its edge. But a soothing voice whispered in her ear, "I know your grief, dear Psyche; but listen to me and you will learn a safe way to make your journey and return." And the gentle voice went on to tell her how one might avoid all the dangers of Hades and come out unscathed. "Just be sure," added the voice, "that when Proserpine has returned the box you do not open it, however much you may long to do so."

Psyche listened well and followed every step the voice had told her and, before long, had made her way safely into Hades and into the palace of its king and queen. She made her errand known to Proserpine, who complied with her request, and soon Psyche found herself in the upper world again, wearied but hopeful. "But I am so worn with toil," she lamented, "that my appearance will no longer be pleasing to my husband. I have come so close to seeing him again, and now he will think me unattractive. Surely Venus cannot need all the beauty I have brought back in this box, and since it is only to please my beloved husband, it might be right for me to take just a little."

So saying, she carefully opened the box. Poor Psyche should have known that the spells and potions of Hades are not for mortal maidens. No sooner had she inhaled the strange aroma that was emitted than she fell down in the middle of the road, without sense or motion, quite overcome with the deepest sleep.

Now it happened that Cupid had recovered from his wound, and he could no longer endure the absence of his beloved Psyche. He slipped unnoticed from his chamber and flew to the spot where she lay. He gathered up the potions and spells that had escaped and sealed them again in the box. "Dearest Psyche," he said, "your curiosity has once again led you near to ruin. But the power of my love will save you." And he knelt beside her and kissed her cheek.

As if from a dream, Psyche awoke and found herself beautiful once again. "Take the box to my mother as she commanded you," Cupid said, "and I will take care of the rest." He spread his rainbow wings once again, and Psyche watched him rise until he was far out of sight. He continued on and up until he reached the heights of Mount Olympus, where all the gods sat feasting, and he begged them to calm his mother's anger and hatred for Psyche. They heard his story and their hearts were touched; the mighty Jupiter himself lent a favoring ear and, shortly thereafter, called Venus to him and persuaded her to accept Psyche as one of her own. Mercury was dispatched to bring the mortal maid up to Olympus, and there she was offered ambrosia [am-BRO-zhuh] and nectar on which to feast. "Take these," Jupiter said, "and become immortal; nor shall Cupid ever be apart from you again." Psyche consumed all that she was given and, thereby, became a goddess. Cupid took her by the hand, and they remained together forever.

A Few Words More

Psyche is the Greek word for "soul," and from this base grew our words *psychology*, which is the study of *(-logy)* the mind; *psychiatrist*, a doctor or healer *(-iatric)* of disorders of the mind; *psychoanalysis*, a technique for analyzing mental processes; and many others. These words are frequently misspelled by students (and adults), but if one merely remembers the spelling of the maiden's name that is at the core of all these words—Psyche— most of the subsequent spelling problems disappear.

In this myth, too, we see Psyche's parents consulting an *oracle* as a means of learning what the future held for their daughter. The word *oracle* comes from the Latin word that meant "to speak" (the same root that gives us *oral* and *orator*). The priestess at an oracle would often go into a swoon or trance, thereby allowing a god to "speak" through her and reveal the future.

Pygmalion and Galatea

About the story:

> *This is the story of a sculptor named Pygmalion, who could not find the "ideal woman" in the real world, and so he "created" her out of a block of marble. The British playwright George Bernard Shaw used this general idea as the theme of his play* **Pygmalion,** *in which a cultured professor of phonetics "creates" a charming and sophisticated lady out of a cockney flower seller simply by teaching her how to speak and act like a lady. Unlike the sculptor in the myth that follows, however, Shaw's professor discovers to his dismay that the soul he had awakened is now independent and no longer caters to his every whim. The play was adapted into one of the world's favorite musicals,* **My Fair Lady.**

Approximate reading time: 14 minutes
Vocabulary and pronunciation guide:
>   **Pygmalion** [pig-MAY-lee-un]
>   **Galatea** [gal-uh-TEE-uh]
>   **Amathus** [AM-uth-us]

*I*n the busy seaport of Amathus [AM-uth-us], on the southern shore of Cyprus, there once lived a sculptor named Pygmalion [pig-MAY-lee-un], whose work meant everything in the world to him. He scarcely knew any other joy but that which came from carving his statues, and that joy came not from the praises that others lavished on his handiwork, either, but just from the sheer exhilaration of creating beauty where none existed before. He did not choose to have friends or companions among the people in the town, although there were many fair maidens who would gladly have married this maker of beautiful statues.

There came a day, however, when, for the very first time, Pygmalion felt lonely and dispirited. From an upper window in his studio, he had been looking out at the busy life of the streets and the wharf, and it made him think that his own life, by comparison, was exceedingly dull and uninteresting. Looking around his quiet studio only increased his loneliness: Of what good were these lovely statues of Minerva or Juno or Diana to him? What companionship could he find in a marble Mercury?

But these gloomy thoughts did not remain with the sculptor very long, for like a shaft of light from the rising sun, an inspiration came suddenly to him, and selecting a block of snow-white marble that had just been brought to his workshop, he began with feverish haste to give form to the shapeless mass. And as his practiced hand wielded the mallet and chisel, he exclaimed, "O Venus, goddess of love, I beseech thee: Direct my hand, and from this stone shall come the figure of a maiden worthy of acceptance in your eyes."

Little could Pygmalion imagine how fully his prayer would be answered. Venus heard his request, and forthwith she filled his mind with a vision of womanly beauty beyond anything he had dreamed, and she gave to his chisel the skill to reproduce it in the lifeless marble that stood before him. As the form took shape beneath his hand, its surpassing loveliness stirred him to the depths of his being, and he gave himself up wholly to the inspiration of Venus.

Each morning he rose early, and, absorbed in his work, he labored ceaselessly as long as the daylight lasted. Night seemed to him but a cruel interruption to his work, and the dark hours were endurable only when brightened by dreams of the maidenly form that haunted his waking thoughts. Once, when the statue was all but completed, he grew ashamed of the eagerness he was displaying, and he decided to leave his studio and spend an entire day out in the woods, hoping that the change of scenery might bring him to a more wholesome frame of mind. But it was all in vain. Never did he spend a more wearisome day in his life. Oh, the countryside was beautiful, to be sure—the gentle West Wind swept over the scented flowers, and the bees busied themselves in the clover—but living things held no interest for Pygmalion that day; all his heart and mind remained back in his workshop with that lifeless form in marble.

Long before sunset, he found himself running homeward, murmuring to himself, "What a fool I was to leave her! What would I do if she were gone when I returned?" And then he paused, somewhat vexed at the realization that he had begun to speak of the statue as if she were a woman of flesh and blood. But this was just a fleeting worry, and he hastened on his way once again.

No sooner had he reached his home than, taking up his chisel, he set to work, with such energy that before daylight had faded he had put the last masterly touches to his statue and was feasting his eyes upon the completed marvel. The image stood with one hand outstretched toward him, and in the other was a beautiful rose. Her lips were parted, but without a smile, and her calm, grave face looked down upon the sculptor with eyes that seemed to harbor something of human love itself.

Now, however, his toil finally at an end, Pygmalion felt only grief, and he sat before his creation and lamented, "What a poor wretch I am. The statue I have fashioned has shown me how deeply I can love, but it is still just a statue. Other men can express their love to real women whom the gods send to them to share their lives, but my love is for no other than this figure in stone. Oh, if I could only perfect my work so that I could give life to this divine figure!"

And as his lips framed the hopeless words, the impossibility of his longing sank into his weary soul. For a time, his grief overwhelmed him, but as he grew calmer, he comforted himself with the thought that at least he had this vision of loveliness to gaze upon for the rest of his days. He then moved the figure to a place of prominence in his home, and he struggled to position it on a small platform, the better that it might be looked upon and idolized. Next he ransacked his chests in search of the costliest ornaments he owned, and finding his best still too poor for the marble maiden, he visited every jeweler's shop in the town until he had collected gems that he felt were worthy enough to adorn his beloved. On the rounded arms and the slender fingers he placed bracelets and costly rings, and he encircled the delicate throat with the rarest of jeweled necklaces. In the morning, still not content with these costly expressions of his devotion, he hurried to his garden and brought bunches of sweet flowers to lay at her feet.

"Dear image of the woman I love," he cried, "although you can never move nor speak, yet I will worship you till the day of my death, and you shall be to me just like the living woman of my dreams." And he did worship her, too, morning and evening, just as though she were a goddess from above. But during the day, he would look upon her as a real woman, and would talk to her, praising her loveliness or reproaching her playfully for her silence. He would tell her how honored he was that she would choose to remain with such a dull companion as he, and he would often take up a book and read to her a lover's tale.

The love that he had been unable to lavish upon any woman thus found a strange outlet in his devotion to the marble maiden. How foolish it was, and yet how natural, that he should find such pleasure even in pretending that his lovely rooms were at last brightened by the presence of a gracious lady.

One morning, Pygmalion was awakened by the singing of townspeople outside his window. When he looked down into the streets, he saw that they were joyously parading behind a statue of Venus—one that his own hands had carved—for this was a day of celebration in honor of the goddess of love. As Pygmalion watched the throng stream past, he recalled many stories of how Venus had come to the aid of wretched, lovelorn men, and how she had often helped those who worshiped her to gain their heart's desire. "But of course!" he cried out. "That is the answer to my loneliness."

Quickly he made himself ready to join the crowd that was following the statue through the streets. He had never before taken part in one of these ceremonies, and so he felt strangely refreshed as he dressed himself in colorful clothes and placed a wreath of flowers atop his head. Then, stooping to kiss the cold white feet of his marble love, he left his house and hastened after the procession, which was wending its way through all the streets in the city.

To the impatient Pygmalion, it seemed that the parade was moving far too slowly, and that it needn't cover *every* street and alley on its way to the temple of Venus. But in due course the procession finally reached the gates of the temple, and the statue was returned to its place on the altar. Praises were sung and priests conducted long and tedious rites to honor the goddess, but eventually the ceremonies concluded and the citizens returned to their town. Only Pygmalion remained in the temple. He crossed the inlaid floor, now thickly strewn with fresh flowers, and, standing before the altar, he threw some sweet incense into the flame, saying, "Venus, Goddess of Love, to whom all things are possible, refuse not my prayer! Show me your kindness, I beg thee, O Goddess! Take pity on one who so madly loves a lifeless form, and grant me my heart's desire. O Venus, I pray you to bestow the gift of life on the one who holds my heart and my soul and all my love."

Pygmalion waited for some sign that his prayer would be answered. He waited still longer, perhaps for a sign that it would be denied. Nothing happened. How foolish he had been, he thought to himself, to ask that marble be changed to flesh and blood. With a sigh of despair, he turned from the altar and passed out through the temple gates and the surrounding orchard. He saw the townsfolk in the streets laughing and making merry with one another, while he alone was walking back to an empty, silent home, without a soul to welcome him.

"Life without companionship—how miserable!" he murmured, thinking of his fate. And although he was eager to look again upon the face he loved, it saddened him to remember that that face could not be moved by his devotion.

Suddenly, as he reached his own threshold, a strange change of feeling came over him. He saw for the first time what madness it was that he should lose his heart to a statue; he realized at last that love and companionship have meaning only if they are returned, and that that is an act only humans can perform. "Thank you, Venus," he exclaimed, as the first glimmers of peace and contentment appeared on his face. "You have given me an answer to my prayer, unlike though it be to the one I had hoped for. Now I know how foolish it was to ask you to give life to a statue, and you have shown me that it is in this world that I must live, not in a dream world of marble images. Will you, O Goddess, someday send me a helpmate of flesh and blood, now that I have learned the sweetness of love for another?"

Then Pygmalion entered the room where his marble maiden resided, for he still took great joy in looking upon her form and face. He raised his eyes to gaze upon her once again, but there was no statue to be seen! "Gone!" he cried out, his heart aching as never before. "The only thing I have ever loved has been taken from me!"

Just then, a low, soft voice fell upon his ears from behind him. "Pygmalion!" it called.

The poor artist turned quickly to the sound, and there, against the western windows, he saw his beloved standing in the golden light of sunset, a statue no longer, but changed to a living woman, whose breath came gently from the lips that he himself had chiseled. Her slim feet, which his lips had kissed so often, were moving toward him; a rosy blush tinged her cheeks; her hair swirled softly from the breeze that wafted through the open casement; and her eyes shone bright from the newborn life within.

Timidly the maiden drew near, and these were the words that fell in silver tones upon the sculptor's enraptured ears:

"Pygmalion, Venus has heard your prayer. She has given me life today, so that I may become your loving and beloved bride."

At first the sculptor could not believe that what he saw and heard was not a dream, but all doubt vanished when his former statue—now loving companion in life—laid her warm cheek against his and whispered, "No, this is no dream, dearest. Will you still speak to me as lovingly as you did when I stood lifeless on that platform in the corner? Will you still read to me lovers' tales, now that we shall be lovers ourselves?"

Then did Pygmalion assure her that it would always be so, and in overwhelming rapture he kissed her and welcomed her to his home.

A Few Words More

The story of Pygmalion is a love story, and so it is fitting that it is based in a city that paid homage to Venus, the Roman goddess of love. The Romans honored and respected this goddess so much that, although we usually associate only the planet Venus and the rather indelicate term *venereal* with her name, the modern word *ven-*

erate, which means "to look upon with respect, to revere," has come to us from the way that Venus was so respected and revered by the Romans.

Venus's son was called Cupid by the Romans, and it is from his name that we get the word *cupidity* [kyoo-PID-ih-tee], which means "avarice, greed, the love of money." (You may recall that it was *cupidity*—the love of money, not money itself—that the Bible describes as "the root of all evil.") The Greeks called this god of love Eros (he was the son of Aphrodite), which was the Greek word meaning "love." From the name Eros we get today's lusty adjectives *erotic* and *erogenous*.

The Story of Theseus

Part One

About the story:

Theseus holds a special place of honor among all the heroes of Athens. Numerous plays and stories were written about his life by Greek and Roman writers alike. These works tell of the many adventures Theseus had throughout his life; for example, he saved the life of mighty Hercules, he was one of the Argonauts who went on the quest for the Golden Fleece, and he befriended Oedipus when everyone else scorned the once-great king. The two tales that follow show Theseus to be strong and brave, to stand steadfast for what he believes is right, and it is these qualities that endeared him to the people of Athens and made him the model for what the ancients thought a ruler should be.

Approximate reading time (for Part One): 12 minutes

Vocabulary and pronunciation guide (for Part One):

Theseus [THEE-see-us *(th* as in *thin)]*
Aegeus [EE-jee-us]
Aethra [EETH-rah]
Sciron [SYE-ron]
Sinis [SYE-nus]
Procrustes [pro-CRUST-eez]

There was once a man named Aegeus [EE-jee-us], who, although he was still a young man, was king of the great city of Athens. Now, because he was still quite young for a king, Aegeus found more pleasure in travel than he did in remaining at home and governing his own people. And it happened that, while he was on one of his lengthy stays in southern Greece, Aegeus met a beautiful woman in a village there, a woman named Aethra [EETH-rah], and they fell in love, and they were married. After some time, Aegeus grew restless, and he longed to return to Athens and govern his own people once again. So, in spite of his love for Aethra, and in spite of the fact that she had just given birth to their infant son, Aegeus decided to leave the village, alone, and to leave the task of raising the child to Aethra.

Before he went back to Athens, though, Aegeus buried his sword and sandals under a heavy boulder, and he said to his wife, "When our boy is old enough and strong enough to lift this stone, let him take the sword and the sandals and make his way to Athens, for then he will be man enough to succeed me on the throne." Then, kissing his wife and baby, Aegeus walked away, never to return to that village again.

Aethra named her son Theseus [THEE-see-us *(th* as in *thin)*], and as he grew, she taught him many things, for she knew that he would someday be a king. Theseus learned the lessons of nature and also the wisdom of the world's great thinkers; he learned to be brave, but he also learned to respect the gods. And all the while Theseus improved his body and his strength, longing for the day when he could lift the giant stone his mother had told him about and thereby prove himself a man.

It was not many years before that day arrived. Theseus had grown tall, and though he was still quite young, his muscles were like iron. He had become an expert swordsman and such a skillful boxer and wrestler that no one in all the land around dared to challenge him. His mother knew that the time had come for him to join his father in Athens, and so, much as she feared losing her son forever, she led him to the massive boulder under which Aegeus had placed the sword and sandals. Theseus put his bulging arms around it, and his hands grasped it firmly on the sides. Then, with his knees bent and his back arched, he gave the huge rock a mighty upward jerk, and up it rose, as though it had been made of paper instead of stone. Theseus raised the boulder above his head and heaved it deep into the surrounding woods. Then he looked down at the sword of bronze, its hilt glittering with gold, and at the pair of golden sandals that had been placed there by his father long ago.

Tears filled Aethra's eyes as she told Theseus that the time had come for him to take the sword and sandals to his father in

Athens. Theseus, too, wept now, for he suddenly realized that, although he had longed for the day when he could join his father, that day would also be the last he would ever see his mother. But Aethra comforted him, saying, "Weep not, my son, for that which has been fated must come to be. We cannot know what the gods intend, and so we must do as they command and try to live a good life as best we can." And then she kissed Theseus one last time, and she began to make her way back to the village. Theseus gathered up the sword and placed the sandals on his feet. Still weeping, he turned and began to walk in the opposite direction, but he never once looked back.

Now, all along his way, Theseus had many thoughts, and some fears, come to him about what it would be like to meet his father. What if the king has other sons whom he loves, thought Theseus, and what if he does not accept me? After all, he has forgotten me since I was born, so why should he welcome me now? What have I done that he would want to look upon me as a son? These thoughts saddened him greatly, until at last he thought of a plan, and he cried aloud, "Yes, I will make my father love me by proving myself worthy of his love. I will win such honor and renown and do such deeds that Aegeus shall be proud of me no matter how many sons he may have!" And so he determined to take the long way to Athens, over the mountains and through many strange lands where he could find adventure and where monsters and robbers preyed upon helpless people. And this is just what he did.

Along his way, Theseus was set upon by robbers who lay hidden behind every turn in the road and by cruel giants that set all kinds of traps to ensnare unwary travelers. First there was Sciron [SYE-ron], a robber who would throw his victims over a cliff where they would be eaten by a giant tortoise who lived at the bottom. Theseus not only wrestled this robber into submission, but then he threw Sciron over the cliff so that the tortoise could put a fitting end to this evildoer. Then there was another savage robber, Sinis [SYE-nus], who was called "the pine-bender" because he tortured his victims by bending down two tall pine trees and tying his prey between them. When the trees were allowed to spring back, the bodies of the poor travelers would be torn to pieces. Theseus rid the countryside of this monster, too, and he gave to Sinis the same death between the trees with which Sinis had tortured so many others.

There were many other monsters and barbarians that Theseus defeated on his journey, too, and all along the way his fame among the people in the surrounding lands grew and grew. He had made the hills safe to live upon and the roadways safe to travel.

Now, as he came ever nearer to the Athenian countryside, he met an old man who was trying to gather a load of driftwood, but his burden was far greater than his weary old bones could carry. Theseus did not ignore the old man's plight, as so many others who had passed along the road had done. And when Theseus picked up all the wood and carried it upon his own shoulders, the stranger blessed him and asked where he was bound. Theseus told him that he was following the road to Athens, and with that a look of terror came over the old man's face as he warned Theseus to beware of a wicked robber named Procrustes [pro-CRUST-eez], who preyed upon people who traveled that road.

"He invites his victims into his home," the old man warned, "and he offers them a bed to rest on for the night. He boasts that this bed fits people of all sizes, and surely it does, but none ever rose from it alive. For if a man be too tall for it, Procrustes lops off the legs of his guest till they fit just right. And if a man be too short, then he is stretched from head and foot until he, too, is the perfect size for the bed. Oh, the pain and horror of it all! Fly from this murderous beast," cried the old man to Theseus. "He will have no pity on you because of your youth or kindness. Even yesterday he brought a young man and a maiden to rest at his house, and he fitted them both upon his bed. The young man's hands and feet he cut off, but the maiden's limbs he stretched until she died, and so both perished in a most miserable way. Turn back, my friend, and do not be another of his victims."

"I have no need to flee," replied Theseus, "now that you have warned me what I may expect from Procrustes. Besides, this land must be rid of such monsters, and I will see to it that it is."

Thus prepared, Theseus was not surprised when he later encountered another stranger along the road, who called to him in a friendly voice and offered him the hospitality of his home for the night. "And might you have a special bed for me as well?" answered Theseus. Then did the face of the stranger, who was none other than Procrustes himself, take on the look of fear, for his would-be victim was not to be taken by surprise. Procrustes reached for his sword, but Theseus leaped upon him and encircled the monster's body with his mighty arms. Tighter and tighter he closed his embrace, all the while accusing and berating Procrustes for the crimes he had committed, until at last, with one powerful constriction, he squeezed the very life out of the vicious beast.

Then he bore the body to Procrustes' home, where he found great wealth and treasure, all of which had been stolen from passersby. He called all the people of the surrounding country together, and he divided up the treasure among them. And then he resumed his journey once again, but his fame and honor became legend among the people, and they spread the word of his heroic deeds far and wide, so that there was no corner of Greece that had not heard of the mighty Theseus or of his many noble achievements.

At last, weary and footsore, but looking like a king's son, every inch of him, Theseus came to the gates of his father's palace. He went up the steep stairs and made his way to the great hall, where he saw many young men feasting and drinking wine. Soon he learned that these were not the king's sons, but the king's nephews, and he was told that because the king had no son to reign after he died, one of these foolish fellows would someday be king of Athens. "It is no wonder," Theseus muttered to himself, "that the land is full of robbers, if the like of these are destined to rule."

Then he strode into the midst of the feast, and he announced that he was Theseus, slayer of many monsters, and he wished an audience with the king. Well, Theseus's fame had arrived in Athens long before he did, and so everyone knew and honored the name as soon as it was spoken. King Aegeus came running from his chamber into the great hall to meet the man who had rid his kingdom of so many evils, and when Theseus saw the king, the young man's heart leaped into his mouth. He wanted so much to hold his father in his arms, but he realized that Aegeus had no idea at all that it was his son who stood before him. And so Theseus took off his sword and sandals, and, bowing low, he presented them to his father, saying, "You left these for me under a large rock long ago, and I have come here to return them."

Aegeus stepped back a pace, and he looked at the lad until

his eyes grew dim, and then he threw his arms around Theseus's neck and he wept, and Theseus wept on his neck, till
they had no strength left to weep anymore. Then Aegeus
turned to all the people, and he cried, "Behold my son, who
has come to me after all these years, a better man than his father was before him." And all the people cheered to see their
king and his son united again, and they made Theseus welcome in their land, which would be his land, too, from this
time on.

A Few Words More

The vicious robbers that Theseus encountered on his
way to Athens each carried out various forms of torture
upon their victims. We can see in this word *torture* the
Latin word *tortus*, which meant "to twist or bend," re-
minding us of the earliest methods of torturing a human
being. But the idea of "twisting" is also apparent in
many other common words as well. A blackmailer
might try to *extort* (*ex-* meaning "from") money by
twisting it from his victim; faces or figures may be *dis-
torted* (*dis-* meaning "away") or *contorted* (*con-* meaning
"with") when they are twisted out of their normal
shape; a clever *retort* (*re-* meaning "back") twists a remark back upon the opponent. Even the *tortoise*, which
we saw as a maneater in this myth, bears the *tort* root in
its name because of the "twisted" appearance of its feet.

The highwayman called Procrustes, who had a most
ingenious method of torturing those who accepted his
hospitality, has given us a word that is quite commonly
used in education, politics, and other fields as well: *procrustean* [pro-CRUST-ee-an]. A procrustean system or
plan forces individuals—no matter how different they
may be—to fit the same mold or to conform to a single
type or pattern. Regulations that ruthlessly or arbi-
trarily attempt to achieve conformity are often criticized
as being a "procrustean bed."

The Story of Theseus

Part Two

Approximate reading time (for Part Two): 12 minutes
Vocabulary and pronunciation guide (for Part Two):

    equinox [EE-quin-ox]: the one day each spring and fall
      when the night and day are each twelve hours long
    tribute: a payment made by one ruler or nation to an-
      other for protection
    Crete [KREET]: the largest of the Greek islands
    Minos [MY-nos]
    Minotaur [MY-nuh-tore]: a monster with the body of a
      man and the head of a bull
    Labyrinth [LAB-uh-rinth]: an intricate maze
    Daedalus [DEAD-uh-luss]
    doleful: mournful; melancholy
    Ariadne [air-ee-ADD-nee]

Theseus stayed with his father all the winter, and when the spring equinox [EE-quin-ox] drew near, all the Athenians grew sad and silent, and Theseus saw this and asked why it should be, but no one would explain it to him. Then he went to his father, and he asked about why the people were sad, but Aegeus turned his face away and wept. "Do not ask, my son, about evils that must come to pass," he said. "It is enough to wait for them and face them when they arrive."

And when the spring equinox did come, there also came to Athens a black-sailed ship, which put into the harbor, and a herald came from the ship and made his way to the market-place. Here he cried aloud, "O people of Athens, hear me well.

It is time for your yearly tribute, so assemble your youths and maidens at once, for we sail with the tide to Crete [KREET]."

Then Theseus went to the herald and said, "I am a stranger here. Pray, tell me the meaning of your message so that I might know why mighty Athens should pay a tribute to anyone."

And the herald related to Theseus the whole story of the war between Athens and Crete, and how King Minos [MY-nos] of Crete had laid siege to Athens and would have let all the people there starve to death if they had not agreed to pay him a tribute each year. But what a terrible price the Athenians agreed to pay for their lives: Every year, at the spring equinox, the people of Athens must send seven youths and seven young maidens to King Minos, who then feeds them, alive, to a terrible monster called the Minotaur [MY-nuh-tore]. So once each year, all the boys and girls of Athens are called together in the marketplace, and there they draw lots to see which fourteen unlucky ones will be sent away to Crete, there to be given to the Minotaur for food.

Now when Theseus heard this incredible tale, he knew why there was so much sorrow in the city, and he went to his father and said, "I will go myself with these youths and maidens, and I shall slay the Minotaur and rid Athens of ever having to pay this tribute again."

But Aegeus shuddered at this and cried, "You shall not go, my son, for you are the light of my old age and the person who must rule this land when I am dead and gone. If you go to fight the Minotaur, you will surely die a horrible death, for the beast is kept inside the Labyrinth [LAB-uh-rinth], which the cunning architect Daedalus [DEAD-uh-luss] built with so many winding and bewildering paths that no one who enters it can ever find his way out again. Here, entangled in the winding corridors, lives a monster who is half man and half bull and who feeds on human flesh. No, my son, I beg you not to give up your life this way."

But Theseus was only the more convinced that it was his duty to slay the horrid beast, and he told his father that somehow he would find a way to kill the Minotaur and escape the Labyrinth as well. Aegeus clung to his son's knees and, weeping bitterly, pleaded for him to stay, but Theseus had made up his mind. Finally, seeing that Theseus would not be swayed from his course, his father asked him one favor, saying, "Promise me that, if you do come back alive and well, you will strike the black sail of the ship and hoist a white one instead, for I will be watching every day from the cliffs, and if only white sails I see, then I will know that you are well and will someday return to my side. Promise me this, my son, and may the gods be with you on your quest."

And Theseus promised he would honor his father's request, and went out to the marketplace where the herald stood, watching the drawing of lots that would decide who was to sail in that doleful crew. And the people stood wailing and weeping as first one was chosen, then the next, and the next. But Theseus strode into the midst, and cried, "Here is a youth who needs not be chosen by lot; I will be one of the seven." Then did the people give a great cheer, for they now had hope that perhaps mighty Theseus could put an end to their yearly misery.

The townspeople followed Theseus and the thirteen unfortunates down to the black-sailed ship, and the herald from Crete was with them and so was King Aegeus. Theseus tried to comfort Aegeus, saying, "Father, I am young and strong, and I have overcome many monsters and giants before this. Fear not, for this Minotaur is not immortal, and if he can be slain, then I shall do it." But his words cheered neither his father nor his companions, for they knew that even if the monster could be slain, whoever accomplished the feat could never find the way back to the entrance of the Labyrinth. So there was much sobbing both on the ship and on the dock as the tide came in and the fairest of all Athens sailed off toward their deaths on Minos's island kingdom.

After several days, the ship reached Crete, and the young people were led into the king's presence. Minos looked at each one to assure himself that the exact tribute had been paid, and then he commanded his guards to take them to a prison cell and lock them up this night, for in the morning they would be fed to the monster one by one. Then Theseus stepped forward and cried, "A favor, O King! Let me be thrown first to the beast, for I came here of my own will, and it is only right that I should precede those who were forced here by lot."

Minos, then, could see that this was no ordinary youth standing before him, and when he learned that it was, in fact, the prince of Athens, he said, "It is wrong that one so brave should meet such an inglorious end, and so I say to you, brave prince, go back to your home this night; the Minotaur will be satisfied with your companions alone."

But Theseus would not leave the others, and he repeated his demand that he be the first of all to face the monster. Now Minos was angered at having his kindness refused, and he said to Theseus, "You have sealed your own fate, rash prince; tomorrow you shall have your wish. Now, guards, away with them!"

It happened that King Minos's daughter, the beautiful and tender-hearted Ariadne [air-ee-ADD-nee], had witnessed this encounter, and her beating heart was filled with love for the courage that Theseus had displayed. "He shall not die, if there is some way I can save him," she said to herself.

Later that night, Ariadne crept down to the dungeon beneath the palace, and she unlocked the cell in which Theseus was being held. "Flee to the ship at once," she said to him, "for I have bribed the guards to look the other way. Take your friends with you, but I beg you to take me, too, for my father will cause me to die a miserable death when he finds out what I have done."

Theseus stood silent for a while, for he was stunned by her beauty. At last he said to her, "Dear princess, I cannot go home in peace until I have slain this Minotaur and avenged the deaths of the youths and maidens he has so cruelly devoured. Help me in this quest and I shall gladly take you home with me in triumph."

Then she loved him all the more, and she said, "Fair prince, you are too bold, but I can be of help to you. Here is a sharp sword for you to carry, so that you won't have to face the beast unarmed. And here is a ball of string, the end of which you must fasten tightly to the gate of the Labyrinth, and the string must unwind without breaking through all the twisting passageways so that, after you have slain the monster, you can follow the string back to the entrance."

Now Theseus smiled, for he knew that he would be safe. He kissed Ariadne for a long while, and she wept for fear that her plan might fail. Then the princess led him, quietly, out of the palace and toward the great Labyrinth that lay some distance away. At the gate, Theseus made sure to fasten one end of the string tightly, and he played out the rest of the ball as he wandered through the many dark and winding passages.

After encountering a seemingly endless set of blind corridors and blocked passageways, and after doubling back his course so many times that he had lost all sense of direction, he at last came into an open court. There lay the Minotaur, fast asleep, for he expected no food until the next morning. Theseus stopped short, for he had never seen such a strange beast. His body was that of a man, but his head was the head of a bull, and his teeth were like those of a lion, so sharp and strong that they could tear apart any prey. The monster sensed the presence of someone nearby, and he awoke with a roar that sent a shiver through Theseus's body and weakened his knees. Still the prince knew his duty, and he raised the sword Adriadne had given him, just as the Minotaur charged headlong toward him. Theseus stepped nimbly aside, avoiding the monster's charge, and he struck the body of the passing beast with his sword, wounding the Minotaur and causing it to bellow even louder. Again it charged, with its head down and its sharp horns ready to rip apart the body of the man who had caused him this pain. But this time Theseus brought his sword above his head with both hands, and as the beast rushed blindly by, down came the blade with such a force that the monster's head was severed completely from its body, and its life's blood gushed out all around.

Now, weary from his adventure, Theseus turned to locate the ball of string he had brought with him, and finding it nearby, he followed its course through all the passageways he had traversed before, until at last it led him to the gate of the Labyrinth. Here, waiting for him, was none other than Ariadne, and Theseus held her tightly in his arms as he whispered, "It is done! The terrible beast is dead!"

Together they returned to the dungeon, where they opened the cells of all the Athenians who had expected to die on the following morning. Then Theseus led them all, including the lovely Princess Ariadne, down to the black-sailed ship on which they had come to Crete. He lifted the anchor, and before morning could alert King Minos to the events that had taken place that night, they were well out to sea and rejoicing at their great good fortune.

Ah, but great tragedy lay just ahead, for in his haste to return to Athens, Theseus forgot the promise he had made to his father, and he did not replace the black sail with a white one. Aegeus, therefore, who watched the sea day after day from high atop an overlooking cliff, straining his tired old eyes to see the color of every sail in the distance, now was filled with terror at the sight of the black-sailed vessel he had feared so. Knowing by this sign that his dear son Theseus had perished in Crete, Aegeus felt that his own life was no longer worth living, and so he leaped from the cliff and fell to his death in the sea below. From that day on, the water that claimed Aegeus's life became known by the name of the old king, and still today it is called the Aegean Sea.

A Few Words More

Although, as we have seen, many modern words have come into English directly from the ancient myths, the tale of Theseus and the Minotaur has enriched our language, not by originating a word, but by giving a new and different meaning to an existing word. Even in Chaucer's time, there was a common English word *clewe*, which meant "a ball of thread or string." Now the story of Theseus's escape from the Labyrinth, and the story of Ariadne's ingenious method for him to retrace his steps, were well known and frequently told among the English people. And because it was the *clewe* of string that guided the hero back to the entrance of the maze, the meaning of the word *clewe* gradually changed, and the word began to be applied to other situations in which it signified not "a ball of string" but "the ball of string that solved a great mystery." Time also worked a change on the spelling of the word, so that today, when we use the word *clue*, we mean "anything that aids the solution to a mystery or a problem," but without the help of Theseus and Ariadne, we might be talking about something entirely different.

Jason and the Golden Fleece

Part One

About the story:

>   This is the story of what was, perhaps, the first great quest in European literature. Like the quest for the Holy Grail, or Don Quixote's quest to restore chivalry to the world, or Luke Skywalker's quest to prevent the take-over of the universe, this is the tale of a courageous hero who must travel far from home and encounter numerous dangers before his determination and goodness finally win the day.

>   The tale presented here refers only briefly to the many monsters and dangers that Jason faces along his journey to the land of the Golden Fleece, and it does not mention his companions by name, though some of them—like Hercules, Theseus, and Orpheus—may be known to readers and listeners alike. It does, however, provide a brief and exciting introduction to one of the most famous adventure stories ever told.

Approximate reading time (for Part One): 7 minutes

Vocabulary and pronunciation guide (for Part One):

>   **Nephele** [NEFF-uh-lee]
>   **Phryxus** [FRIX-us]
>   **Helle** [HELL-ee]
>   **Ino** [EYE-no]
>   **oracle** [OR-uh-cull]: a temple where a priest or priestess would issue prophecies and answers to questions
>   **Colchis** [KAHL-kiss]

L ong, long ago there lived in Greece a proud king who had a beautiful wife named Nephele [NEFF-uh-lee]. Now *Nephele* means "cloud," and there was something about this fair young queen that made one think of soft pink-and-gold-edged clouds on a summer's evening.

The king and queen had two children, a boy named Phryxus [FRIX-us] and a girl named Helle [HELL-ee], and they brought such pleasure to their parents that the whole family lived each day and night in happiness. Only one thing marred their joy, and it was a strange thing indeed. For in the hot summer days, when the sky was cloudless and the air was dry and still, Nephele would grow thin and pale, and then she would leave her home for a long time, and come back only when the soft rainclouds were again in the air. Now some people said that the clouds were her sisters, and that when they left the sky, she had to travel far away with them. But no one really knew where Nephele went, or why.

As you can imagine, there came a time when the king began to grow tired of his wife's long and mysterious absences, and there was, as well, a beautiful, dark-eyed lady in town who encouraged his anger, for she had long been in love with the king, and she saw this as a chance to have him for herself. The lady's name was Ino [EYE-no], but there was precious little lady in her, for in truth she was a witch with strange and magic powers. Before long, Ino had made the king forget all about Nephele, and had even talked him into marrying herself instead.

Now Ino hated Phryxus and Helle because they were not her own children, and because they were beautiful and good. Soon she began to mistreat them in terrible ways. She took their fine royal clothes and made them dress in rags. She wouldn't allow them to live in the palace, and instead they had to live with the shepherd's children in a tumbledown old cottage, and they had to work all day long guarding the shepherd's flocks on the hillsides.

But, if the truth were known, Phryxus and Helle were really not very unhappy, for they loved to frolic in the green fields all day and besides, they did not care much about what they ate or wore. Their only grief was at the loss of their lovely young mother, Nephele.

Nephele had now been gone a long, long while. The sky was cloudless day after day. Not a drop of rain fell, the fields became parched and dry, and all the crops withered away. There was not enough food for the people, and everywhere they were dying of hunger.

The king at last sent messengers to an oracle [OR-uh-cull] in a distant city, asking what he must do to bring back food and health to his people. But his wicked wife, Ino, who was now the queen of the land, saw this as a chance to rid herself of the king's two children once and for all. And so she secretly bribed the messengers and told them that, when they returned, they were to announce that the oracle had said Phryxus and Helle must be killed before rain would once again fall upon the land.

Now these messengers were eager for the gold that the queen offered, and so they did just as they were told. In a few days, they came back to the king with their false report, and they announced to all the nobles who were assembled at the palace that only when Phryxus and Helle were dead would comfort and plenty come back to the people of the kingdom. The king was very sorrowful at this news, but he knew that he could not disobey the gods, and, with Ino's encouragement, he ordered that the sacrifice be carried out with all possible haste.

Everything was prepared, and the children were brought from the hills to the courtyard of the palace and decked out in white robes and flowers, as was the custom in those days for adorning things that were about to be sacrificed. Here they were to be tied and placed on top of a huge pile of logs that would soon become a raging bonfire. But just as they neared the spot where they were to be put to death, suddenly there came flying from the heavens a golden-fleeced ram, which the gods had sent in answer to Nephele's prayer. Nephele, you see, only seemed to be far away; in truth, she had been watching over her children from above all the while. Quick as a flash, Phryxus sprang upon the ram's back with Helle behind him, and the next minute they were flying high above the courtyard, far beyond the reach of the astonished people below.

Over land and sea flew the golden ram—faster and faster every moment, until Helle became so weary of the dizzy flight that she loosened her grip from the ram's golden fleece, and she fell down and down through the air until she splashed into the water of a narrow sea that they happened to be flying over at the time, and she was drowned.

But Phryxus clung to the ram's back, and they flew on over the great Black Sea until they reached a country called Colchis [KAHL-kiss]. There the ram glided gently down to the ground, so tired and weary from this long and difficult journey that it soon died. Phryxus stripped the beautiful Golden Fleece from the ram's back, and he hung it on an oak tree in a dark forest. And there it was guarded by a monstrous dragon that never slept—neither during the night nor during the day—so that nobody dared go near the fleece. And Phryxus remained in that land and married the king's daughter, and they lived happily together for many years until Phryxus died. And all this time the wondrous Golden Fleece hung on the branch of that same oak tree, guarded over by that same dragon, and for many years thereafter the legend of the Golden Fleece spread to all parts of the world. No one was able to steal the fleece or to deceive the dragon who guarded it.

A Few Words More

Had it not been for the ram with the Golden Fleece, both Phryxus and Helle would have been burned to a crisp on a bonfire. Although the word *bonfire* came into our language from the Scots, and much later than the time of the classics, its tie to this tale comes from its original meaning: a "bonefire" was a fire that was used for the burning of corpses.

It may also be interesting to know that the narrow sea in which Helle was drowned was for centuries referred to as the *Hellespont,* meaning "the sea of Helle." Today, this strait, which is in the northwestern part of Turkey, is called the Dardanelles.

Jason and the Golden Fleece

Part Two

Approximate reading time (for Part Two): 8 minutes
Vocabulary and pronunciation guide (for Part Two):
> **Aeson** [EE-son]
> **Chiron** [KYE-ron]
> **centaur** [SEN-tore]: a creature that was half human and half horse
> **lyre** [LYE-er]: an ancient stringed instrument, some-what like a guitar without a neck
> **Juno** [JEW-no]: queen of the gods; wife of Jupiter
> **Pelias** [PEE-lee-us]
> **bade** [BAD]: offered, invited; the past tense of *bid*
> **prow:** the fore part of the hull on a ship; the bow

*L*ong after Phryxus had died, there lived in a certain country a king and queen who had but one child, a boy named Jason. The king, whose name was Aeson [EE-son], was a good-natured man, but a rather weak king. He could not defend his kingdom, and after a while his own brother, Jason's uncle, came to Aeson's kingdom with a large army, and he drove King Aeson and his family out of the land and seized the throne for himself. Thereafter, Aeson was forced to live far away, in poverty and without friends.

Aeson always wanted the very best for his son, however, and so he sent his boy, Jason, away to be educated by Chiron [KYE-ron], who was thought to be the wisest person in the world. Chiron might be called only half a person, for Chiron was a centaur [SEN-tore], and while centaurs had heads and arms like those of men, their bodies and legs were like those of horses. Although centaurs were, for the most part, savage and monstrous creatures, Chiron was a much different sort altogether. He was a scholar and was famed for knowing more about everything than anyone else in all of Greece. He knew about the stars, and about which plants could cure diseases; he was a great archer, and he could play the lyre [LYE-er] and sing songs and tell stories better than any human in all the land, and that is why many kings sent their sons to him to be educated.

So little Jason went to the centaur's cave on the mountaintop, and he spent his youth there learning to hunt and to fish and to use the sword and the spear and, what was better still, to be truthful and kind.

But at last Jason grew to be a man, and then Chiron told him that his father, Aeson, was not just a friendless pauper, but had once been a king. He explained to Jason how Aeson's throne had been taken from him, and he told the boy that his duty now lay in reclaiming the kingdom that was rightfully his father's own. When the time for parting came, Chiron went with Jason to the foot of the mountain and said, "Forget not the lessons I have taught you. Always speak and act the truth, and be kind to all who need your help."

So Jason started on his journey. When he had gone some distance, he came to a stream that had been flooded by the spring rains. On the bank there stood an old woman looking for some way across. Mindful of what the centaur had said, Jason spoke to her and offered to carry her across the swollen stream. The old woman gladly accepted the offer, and Jason lifted her upon his shoulders and entered the rushing river. The water dashed against him with great force; he had to struggle with all his might, and he was out of breath when he landed his companion safely on the other shore. But you can imagine Jason's surprise to see not the old woman he had carried across, but the stately form of the goddess Juno [JEW-no], queen of all the immortals, standing before him.

"Young man," said she, "you have a good and brave heart, and you shall not regret your kindness to an old woman." And in the next instant she vanished.

When Jason recovered from his surprise and started to go on his way, he saw, to his dismay, that one of his sandals had been lost in the rushing water, and so he had to walk the rest of the way with only one shoe. He came at last to the palace of his father's brother, whose name was Pelias [PEE-lee-us], and he was taken straightaway to see the king.

The king turned pale with fear at the sight of Jason, for an oracle had foretold that his kingdom would be taken from him by a youth wearing only one sandal, and one of Jason's feet, as you know, was bare.

But the crafty king pretended to be very glad indeed to see his nephew. He bade [BAD] him sit down and rest himself, and he placed food and drink before him. While they were eating, the king told many stories of brave men who lived long ago. "Ah, those were the days," he sighed. "But such heroes do not live in our times."

"You are wrong!" cried Jason. "There are many heroes waiting only for the chance to do great deeds."

At this the king laughed out loud. "You are a foolish lad," the king chided, "but it is time that I find out who you are, and why you have come to this kingdom."

"I am Jason, son of the rightful king, Aeson," he replied, "and I have come to take back my father's kingdom."

Then Pelias grew pale again, but he was cunning, and he leaped up and embraced the lad, and made much of finding him after all these years. And he said that it was good for the kingdom to have a new ruler, for he himself was old and was tired of the responsibilities of being king. "But that can never be," the king lamented, pretending to be sorrowful at the thought. "For there is a curse upon this kingdom—that it shall not be ruled by another until the Golden Fleece is brought here from the land at the end of the world." And then he told the story of Phryxus and Helle, and of the Golden Fleece hanging in the woods, guarded by the dragon who never sleeps.

When he had finished, Jason sprang to his feet and cried, "I will prove to you, O King, that the race of heroes is not dead. I will bring you the Golden Fleece, or die in the attempt."

This, of course, was exactly what the king wanted to hear, for he knew there was very little chance of Jason's ever returning from such a journey. But, of course, he did not show how pleased he was.

Jason then proceeded to construct a good, strong ship, which he called the *Argo,* and he sent out messengers all over Greece to his friends who had been schooled with him in the centaur's cave. He warned them that there would be fighting and danger and even a dragon to kill, but they all came, for they were eager to help Jason regain his kingdom. They gathered by the shore and helped in fitting out the *Argo* for the voyage, and they called themselves the Argonauts.

Now it happened that the great goddess Juno had sent to Jason a gift to show that she had not forgotten her promise to help him. It was a wondrous piece of sacred oak, carved into a figurehead and fitted onto the prow of the *Argo*. And truly wondrous it was indeed, for the greatest wonder of it all was the fact that this piece of wood could actually speak! Many a time during the long voyage, when Jason was in great danger and did not know what to do, he consulted that figurehead, and he always received good advice. But that is getting ahead of the story.

When the *Argo* was finished and all the provisions had been put aboard, the Argonauts waited for the tide and at last set sail. High atop his mountain home, old Chiron saw the swift ship depart with his best and brightest boys on board, and he waved his mighty arms and prayed that their courage and wisdom would bring them home safely once again.

A Few Words More

The word *Argonaut* means "a sailor on the *Argo*," its last syllable coming from the Greek word *nautilos*, which meant "sailor." Not only do the words *astronaut* ("star sailor") and *cosmonaut* ("sailor of the cosmos") come from this Greek root, but so does the word *nautical*, which means "having to do with the sea."

The Greek word meaning "ship," *naus*, provides the root for the modern word *nausea*, which is rather like the seasickness one experiences on a ship. The Roman word for "ship" was similar to that of the Greeks, *navis*, and from it we get such common words as *navigate* and *navy*.

Jason and the Golden Fleece

Part Three

Approximate reading time (for Part Three): 10 minutes
Vocabulary and pronunciation guide (for Part Three):
   Harpies: winged monsters each having the head of a
      woman, but the body and claws of a giant bird
   Aeetes [ee-EE-teez]
   Medea [meh-DEE-uh]
   brazen [BRAY-zen]: made of brass

*F*or many weeks and many months, Jason and his crew of
bold adventurers sailed on the *Argo,* and when the wind
failed or when they were in dangerous waters, they took
to their oars, and they guided the ship through each perilous
situation. They visited many islands and encountered many
strange creatures along the way. They fought with a band of
hideous giants, each having six hands; they escaped from the
water nymphs who wanted to imprison them in their crystal
caves; they slew the vicious Harpies, those frightful flying creatures with hooked beaks and iron claws and shrieking cries;
and they navigated their way through the treacherous Wandering Rocks, which would suddenly crash together when a ship
tried to pass between them.

   After all these, and other adventures as well, the Argonauts
finally arrived in Colchis and were brought to the palace of the
king. Now the king, whose name was Aeetes [ee-EE-teez], had
two children, a little boy of whom he was very fond, and
a dark-eyed, dark-haired teenage daughter named Medea
[meh-DEE-uh], who was a witch and had many magical ways
about her.

   Aeetes was seated on his throne, with his little son at his feet and Medea at his right hand, when the Argonauts were brought before him. Jason was asked what his business was in Colchis, and when he answered that he had come to take the Golden Fleece back to Greece, the king laughed aloud and said, "You have come on a very bold mission, but the Fleece of Gold can be won only by those of great courage. If you can perform three tasks I set out for you, only then will I know that such courage is yours, and only then will I allow you to carry away the Fleece."

Now the tone in which the king made this challenge showed that he was not afraid of losing the Golden Fleece, but Jason was not discouraged, and he asked the king to tell him about the three tasks that he must perform.

"The first task," the king replied, "is to yoke two fierce, fire-breathing bulls to the plow, and with them to till four acres of land. The next is to sow the field with dragon's teeth and to conquer all the armed warriors that will then spring up out of the earth from these teeth. And the third is to kill the fierce dragon that guards the Golden Fleece in the woods, but who never sleeps by night or by day. When you have succeeded in doing these three things, you may take the Golden Fleece back with you to Greece." Having said this to Jason, the king dismissed all the Argonauts with a wave of his hand.

Although Jason would not let the king see it, he was just a little discouraged when he heard what the tasks were. He walked away from the palace, down toward the shore where the *Argo* was anchored, and he thought of Juno's promise and wished that she would help him now.

When he came to the ship, he found that there was help awaiting him. For Medea, the king's daughter, had fallen deeply in love with him, and had come to talk with him and offer him her aid. She promised to tell Jason certain secrets that would help him to do the tasks that seemed so impossible, if, in return, he would make her his wife and take her back with him to his home in Greece.

It may seem strange that Medea was willing to leave her home and all the people who loved her, to go so far away with this stranger. Indeed, the girl herself hardly knew why she did it. But the truth was that Juno had not forgotten her promise to help Jason, and the only way she could do it was by making Medea love him so much that she would be willing to give up everything for his sake. And so it really was Juno who was helping Jason.

The king's daughter gave Jason a magic potion that had the power to protect whoever was anointed with it from harm by either swords or fire, and then she told him just what he must do to overcome the fierce bulls and the armed men. After she left him, he paced up and down the seashore for a long time, thinking about Medea and about the tasks the morrow would bring.

The next morning all the people of Colchis went in a great crowd to the field where Jason was to meet his death, as they thought. In the midst of them sat King Aeetes himself, with Medea at his right hand. In all that vast crowd, she was the only one who dared to hope that Jason would be successful.

As soon as Jason entered the field, the two bulls came snorting and bellowing toward him. If you could have seen the creatures, you would have believed, as all the people did, that Jason's last hour had come. They were great ugly creatures, with hoofs of brass and horns pointed with iron. As they came trampling along, making the ground tremble at each step of their brazen [BRAY-zen] hoofs, they breathed out curling flames from their nostrils, so that the fields and the air itself seemed to be on fire.

But Jason did not feel the heat of the flames, thanks to Medea's magic potion. He went up close to the angry creatures and, seizing them by the horns, dashed their heads quickly together until the bulls were stunned. Then he swiftly slipped the yoke over their heads. The bulls were now as gentle as cows, and Jason plowed the four acres in straight ridges and furrows.

Next he was given a sack of dragon's teeth, and he sowed these teeth, on the left and the right, in the soil he had just turned up. In less time than it takes to tell, a mass of helmets began to show above the ground, just as the little leaves pierce through the soil in the springtime. But, whereas the leaves are followed by pretty blossoms, these helmets covered a very ugly crop of fierce, armed soldiers who leaped out of the furrows, all furious for battle, and all rushed to slay Jason. Remembering Medea's advice, he picked up a large stone and threw it into their midst, which caused each of the soldiers to think that his neighbor had thrown the stone. They turned their attention away from Jason, and instead they turned upon each other with their spears and swords. In a few minutes, they were all fighting and struggling in a confused mass, and they fought so fiercely that in a short time the field was strewn with the dead bodies of the men who had sprung up from the dragon's teeth.

Of course, the people all rejoiced at Jason's success, but the king looked angry and sullen. He knew very well that Jason could not have succeeded except by the aid of magic, and he suspected that in some way Medea had helped this stranger. Therefore, when Jason asked for leave to begin his third task, the king answered that he had done enough for one day, and that he should rest until tomorrow.

But that evening, Medea, who could see that her father suspected her, came to Jason and told him that he must kill the dragon that very night and then sail for home. She said that she feared her father would put her to a cruel death and that he had planned for some harm to befall the Argonauts as well. She gave Jason a drug that would put the dragon to sleep, and Jason made his way alone into the dark forest.

He had not gone far when he noticed a golden light among the forest trees, and he knew that he must be near the treasure he was seeking. So he went along carefully, and when he came within sight of the dragon, he doused his spearhead with the magic drug, and he cast his spear with a mighty throw, just as Chiron had taught him. The point embedded itself in one of the dragon's eyes, and the beast hissed and roared so loudly that all the people in Colchis were shaken from their beds. Soon the drug took effect, and the wounded dragon lay down fast asleep. Now Jason climbed up on the neck of the beast, and he hewed off its head with one mighty stroke of his sword. He seized the Golden Fleece from the branches of the sacred oak tree where it hung, shining like a golden cloud at dawn, and he then hurried back to the ship.

The Argonauts were very glad to see him, and Jason—taking Medea in his arms and carrying her aboard the *Argo*—called for the anchor to be lifted and the sails unfurled at once. The ship slowly began to pull away just as the people of Colchis came running down to the shore, and they launched volleys of arrows out into the bay, but these were deflected by the shields of the Argonauts, and soon the ship was far out to sea, heading toward home, carrying the Golden Fleece.

After a long and hard journey, filled with even more adventures, they at last reached their homeland. Jason banished his uncle from the kingdom, and set his father back on the throne. Thus, he fulfilled his vow, and the Argonauts had shown that there truly were heroes still alive in the land. As for King Aeson, he had grown young again because of all his happiness at his son's return, and he ruled his kingdom in peace for many, many years.

A Few Words More

The Greeks placed great value on wisdom, and in those who were wise, like Chiron; although he was of a half-human race of monsters, he was given the care and training of the land's royal children. *Sophos* was the Greek word for "wise," and we can see it still in our modern words *philosopher* ("one who loves wisdom") and *sophisticated* ("cultured, worldly-wise"). It can also be seen in combination with its Greek opposite, *moros*, which meant "a fool." One who is a "wise fool" might know only part of what true wisdom requires, and so would know just enough to get himself in trouble. Does this description remind you of a *sophomore?*

Listening Level II

(Ages 8 and up)

*Most of this section is devoted to the telling of stories from three of the world's most famous epics: the **Iliad**, the **Odyssey**, and the **Aeneid**. These stories are presented in segments or chapters, each of which can be read aloud in one sitting, and because they tell each epic roughly from start to finish, the chapters should be read in order.*

*I have said in previous collections that the masterpieces of our literary culture—novels as well as poems and short stories—can be listened to with enjoyment by children of elementary-school age, if those works have been previewed and edited by a teacher or parent. This elementary-school age is, in fact, **the best time** for introducing great literature to children, because the provocative questions and themes that define "great" literature are just now beginning to have very real applications in a child's life. Children simply should not be forced to wait until junior high or high school before they are given the opportunity to see that their own questions and troubles have been questioned and troubled over by children and adults for centuries.*

Here, then, are stories in which characters struggle with the conflict between their desires and their duty; they sulk when they don't get their own way; they feel envy, anger, remorse, fear, pride; they win great victories, and they suffer humiliating defeats. Here, too, you will find the characters, the events, and the vocabulary that will help you to discuss the struggles your own children have with their world, both now and for many years to come.

Perseus and the Gorgon's Head

About the story:

> *The version of the Perseus myth that follows does not include all the many adventures that happened to the hero on his return home. Instead, it focuses on two escapades that are among the most imaginative in all of classic literature. Young listeners will certainly stretch their creative powers in trying to picture a monster as hideous as Medusa and a trio as strange as the weird sisters described in this tale.*

Approximate reading time: 15 minutes

Vocabulary and pronunciation guide:

Perseus [PER-syoos]

Medusa [meh-DEW-suh]

Danaë [DAN-aa-ee]

Jupiter: king of all the Roman gods; he was called Zeus by the Greeks

writhed [RYTHD]: squirmed; twisted

brazen [BRAY-zen]: made of brass

Pluto: god of the dead; he was known to the Greeks as Hades

Minerva [mih-NERVE-uh]: the Roman goddess of wisdom; the Greeks called this goddess Athena

whence: from where

Once there was a princess named Danaë [DAN-aa-ee], who was so beautiful that mighty Jupiter himself had fallen in love with her, and Danaë bore him a son whom she named Perseus [PER-syoos]. When the boy was only a few weeks old, Danaë's father, who was a very cruel and wicked king, learned from a soothsayer that his own death would come at the hands of his grandson, and so he sealed both Perseus and his mother in a large trunk and cast them out into the sea, there to meet whatever death awaited them.

They floated about for many days, and Danaë held her little boy close, and she sang him sweet lullabies, both to keep him from crying and to hide her own fear of the great waves that crashed over the trunk. But the wooden chest did not sink, and one day it was washed up on an island, where it rested on the sloping shore. There some kind people found them, and they gave Danaë and her little boy a home. Both mother and son lived in peace and happiness there for many years, until Perseus was no longer a boy, but a brave and fearless young man.

Now it so happened that the island on which they landed was ruled by still another wicked and cruel king, perhaps even more heartless than Danaë's father, who had condemned his own daughter and grandson to what he presumed would be a watery grave. When this island's king heard of Danaë's beauty, he wanted to have her as one of his palace slaves, so that she would always be near him, and so that he could punish her if she refused to do his bidding. So the king thought long and hard about some means of getting Perseus out of the way, for he knew that, if the boy were gone, the king could easily do what he liked with the mother.

At last he thought of an adventure that would please Perseus and, at the same time, would be so dangerous that the youth, he felt sure, would never return from it alive.

On another island, far away and in the middle of the ocean, where fierce waves beat against the shore all day long, there lived three terrible monsters known as the Gorgons. They were half woman and half dragon. They had beautiful faces, but their bodies were so hideous that one could think of them only as ugly monsters. Instead of skin, they had large scales, like fish; their hands were made of brass; but most horrible of all, in place of hair on their heads, there writhed [RYTHD] hundreds and hundreds of poisonous snakes, with open mouths and hissing tongues.

These were truly not very pleasant creatures to meet, as you may well imagine. With one blow of their tails or of their brazen [BRAY-zen] hands, they could have crushed poor Perseus like a grape. But worse than that, worse even than the deadly bite of the snakes on their heads, was the power of their fierce eyes, for whoever looked a Gorgon in the face was immediately turned to stone!

Of the three, the most terrible was Medusa [meh-DEW-suh], and the task that the king had thought of giving Perseus was nothing less than cutting off Medusa's head, snakes and all. Since merely looking at Medusa would turn Perseus to stone, and he could not very well cut off her head without looking at her, the king was pretty safe in thinking that this was an adventure from which Perseus would never return.

So he sent for the young man, and when Perseus stood before him, the king began to praise his boldness and courage, which, he said, had been the talk of the island. Perseus, of course, was flattered by these words of praise and replied, "Indeed, O King, I think there is no task from which I would shrink in fear."

The king was delighted to hear this, and he said, "If I thought that, my boy, I would let you undertake a task that I am saving for the bravest man in all my kingdom."

"And do you think me worthy of this honor?" cried Perseus, in great delight.

"Well, you may try it if you like," answered the king. "It is to bring me the head of Medusa, complete with its snaky black hair."

Perseus gladly agreed, and he left the palace. Oh, how the wicked king chuckled over the success of his plot! In seeming to do the boy an honor, he was really sending him to his death.

Now, after poor Perseus left the palace, he began to think over his promise, and somehow the plan did not seem nearly so pleasant nor so easy as it had when he was talking with the king. In fact, the more he thought about it, the less he liked the idea. In the excitement of the moment, he had promised to do something that would surely cost him his life.

When he had passed the gates of the city, he sat down under a tree by the roadside and began to think of how he could accomplish what he promised to do, but the more he thought, the more hopeless did his task seem.

Perseus was a very brave man, to be sure, but the bravest person in the world would rather be alive than be turned to stone, and the thought of what would probably happen to him made him so sad that he could not keep the tears from his eyes.

Suddenly a voice said, "Perseus, why are you weeping?" Perseus raised his head in surprise, and he saw a strange-looking little fellow, with an odd-shaped cap and wings on his shoes. It was none other than the swift-footed god Mercury, but Perseus did not know this. Still, there was something so kind and comforting in the tone in which the stranger asked the question that, almost before he knew it, Perseus was telling him the whole story.

When he had finished, Perseus waited for the stranger to say something, but Mercury sat silent for a few moments, lost in deep thought. Finally he said, "My boy, you have undertaken a dangerous task, yet with my help you may still succeed. But first of all, you must promise to do, in all things, just as I tell you." This Perseus promised to do, and Mercury then began to rummage through a large bag he had brought with him, removing its contents one at a time.

Mercury revealed his identity to Perseus and told him that the gods and goddesses had been watching over him since his birth, and that it was they who had guided the chest carrying Danaë and him to safety. Now they had given to Mercury some of their own possessions to lend to Perseus so that he could accomplish his dangerous task. Pluto, who reigned over the dead in the land below the earth, had lent him his wonderful helmet, which made whoever wore it completely invisible. Minerva [mih-NERVE-uh], goddess of wisdom and warfare, sent down her shield, which shone like gold, so bright that it reflected every image like a mirror. Last of all, Mercury pulled out of the bag his own sword—with its sharp, crooked blade—which could cut through anything in a single stroke, even the armorlike scales of the Gorgons. And finally Mercury added one other gift: his own wingéd shoes with which Perseus could fly more swiftly than the fleetest bird.

Now all that Perseus had to do was find out the way to Medusa's island home. Mercury told him that the only people in the whole world who knew where that was were three sisters who lived together in a cave. They were truly the oddest sisters you could ever imagine, but the strangest thing about them was that instead of having two eyes each, as you would think, there was but one eye for all three of them! They took turns in using that single eye, so that while one of them had the eye, the other two could see nothing at all. And while they were passing the eye from one to another, all three sisters were, for the moment, completely blind.

It may have been only a single eye, but, oh, what an eye it was—worth much more than any other six eyes put together. With it the sisters could see what was going on in the farthest parts of the earth, and that was how they knew the way to Medusa's home.

To this cave, in which the three sisters lived, Mercury led Perseus, and after giving him some parting advice, hid himself in the grove nearby, while Perseus stood just outside the cave, behind a bush, and waited.

By and by, one of the women, with the wonderful eye in her forehead, came to the door of the cave. As she led her sisters by the hand, she told them of everything that she was seeing with the eye—strange things that were happening in countries far away. They were interested for a while, but one of them began to grow impatient and said, "Sister, it is my turn to use the eye now. Give it to me." And the third sister said quickly, "No, that's not true. You had the eye last; it is my turn now." And the middle one, who had the eye, cried out, "Please, sisters, just let me keep it a little longer. I think I see someone behind that thick bush just beyond the door."

When Perseus heard this, he trembled in his wingéd shoes. However, he need not have been afraid, for the sisters continued to quarrel over the eye until, at last, the one who had it was forced to take it out of her forehead. Now, at that instant, all three of the sisters were blind, and Perseus, seeing his chance, darted out and seized the eye. Then began a dreadful hubbub, each one of the three insisting that the other had taken the eye, and these accusations went on and on until, at last, Perseus spoke up. "My good women," he said, "do not be frightened. Your eye is safe, for I hold it in my hand this very moment."

With a cry of anger, the three sisters darted in the direction from which the voice came. But Perseus was too quick for them. On his wingéd feet he rose high in the air, and then, from a safe altitude, called out, "You shall not have your eye back, my friends, unless you tell me exactly how to find the island on which Medusa lives."

This was a secret that the sisters did not wish to divulge at all, but the prospect of losing their precious eye was a thing too terrible to think of. So, after a few minutes, they told Perseus all he wanted to know, and he set their hearts at rest by clapping the eye into the forehead of the sister standing nearest to him. He flew at once back to the grove where Mercury was waiting, and Perseus thanked him for all his help. Then, bidding the god farewell, he started out alone on his errand.

He soared over many lands and seas, until at last he came to the island where the terrible Gorgons lived. He dared not look down, even for an instant, for fear of being turned to stone. But Minerva's bright shield served as a mirror, and, reflected in it, he saw the three monsters lying fast asleep on the shore beneath him. A less noble youth would have fled immediately at such a terrifying sight, but Perseus had a brave heart. So, taking his sharp, crooked sword in hand, and fixing his eyes on Medusa's image in the shield, he darted down. With one mighty stroke, he decapitated the sleeping Gorgon, his sword passing completely through her neck and separating her snaky head from her scaly body. Then, still keeping his eyes fixed upon the picture in the shield, Perseus quickly wrapped up the fallen head in a goatskin bag he had brought along for this purpose. The snakes hissed so loudly that they awakened Medusa's two sisters, and these monsters stretched their dragon's wings and tried to follow Perseus as he rose in the air. But on account of Pluto's magic helmet, which Perseus wore, they could not see him, and he escaped with the head of the snaky-locked Medusa tucked securely in the goatskin bag.

Back over land and sea he flew, and he had many strange adventures along the way. At last he reached the island where his boyhood had been spent, and he learned the sad news that his mother had been bound in slavery by the evil king. Now Perseus was full of rage, and he hastened to the palace at once to demand his mother's freedom.

The king was more surprised than pleased to see Perseus, for he thought the boy must surely have died long ago. "Ah-ha, Perseus!" he cried. "So you have come back without doing what you promised to do. Your courage is not so great as you would have us believe."

"Nay, your majesty," answered Perseus, "I have slain Medusa and have brought you back her head."

"That you must prove by showing us the head," said the

king with a sneer, for, of course, he did not believe Perseus at all.

"Since your majesty insists," Perseus cried, "behold the head!" And, drawing the head from the bag at his side, he held it aloft in all its horrid beauty. The king gazed at it for an instant, with the sneer still on his face, and then froze motionless—turned to solid stone, sneer and all.

When the people heard what had happened, there was great rejoicing, for they had all feared and hated the cruel king. Perseus chose a better ruler for them, under whom they lived in peace and happiness.

Perseus knew that he owed his success to the help that Mercury and the other gods had given him, and he never forgot the debt he owed them. The head of Medusa he gave to Minerva. She was much pleased with the gift, and placed it in the center of her bright shield. From that time on, wherever Minerva was seen in battle, her radiant shield glistened with the head of Medusa, turning to stone all who gazed at its horrid beauty.

A Few Words More

In order to prove that he had killed the terrible Medusa, Perseus was required to bring back the head of the monster, for that was its most vital part. The Latin word for "head" was *caput*, and it is from this source that we have gotten our word *capital*, both the city that is the "head" of a country or state and the large letter that stands at the "head" of a word. When we speak of *per capita* income, we mean individual earnings, for we are counting "by heads." With one stroke of Mercury's magic sword, Perseus *decapitated* (the Latin prefix *de-* meant "away from") the hideous monster. The term "*capital* punishment," in fact, was created in the fifteenth century to be a more delicate way of describing a beheading, for that was the common method of execution at the time.

While we're on the subject of cutting things, you might think about the many words we use today that are based on the Latin word *caedo*, which meant "to cut" and which has come down to us in the form *cis*. For example, an *incision* is a "cut into" something, which we might do with the teeth we call *incisors;* we "cut very close" if we are being *precise;* we "cut off" further debate when we make a *decision,* and we do it in a *decisive* manner. By knowing the meaning of this root, you can now see why it is necessary to include the letter *c* when you spell the word *scissors.*

The Riddle of the Sphinx

About the story:

The story of Oedipus was well known to the citizens of Athens long before Sophocles [SOFF-uh-kleez], in the fifth century B.C., used it as the subject of his tragic play Oedipus the King. *Therefore, it was not the twists and turns in the plot that made the play so captivating to the audience, but it was, instead, the struggle of this basically good and well-intentioned hero against his own unalterable fate, that led people to identify with it so. Aristotle considered* Oedipus the King *to be the most perfect example of a tragedy ever written, and, to many scholars, it still merits that honor today.*

Approximate reading time: 22 minutes

Vocabulary and pronunciation guide:

Sphinx [SFINKS]

Oedipus [ED-uh-pus]

Thebes [THEEBZ]: an ancient city in Greece

Laius [LAY-us]

Jocasta [jo-CAST-uh]

Polybus [POL-ih-bus]

Merope [MARE-oh-pee]

Phoenicia [fuh-NEE-sha]: an ancient country that lay along the eastern coast of the Mediterranean Sea

Delphi [DELL-fie]: an ancient town in central Greece, famed for its oracle at the temple of Apollo

agèd [AA-jid]: advanced in years

Tiresias [tie-REE-see-us]

brooch [BROACH]: a decorative pin

Antigone [an-TIG-uh-nee]

*L*ong, long ago, in the city of Thebes [THEEBZ], there ruled a king named Laius [LAY-us] and his queen, Jocasta [jo-CAST-uh]. They were much loved by the people of the city, and they ruled fairly and wisely for many years, yet their one great disappointment was that they had no children to guide in the ways of rulers and to follow them on the throne. At long last the queen gave birth to a handsome baby boy, and the king, with a father's pride, took the child to the temple of Apollo so that the priest could bless his birth and foretell the glorious deeds that this prince would perform.

But, in an instant, this new father's joy was turned to grief when the priest revealed a prophecy that the child would one day kill his father and marry his mother. Oh, the sadness and disappointment that befell the royal couple, and what were they to do? They could not allow the child to fulfill his destiny, and so, in the depths of misery and despair, they agreed that the boy's life must be ended. Laius called his most trusted servant to him, and, with tears streaming from his eyes, he gave instructions that the child be taken secretly out of the city and put to death. The servant did as his king commanded and wrapped the child in a blanket and carried him out into the hills far away from Thebes. But the farther he journeyed, the more his monstrous task tortured his mind, for although he wanted to obey the orders of his king, he had not the stomach for murdering a babe. At last he reasoned a way out of his dilemma: He would leave the child out in the wild, unprotected, and whether the boy die from starvation or be devoured by animals (for surely he could not survive such an ordeal), at least the death would not have come directly by the servant's hands. And to ensure that the child would not be able to crawl to safety, the servant pierced the boy's ankles with a sharp rod and then suspended the child from a tree limb by attaching a leather thong to the rod. And so the tiny baby boy, crying a tiny baby's cry, swung in the breeze as the servant made his way back to Thebes. There he told King Laius that the appointed task had been accomplished and the child had been put to death.

Now it happened that, shortly after the servant left the baby to die in the wild, a shepherd who was searching for a lost sheep heard the baby's cry and followed the sound. At the sight of this babe swinging by his little ankles, the shepherd immediately cut the boy down from the tree and removed the rod that joined his feet. He tended the wounds and fed the boy some of the goat milk he carried, until it appeared that the child might survive, and the shepherd gave thanks to the gods for helping him to spare the infant's life.

Now this shepherd was not a man of Thebes, but of Corinth, a great city that lay some distance away. And it so happened that the gods had not granted any children to Polybus [POL-ih-bus], king of Corinth, and Merope [MARE-oh-pee], his wife, though they had prayed every day for a child to comfort them and to bring happiness to their lives. The shepherd, out of love for his king and queen, decided that they should be allowed to raise this foundling babe as their own, and when he brought the boy to them, and when they saw the child's uncommon beauty and his noble form, they believed that this was a gift from the gods. Their happiness knew no bounds, and they joyously celebrated the arrival of this boy who would be reared in the palace as their own son, the prince of Corinth.

The child was given the name Oedipus [ED-uh-pus], which meant "swollen foot," because his ankles were still swollen from the rod that had pierced them, but as he grew up, there were no lingering signs of his torment. He became a tall and handsome youth, with a strength and vigor unmatched by any lad in the kingdom. "The gods are gracious," the people would say, "to grant the king and queen such a son, so mighty a prince, to rule over Corinth in the days to come." You see, no one but the shepherd knew that the prince was a foundling, and not the true heir to the throne.

As the child grew, he became so skilled in wrestling and boxing that no one could stand against him, and he took much pride in his athletic skills. Not a day would go by but he would practice and exercise and increase his strength even more. Until his mother, Merope, took him up one day to the bluff that overlooked the city, and from this point they could see the harbors below where ships from many lands came to Corinth. Here they saw sailors and merchants unloading their goods and trading in the great marketplaces that lined the shore. "From far away they come," said Merope, "and they bring not only their merchandise and wares, but the knowledge of their countries as well. Think not, my son, that a lion's heart and a fool's head can ever be a match for the wisdom of Egypt or the cunning of Phoenicia [fuh-NEE-sha]."

Then Oedipus understood, and he said, "Until now I have wrestled and boxed and run races all day, and none can beat me. But these are not the skills I will need to rule wisely. Henceforth I will sit in the marketplace and talk with the foreigners who come there, and I will learn from them so that, when I am called upon to rule, I will be the wisest in the land." And this he did, and he learned many strange things about many strange lands; he acquired the wisdom of Egypt and the cunning of Phoenicia, but still he retained his strength and physical skill.

As Oedipus grew to manhood, there were some rumors about him that were whispered from time to time around Corinth, though no one knew how they got started. The rumors said that Oedipus was not the true son of Polybus and Merope, and that because his parentage was uncertain, he was unfit to be the next ruler of Corinth. As well you might expect, any mention of such a vicious tale would send Oedipus into a rage, and when an enemy or a defeated opponent in a boxing match would repeat the rumor in his presence, Oedipus's violent temper, combined with his strength and swordsmanship, would bring about such swift and summary justice that the offender was unable to libel the prince ever again.

Still the rumor persisted, and after slaying still another of his accusers, Oedipus was at last driven to confront his mother with the question of his parentage. "Am I truly your son?" he asked. "Just call me your own and I will know I was right to silence the liars who have cast dishonor upon my father's name and upon you."

But Merope looked at him sadly and longingly through her tears, and she spoke only in riddling words: "The gods, my child, sent you to your father and to me in answer to our prayers. We are truly your kin in the spirit of goodness and of love." But Oedipus was troubled, for she would say no more; as he withdrew his hand from her grasp, it was wet with tears. "Surely my mother would not weep so if there were nothing in the tale," he said to himself. "I will find the answer, though, for I shall journey to far-off Delphi [DELL-fie] and seek the truth from the oracle there." And this is just what he did.

Oedipus set out alone on his pilgrimage, and after several days he arrived at Delphi and proceeded to the great shrine of Apollo, where he put his question to the god and waited for an answer. Through the dim darkness of the temple he saw the priestess, veiled in a mist of incense and vapor, and as the power of Apollo came upon her, she beheld the future and revealed the hidden secrets of Fate. She raised her hand toward him, and with pale lips spoke these words and nothing more: "Oedipus, ill-fated thou art, for thine own father thou shalt slay, and thine own mother shall become thy wedded wife."

Long after the priestess had finished speaking, her words swam round like a whirlpool in his head, and his heart seemed to turn to stone. How could this be, and how could the Fates possibly believe that he would allow himself to kill his own father and marry his own mother? Yet it had been decreed, and so it must come to pass. With a loud and bitter cry, he rushed from the temple, through the thronging crowd of pilgrims, out into the crowded streets, and the people moved out of his path like shadows. Blindly he sped along a stony road, like some hunted animal, turning neither to the left nor the right, while on every side the mountains frowned down upon him and seemed to echo the doom that the priestess had foretold. He tried to flee as far from Corinth as possible, for rather than commit these awful crimes upon the people he loved, it would be better never to see his parents again.

As he neared a place where three roads came together, he met an old man approaching rapidly in a chariot, accompanied by two servants. "Stand by and let this chariot pass, you madman!" one of the servants cried out to Oedipus, but Oedipus, having been raised as a prince, was not accustomed to being ordered about, and he refused to obey. Incensed at such impudence, the servant laid his whip on Oedipus's back, but that was a fatal mistake. The rage that had built up in the young prince since hearing his fate foretold now rushed through his muscles, and he grabbed the whip in his bare hands and, pulling the servant to him, killed him with a single blow. The old man in the chariot attempted to intercede, but Oedipus knocked him backward out of the cart, where he fell onto the roadway, striking his head on a large rock, spilling his life's blood and quenching the feeble spark of life within him. The other servant fled quickly into the woods that bordered the roadside, but Oedipus did not give chase.

Oedipus then proceeded upon his way, never realizing that the first part of the prophecy had already been accomplished, for the agèd [AA-jid] man in the chariot was none other than Laius, his true father, who had been journeying to Delphi himself, there to consult the oracle. Now Laius lay dead in the road, his life extinguished by the hands of his own son.

On and on went Oedipus, over many a hill and across many a mountain stream, until at last he came to the great city of Thebes, where he found all the citizens in great distress and mourning. It seems that their kind and good king, Laius by name, had been slain by robbers on the way to Delphi, at a point where three roads meet. Worse still, the city was plagued by a hideous monster called the Sphinx [SFINKS], which had the head of a woman, the wings and claws of an eagle, and the body of a lion. This terrible demon had taken up a station near the city gates and would not allow anyone—man, woman, or child—to pass either in or out of the city without being confronted by a riddle that the Sphinx would tell. If a person failed to answer the riddle correctly, or even hesitated in making an answer, the Sphinx would devour him—or her—immediately, and await the next passerby. The wisest and bravest citizens in all of Thebes had tried to answer the riddle, but each had been torn limb from limb, and so none had returned to reveal what this most difficult riddle might be. Now with King Laius dead, the noblemen had given orders to announce throughout the city that whoever would answer the Sphinx's riddle and drive this monster from the land would be rewarded with the crown of Thebes, and would have Queen Jocasta for his wife thereafter. But none of the townspeople who had gathered at the market to hear this proclamation would even think of risking their lives in such a foolish venture.

Then Oedipus stepped forward and announced in a strong voice: "I will go up and face this monster. It must be a hard riddle indeed if I cannot answer it."

"You are overbold and rash, stranger," said the people who heard his boast. "What makes you think that you can succeed where so many others have failed?"

"I have no city to call my own anymore," replied the prince, "for to return there would only bring shame and suffering to my parents. Therefore, this shall be my city, if I succeed, and if I fail, it will make as good a grave as any other."

The people were puzzled by his answer, but they dared not question him any further. Seeing that nothing would turn him from his purpose, they showed him the path to the Sphinx's perch, and they sent him on his way with their prayers and blessings. They left him at the city gate, for he who goes up to face the Sphinx must go alone, and none can stand by and provide him any help. So Oedipus walked on by himself, praying to Athena, the gray-eyed goddess of wisdom, and she took all the fear from his heart.

Suddenly the hideous figure of the Sphinx loomed ahead, peering down at him from her perch atop a thin spire of rock, and when she saw him coming near, a greedy fire lit up her eyes, and she put out her cruel claws and lashed her tail from side to side like an angry lion waiting to spring upon some helpless prey. Although his heart began fluttering in his chest, Oedipus spoke to her in a soft voice, saying: "O lady, I am come to hear thy famous riddle and answer it or die."

"Foolhardy boy," the monster responded, licking her cruel lips. "What a dainty morsel the gods have sent me to dine upon this day! But first, answer me this, if you can: What animal is it that goes on four feet in the morning, on two feet at noon, and in the evening upon three?" This she chanted slowly, and her eyes gleamed cruel and cold.

Then thought Oedipus to himself, "It is now or never for me, and all my learning and wit must avail me here, for surely the time I spent discoursing with the wise travelers of the world cannot have been in vain." And the light of understanding flashed into his heart, and boldly he replied: "What can this creature be, O Sphinx, but man? In the morning of life, as a helpless babe, he crawls on his hands and knees; at midday of his span, he walks erect in the strength of manhood; and in the evening of his days, he supports his tottering limbs with a staff. Have I not answered your famous riddle correctly?"

The Sphinx answered not a word, but realizing her defeat and with a loud cry of despair, the great beast sprang from her perch and hurled herself over the adjoining cliff into the deep gulf beneath, dashing her body on the sharp rocks at the bottom. Far away across the plain, the people heard her cry, and they poured out from every door in the city, rushing to the edge of the cliff so that they could see with their own eyes the monster's twisted and lifeless body on the rocks below. A great cry of joy arose, and Oedipus was raised upon the shoulders of the people and carried back to the city, where he was praised with songs of triumph, and where he was crowned king of Thebes. Jocasta, as his queen, became his wife, and together they ruled the city wisely and well for many years, though neither of them suspected for a minute that the second part of the prophecy had come to pass.

There came a day, however, when a terrible pestilence broke out in Thebes, and people died by the hundreds, and there was nothing anyone could do to end or lessen the dreadful plague. King Oedipus then sent messengers to consult the oracle at Delphi to learn from Apollo why the gods had become so angry with the people of Thebes as to visit this terrible plague upon their city. When the messengers returned, they reported that the plague had been sent because the murderer of the former king, Laius, had never been found, and that the dying would continue until the evildoer had been punished.

Oedipus now conducted an investigation of the murder, calling upon everyone who had any knowledge of it to appear before him and give whatever evidence he could. He also sent for the blind seer Tiresias [tie-REE-see-us], the oldest and wisest of all mortal men, and when the agèd prophet was brought to the palace, Oedipus said to him, "Old man, you see more with no eyes at all than others who have the sight of eagles. Tell me, then, who it was that so cruelly murdered poor Laius, for only when he is found will this curse be lifted from our land."

But Tiresias would not reveal what he knew, and he begged the king not to question him further. At this, Oedipus rebuked the old man, saying that if he had any care at all for the people of Thebes, he would surely not protect a man who had brought upon them such suffering. Tiresias was stung by this accusation, and he could hold his tongue no longer. "It is you, O King, that murdered Laius!" the prophet cried out. "You yourself have brought this stain upon the land!"

Oedipus only laughed, and he chided the prophet for accusing him falsely. "I know not even the face of Laius," Oedipus said, "much less had I any cause to do him harm." And Queen Jocasta comforted her husband, saying, "Believe not this man, my lord, for it was he that long ago prophesied that Laius would be slain by the hands of his own son. That innocent child, though, met his death before he could grow to manhood, and we know that Laius was slain by robbers at the place where three roads meet. He is a false prophet, my king, an enemy who cannot be believed."

But her words brought little comfort to Oedipus, and a dreadful fear came into his heart, like a cold, creeping snake, as he listened. For he began to recall his journey from Delphi, and how he had, in a frenzy, struck down an old man and his servant at a place where three roads meet. He summoned before him the servant who had brought the news of Laius's death back to Thebes, and it so happened that this was the same trusted servant that Laius had long ago commanded to kill his infant son. Now the tangled story began to unravel, and before long it was learned that not only had Laius and his driver been slain by a single assailant, but that the infant who was prophesied to kill his father and marry his mother had not been slain after all, but had been left in the hills to starve.

Oedipus felt a chill come over him when he heard this prophecy, for he recalled that the same fate had been predicted for him at Delphi. But surely it could not be he who was hung from a tree and left there to die, for he had been born in a palace, to the king and queen of Corinth. Oh, the torment that ensued and the wailing that could be heard throughout the palace when the shepherd who had saved the baby on that hillside long ago at last revealed what he knew. Now the awful truth came crashing down upon Oedipus, as an avalanche buries the unsuspecting beneath its ever-deepening mass. Not only was he the true son of Laius and Jocasta, but it was, indeed, his own father that he had slain on the road from Delphi.

Oh, the foolish hearts of mortals, to think that they can escape the doom that Fate has decreed.

Jocasta now walked in a daze back to her palace chamber, and there she put an end to her life. And Oedipus, who arrived too late to prevent her death and found the sight of her lifeless form more than he could bear, took from her a brooch [BROACH], and in his shame and misery he stabbed out the sight from both his eyes. This was not the end to his torment, though, for he was scorned by the people of Thebes, and he wandered about the land as a blind beggar for many years. No one would give him comfort except his daughter, Antigone [an-TIG-uh-nee], who remained faithful to him all the rest of his days, and who guided him and cared for him until, at last, he laid himself down in a peaceful grove and drifted from this world into the land below.

A Few Words More

The spot "where three roads meet" played an important role in this tale, and similar crossroads also provided us with the origin of a modern word that is quite popular today. The point at which three roads converged became a convenient meeting place for people on their way home from market. Here they could discuss the gossip of the day and exchange the "small talk" that is common at such gatherings. The Romans combined their prefix *tri-*, meaning "three," and the word *via*, which meant "way or road," and created the Latin word *trivialis* for the trifling matters that would be discussed "at the crossroads." Today, we still refer to insignificant matters as being *trivial*, even though a knowledge of *trivia* itself has risen to some importance.

The Story of Helen of Troy

The six tales that follow form a story that has endured for thousands of years—a story that is well known to adults and children throughout the world. It is the story of the great Trojan War, which took place around 1250 B.C., but it is also a story about the passions and follies of human beings, and for this reason it seems in many ways to be as modern as the current dramas we see on television.

The story was memorized and recited by poets and minstrels during a period of several centuries when Greece had no written language. Around 800 B.C., it was put down in writing by a poet whom we call Homer, although we know virtually nothing at all about him. Homer's epic poem titled the *Iliad* [ILL-ee-ad] focuses on the last year of the ten-year siege of Troy by the Greeks, and so we must learn the story of the stealing of Helen and the destruction of Troy from other sources.

I hope that you will read these six tales to your children in the order presented here, so that they (and you) might become better acquainted with the characters and better accustomed to the pronunciations of their names. Such a reading, over several sessions, will also allow your children to see this epic tale as a series of connected events, rather than as isolated myths about specific characters and happenings. To aid you in your storytelling, I have provided below a list of the pronunciations and identifications of names that appear frequently throughout the six tales. Each pronunciation, however, will be given again the first time that name appears in each story.

Pronunciation guide (names that recur frequently in the story):
    Aegean Sea [ih-JEE-an]
    Hecuba [HECK-you-bah]
    Thetis [THEE-tiss *(th* as in *think)*]
    Hera [HAIR-uh]
    Athena [uth-EE-nuh]
    Aphrodite [aff-row-DYE-tee]
    Hermes [HER-meez]

Ulysses [you-LISS-eez]
Agamemnon [agg-uh-MEM-non]
Menelaus [men-uh-LAY-us]
Achilles [uh-KILL-eez]
Patroclus [puh-TRO-klus]

The Judgment of Paris

About the story:

Troy was a very real city, or perhaps I should say that it was several cities, for archaeologists have uncovered the ruins of about ten kingdoms, each built on the ashes of its predecessor, at the site on the coast of western Turkey where this epic places the location of Troy. The Greeks called the city Ilium [ILL-ee-um], and this is the reason that Homer's poem is called the **Iliad.**

In this opening adventure, we see that the struggle begins, as it does in so many ancient myths, with the gods. Yet, it is their petty and very human frailty—vanity— that sets into motion the events that lead ultimately to the destruction of an entire civilization.

Approximate reading time: 6 minutes

Vocabulary and pronunciation guide:

benevolent [ben-EV-oh-lent]: kind; caring

Priam [PRY-am]

Peleus [PEE-loose]

Thessaly [THESS-uh-lee]: a province in northern Greece

nymph [NIMFF]: a beautiful female nature spirit

Muses [MEW-zez]: the nine sisters, all daughters of Zeus, who presided over the arts

Eris [EAR-iss]: goddess of discord; sister of Ares (the Greek god of war)

There was once—long, long ago—a mighty city that lay across the Aegean [ih-JEE-an] Sea to the east of Greece, a city of high towers and strong walls, a city that stood on a hill overlooking the seashore, a city of proud people ruled by a benevolent [ben-EV-oh-lent] king named Priam [PRY-am], a city known as Troy. Now Troy was a city well favored by the gods, and its position and power brought it many riches, including much gold, fine statues, and the swiftest horses in all the land. King Priam, too, was much blessed, not only by having the love of his people, but also by having a son who was the strongest and bravest warrior in all of Troy, and this warrior's name was Hector.

But Hector was not Priam's only son, for when the king was well into his years, his wife, Queen Hecuba [HECK-you-bah], bore him another son, a babe of such beauty that neither his father nor his mother could understand the prophecy that the oracle gave at the birth of the child. The prophecy was that Hecuba would give birth to a burning torch that would one day set fire to the city and burn the topless towers of Troy to the ground. Though they did not understand, they knew that the prophecy would come true, unless they could prevent the destruction of their city by destroying this beautiful child first. And so, with very heavy hearts, they directed one of their servants to take the child into the woods on Mount Ida and leave him there to starve or to be killed by wild animals, and this the servant did.

Somehow the baby survived for five days, until a shepherd found him and took him home, where the baby was raised as the shepherd's own child. As he grew toward manhood, the child's wondrous features grew also, so that all who had ever seen him tending flocks on the mountain slopes agreed that this youth, whom the shepherd had named Paris, was the most stunningly handsome mortal man in all the world; moreover, he was also the best runner and the best hunter and the best archer among all the country people who lived in the lands near the mountain. And here Paris stayed, not knowing of his royal parentage, until one fateful day when he was summoned by the gods. And it happened this way.

A wonderful wedding was about to take place on a high mountain in Greece; King Peleus [PEE-loose] of Thessaly [THESS-uh-lee] was marrying the beautiful sea nymph [NIMFF] named Thetis [THEE-tiss (*th* as in *think*)], who was much loved by the gods. Indeed, all the gods and nymphs and Muses [MEW-zez] were in attendance—all except for Eris

[EAR-iss], the goddess of discord, for she alone had not been invited. This exclusion enraged Eris, and in her anger she decided upon a plan that would disrupt the entire ceremony. When all the guests had gathered, Eris secretly entered the hall and set down in their midst an apple made of the brightest gold, with an inscription saying simply: FOR THE FAIREST OF ALL.

Well, it did not take long for that golden apple to be claimed, but just as Eris had hoped, there were several in the assemblage who thought it should rightfully be theirs—each thought that she was the most beautiful of all. Hera [HAIR-uh] (the wife of Zeus), Athena [uth-EE-nuh] (the goddess of wisdom), and Aphrodite [aff-row-DYE-tee] (the goddess of love) each claimed that she was the fairest of all and, therefore, should have the apple. The mighty Zeus, who would usually settle such disputes swiftly and decisively, knew well that to give the prize to one of the three claimants would offend the other two, and so he chose not to be the judge in this case, but to have another assume the role. In a commanding voice he announced, "My messenger, Hermes [HER-meez], will fly all three of you over the sea to Mount Ida, where there dwells the handsomest of all mortals, who is known as Paris. He shall judge which of you is most beautiful and deserves to have the golden apple for her own."

You can imagine how surprised young Paris was as he sat on the mountain slope watching his flock, when, as if in a flash, Hermes appeared before him with his three immortal companions. The goddesses were all so lovely that when they asked Paris to say which was the most beautiful, he became perplexed and could not decide. Thereupon, each goddess took him aside separately and made him certain promises in the hope that he would decide in her favor. Hera, for instance, promised to make him the most powerful of kings if he would choose her as fairest. Athena offered to make him the wisest of men if he would select her. Aphrodite, though, promised to give him the most beautiful woman in the mortal world for his wife, and the mere thought of such a gift so appealed to Paris that he, then and there, awarded the apple to the goddess of love. Of course, Hera and Athena were greatly offended, and they secretly vowed to punish the youth for his rash judgment, but Aphrodite had become his ally and would watch over him and protect him with all her power from this time on.

The gods then left as suddenly as they had arrived. Over the next several days, with the urgings and guidance of Aphrodite, Paris made his way to the city of Troy, where he was quickly recognized by King Priam and Queen Hecuba as their own son, who they thought had perished long ago. In spite of the prophecy that Paris would one day bring about the destruction of Troy, they welcomed him to the city and back into their royal family as the youngest prince of Troy and the brother of the brave and powerful Hector.

A Few Words More

The *Muses* who attended the wedding of Thetis and King Peleus were goddesses who had the special duty of overseeing the production and performance of the fine arts. Each of the nine sisters was responsible for a specific field; you will recall from the story of Orpheus and Eurydice (page 68), for instance, that Calliope was the Muse of epic poetry. If a mortal wished to create a dance or a song or a play, he would pray to one of the Muses, and she would provide him with the necessary inspiration and perseverance. The Greek name for the place where the Muses studied their arts has come down to us in the word *museum*. Even our word *music* comes from a Greek word that meant "belonging to the Muses."

The Muses were all daughters of Zeus and Mnemosyne [nee-MAHS-uh-nee], who was the goddess of memory. The strange silent letter *m* that appears at the beginning of this goddess's name also appears (and still is not sounded) in a modern word that comes from her name: *mnemonic* [nee-MAHN-ik]. A *mnemonic* is any device that aids the memory, such as tying a string around your finger, for example. The way many people remember the Great Lakes is by remembering just the mnemonic "HOMES" (Huron, Ontario, Michigan, Erie, Superior). Now, if we add the Greek prefix *a-*, meaning "without," to the name *Mnemosyne*, the words that result should mean, literally, "without memory," and when this prefix is attached, the previously silent letter *m* in *Mnemosyne* becomes pronounced. Our word *amnesia*, for instance, describes "a loss of memory," and when we grant *amnesty*, we actually "forget" that the crime was ever committed.

The Stealing of Helen

About the story:

Here we are introduced to many of the major characters who will fight for the Greeks in their war with Troy, and these names seem quite unlike any of our common names today. In fact, the only woman's name from Greek mythology that is still popular throughout Europe and America today is that of Helen. Girls who are known as Ellen or Elaine or Eleanor or Ella will also be interested in knowing that their names have descended from that of the woman who was thought to be the most beautiful in all the world.

Approximate reading time: 11 minutes

Vocabulary and pronunciation guide:

King Tyndarus [TIN-dah-russ]
Diomedes [dye-oh-ME-deez]
Mycenae [my-SEE-nee]: an ancient Greek city, which Agamemnon ruled as king
Laconia [luh-CONE-ee-uh]: a province in ancient Greece; Sparta was its capital
Ithaca [IH-thick-uh]: an island kingdom off the north-west coast of Greece
Penelope [pen-EL-oh-pee]
Telemachus [tell-EM-uh-cuss]
emissaries: ambassadors, agents sent on a mission
feigning [FAY-ning]: pretending
Iphigenia [if-ih-jen-EE-uh]

Not long after Paris returned to Troy, the news came to that city about a woman in Greece whose beauty was unsurpassed. She was a princess—Helen by name—and she was so fair of face and stature that all who saw her fell in love with her and wanted to marry her. When young Paris heard these reports, he knew that this was the woman he must have for his wife, and so he prayed to Aphrodite [aff-row-DYE-tee] that she would keep her promise and grant that, if this Helen proved to be the most beautiful woman in the world, then Paris could have her for his bride. And Aphrodite was true to her word, vowing that if this was the woman Paris chose, then nothing would stand in his way. This so inspired the young prince that he sailed that very day with a few companions to see this beauty for himself and return with her to Troy.

The trip was a long and difficult one, for the winds were not favorable and many dangers had to be overcome along the way. And while this crew was still at sea, fair Helen was wed to another man, and this is how it happened.

Helen's father, King Tyndarus [TIN-dah-russ], had been besieged for several months by the many noble princes who all sought the hand of his daughter, and he knew that the time had come for him to select one of these suitors to be Helen's husband. He also knew that no matter which of the suitors he chose, the others would be greatly disappointed and might try to take by force what they could not have by right. And so the king demanded that all the princes take an oath to stand by the man whom he chose and, no matter who Helen's husband was to be, that all the others should come to his aid if Helen were ever taken from him. And this they vowed, each man among them.

It was not an oath to be taken lightly, and those who took the oath were men of honor, including such heroes as the wise Ulysses [you-LISS-eez] from Ithaca [IH-thick-uh]; Diomedes [dye-oh-ME-deez], king of Argos; Ajax, the tallest and strongest of the Greeks; Agamemnon [agg-uh-MEM-non], king of the rich city of Mycenae [my-SEE-nee], and other chiefs from kingdoms many miles away. From all these suitors, King Tyndarus chose Menelaus [men-uh-LAY-us], King of Laconia [luh-CONE-ee-uh], to be Helen's husband. Menelaus was not the wealthiest of the Greeks, nor was he the wisest or the most handsome. Indeed, it was Menelaus's own brother, Agamemnon, who was the leader of all the chiefs and the general of all the Greeks in war. But Menelaus was both brave and kind; he loved and honored the fair Helen, and would do so all the days of his life.

Helen and Menelaus had not been married long before Paris and his companions came to their palace in Laconia, and the travelers were welcomed with kindness, as would befit a prince and his friends from a faraway land. King Menelaus provided them with meat and wine, and they discussed their journey as they dined. While they were talking, Helen came forth from her fragrant chamber, like a goddess, her maidens following her, and she sat and listened as Paris told how the talk of her beauty had spread even to Troy and how he had traveled so far to witness it for himself. He did not say that he intended to have her for his wife, but he had never seen a lady so lovely and gracious as she, and he knew that he would not return to Troy without her.

Later that evening, Paris prayed again to the goddess Aphrodite to help him in his quest. Paris was more handsome than any of Helen's suitors, it is true, and Helen was, indeed, attracted to him. But she had a husband whom she respected and admired, and she would remain by his side no matter what earthly temptation was placed before her. Ah, but earthly temptations have little allure compared with those that can be concocted from above, for when Aphrodite put Helen into a trance whereby she could be carried away by Paris and his countrymen in the middle of the night, Helen was helpless to resist.

When the rosy dawn appeared, Menelaus found that his beautiful bride had been stolen by those to whom he had shown kindness and hospitality. No crime could be greater than this, and none called so urgently for revenge. Still in grief and shock, Menelaus called upon all the chiefs of all the kingdoms in Greece to honor their pledge and to take up his cause as their own. Helen, he urged, must be returned to Greece, and her wicked Trojan captors must be punished by the Greeks sacking the city of Troy and burning it to the ground.

And so it was that a vast army was gathered from all over Greece, for not only did the suitors keep their pledge and bring with them many soldiers and many ships, but other chiefs as well brought their warriors, each man determined to bring back the honor of Greece or die in the attempt. Each prince came without hesitation, save only two.

Ulysses, who had sought Helen's hand himself and who had taken the oath to come to her defense, was not to be found among the chiefs who were planning for the invasion of Troy, and the others knew that they needed the wisdom of Ulysses if they were to devise a plan that would succeed. Ulysses, however, remained in Ithaca with his wife, Penelope [pen-EL-oh-pee], and his young son, Telemachus [tell-EM-uh-cuss]. Penelope, you see, was Helen's cousin, and although quite beautiful herself, her charms could not compare with fair Helen's. Penelope knew that her husband had been in love with Helen once, and she saw no reason for him to fall under the power of her beauty again, and so she urged him to stay out of the war and to remain a husband and a father instead.

When two emissaries from the gathering princes came to Ithaca, they were astounded to find Ulysses apparently insane, for he was plowing the seashore and seeding the sand with salt! One of the ambassadors, though, suspected that Ulysses was only feigning [FAY-ning] madness, and he picked up the boy Telemachus and laid him down on the sand directly in line with the furrow that Ulysses was plowing, so that if Ulysses continued, his sharp plowshare would cleave the boy in two. But Ulysses turned the plow aside before it neared the child, proving that he was not insane at all. He apologized for not keeping his pledge, and he said that now he saw his responsibility very clearly and was ready to do whatever was necessary for the honor of his homeland. Kissing his wife and child, not knowing when or whether he would see them again, Ulysses put on his battle attire, gathered together as many of the men from Ithaca as would follow him, and went off to war.

There was but one other chief who was missing from the gathering of princes, and that was the best fighter in all the land, Achilles [uh-KILL-eez]. Now Achilles was the son of Thetis [THEE-tiss (*th* as in *think*)], the sea nymph, and therefore he was a mortal with some very godlike qualities. He was the most handsome man of all the Greeks, and his speed and skill with weapons was unmatched. When he was a child, however, his mother learned of a prophecy that said that if Achilles ever went off to war, he would achieve great glory but would die very young and never see his mother again. Not wishing this end for her son, Thetis sent him off to a remote island where he would be concealed in the disguise of a maiden among the daughters of the king.

It happened that Ulysses was sent by the chiefs to locate Achilles, and when Ulysses learned of the prince's whereabouts and disguise, he went to the island and masqueraded as a merchant from a far-off land. He carried with him a peddler's sack, filled with ornaments, dresses, scarves, jewelry, and one sword—its handle studded with golden nails. While the king's daughters were engrossed with the other contents of the merchant's pack, Achilles reached right for the sword and thereby betrayed himself to the keen eye of Ulysses, who found no great difficulty in persuading him to disregard his mother's advice and join his countrymen in war.

With the arrival of Achilles and his friend Patroclus [pah-TRO-klus], the Greek chiefs were now all assembled, and they prayed to the gods to grant them fair winds across the Aegean [ih-JEE-an] and a decisive victory at Troy. But the winds did not come, and sickness spread through the Greek warriors who waited and waited for a signal that the gods would be on their side and help them avenge the stealing of Helen. The men grew restless and their spirits sank so low that the leaders became worried. Then, a soothsayer announced that the gods would not grant their blessing unless Agamemnon, the commander-in-chief of all the Greek warriors, sacrificed his daughter, the beautiful and innocent Iphigenia [if-ih-jen-EE-uh], at the altar of Diana, the virgin goddess of the hunt. Though he loved his daughter more than anything in the world, Agamemnon knew that he must give her up in order to save his country and his countrymen, and so the girl was brought to the altar and taken away to the heavens in a cloud of mist. Almost immediately, the west wind quickened, and the fleet of more than a thousand ships, each with more than fifty armed warriors, set sail for Troy and for what would be forever known as the Trojan War, to return the beautiful Helen to the husband who loved her.

A Few Words More

Menelaus was the king of a region in Greece called Laconia, whose capital was the city of Sparta. The Spartans were famous for their self-discipline and for doing without the luxuries or adornments common in other cultures; their severe and rigorous ways are reflected in today's adjective *spartan,* which describes "an austere life-style or anything that lacks ornamentation."

The people of Sparta and of the region of Laconia also were noted for their brief and pithy speech; they would use as few words as possible to get their point across— again, language without any ornamentation. This type of speech is reflected in the story about the time that Philip of Macedon threatened to invade Sparta and announced to the Spartan leader, "If we come to your city, we will raze it to the ground." To which the Spartan replied simply, "If." Today, the word *laconic* [luh-CONN-ick] is used to describe such terse or concise speech.

The Quarrel

About the story:

The Iliad, *Homer's epic poem about the Trojan War, begins after the Greeks have already laid siege to the city for nine long years. Therefore, it opens "in the middle of things," a literary device described by the Latin phrase* in medias res *[in MAY-dee-us RACE] and somewhat akin to the use of "flashbacks" in today's movie and television scripts.*

Just as the stealing of Helen and the resulting massing of armies grew out of something as petty as the vanity of three goddesses, in this tale we see how another very small incident mushroomed into one of gigantic importance, simply because it involved the very human trait of pride.

Approximate reading time: 10 minutes
Vocabulary and pronunciation guide:

    Ilium [ILL-ee-um]
    Chryseis [cry-SEE-iss]
    Calchas [KAL-cuss]
    prophesy [PROFF-uh-sye]: to predict; the word meaning "a prediction" (*prophecy* [PROFF-uh-see]) is spelled with a *c*.
    Briseis [bry-SEE-iss]

The city of Troy (or Ilium [ILL-ee-um], as it was called by the ancient Greeks) was built on a hill, overlooking the clear river and the wide plain that separated the city from the seashore. From the top of the city's massive walls and high towers the Trojans could see any ship that approached, and their arrows and spears could easily drive back any enemy who tried to cross the plain and storm the city. And this is exactly what they did when the mighty Greek armada arrived at the shore, and the invaders crossed the plain and launched repeated attacks against the city's defenses. Each assault was repelled by deadly volleys of spears and arrows, so that the Greeks were unable to come near the city gates. They soon realized the futility of their efforts and decided, instead, to lay siege to Troy. They erected huts and tents all along the shore, between the wide plain and their ships, and here they lived for nine long years, plundering all the cities and villages for miles around, and fighting little battles with any Trojan forces that came out onto the plain, but the Greeks were always driven back whenever they approached the city itself.

By now the Greek soldiers were weary of the siege, and they longed to see their wives and families again. They were no closer to recapturing fair Helen and punishing her abductor, Paris, than they had been when they set sail nine long years ago. But in the tenth year of the siege an event took place that seemed to be a mere trifle at the time, but changed the course of the entire war, and this is how it happened.

By capturing the neighboring cities, the Greeks were able to take what they wanted: cattle, wine, grain, and women—who were held in slavery. All this plunder was divided among the chiefs, each taking his choice, with Agamemnon, as the leader of the Greeks, being given first choice. Now it happened that among the spoils from one conquered city was a lovely girl named Chryseis [cry-SEE-iss], and it was she that Agamemnon chose for his prize and carried away to his tent to serve him as his slave. Her father could not bear this to be his daughter's fate, and so he came to the Greek camp bringing much gold with which he wished to buy back his daughter. He begged the chiefs, and especially Agamemnon, to take the gold and give him back the girl. He was, after all, a priest at the temple of Apollo in his city, and he assured the chiefs that, if they returned his daughter, Apollo would help them take the city of Troy and return safely to their homes.

All the chiefs were willing, but Agamemnon cried, "Away with you, old man. Do not linger here now, and do not come again, or it will be the worse for you, even though you are a priest. As for your daughter, I will keep her with me even after I have conquered Troy, and I will take her back with me to my home."

So the old man went away in great fear and sorrow, and he prayed to Apollo to help him. And Apollo heard him and was very angry that his priest should suffer such things. The god came down from his palace on top of Mount Olympus, and in the nights to come he shot his arrows of death into the horses and dogs of the Greeks, and then into the warriors themselves. For nine days a plague came over the Greek camp, and the Greeks died in large numbers. Every morning the bodies of the dead were buried in large mounds on the plain near the shore, and on the tenth day Achilles called for a council of all the chiefs.

When the leaders had gathered together, Achilles spoke to the assembly, saying, "It would be better that we went home than to die here from Apollo's invisible arrows. Let us ask the prophets why it is that Apollo is so angry with us."

Then Calchas [KAL-cuss], the soothsayer, stood up. "You wish to know why Apollo is angry," he said. "I will tell you, but first you must promise to stand by me, for King Agamemnon will be angry when he hears what I have to say."

"Speak on," cried Achilles. "No man shall harm you while I live—no, not even Agamemnon himself."

Then Calchas told the chiefs that he had consulted the stars and had seen in them the reason for the plague. "Apollo is angry because, when his priest came to buy back his daughter, Agamemnon would not listen to him. Now you must send back the girl, taking no money for her, and with her you must also send a hundred head of cattle before Apollo's anger will cease."

At this, Agamemnon stood up in a rage and cried, "You always prophesy [PROFF-uh-sye] evil, old man, and though you are a bad prophet, I will send the girl back, for I do not want the people to die. But hear this: I demand another to replace her; I will not go without my share of the plunder."

"You think too much of gain, King Agamemnon," said Achilles. "Surely you would not take from any man that which has already been given him. Wait until Troy has been conquered, and then we will make up to you what you have lost many times over."

"Do not try to cheat me in this way," answered Agamemnon. "My share I will have at once. If the army will give it to me, well and good; but if not, then I will take my choice from the spoils given to one of the chiefs—perhaps even from you, Achilles."

Then Achilles became furious and carried away with rage. He cried, "Never was there a king so shameless and so greedy for gain. Why, the Trojans never did harm to me or mine, yet I have been fighting against them for your sake and for your brother's. And now you say you will take away the small treasures that have been allotted to me. I will not stay here to be shamed and robbed. I will go home."

"Then go," said Agamemnon, "and take your people with you. I have other chiefs as good as you, and they are ready to honor me, as you are not. But mark me well, Achilles, the girl Briseis [bry-SEE-iss], who was given to you as your share of the spoils—she shall become mine to repay me for my loss. You must learn, Achilles, that I am master here."

Achilles was so filled with anger that he half drew his sword from its scabbard, but he held himself back from acting on his rage, and he stared at Agamemnon and shouted, "You drunkard with the eyes of a dog and the heart of a deer, hear what I tell you now. One day the Greeks will miss Achilles. And you, when you see your people dying on the swords and spears and arrows of the Trojans—you will be sorry that you have done this wrong to the bravest man in your army. What the Greeks gave me, let them take away if they will. But mark this: If *you* lay your hands on anything that is mine, that hour you shall die!"

Then Achilles stormed out of the council, and the assembly broke up. Agamemnon called to him a company of soldiers and he said to them, "Go now to the tent of Achilles, and fetch from it the girl called Briseis. And if he will not let her go, say that I will come with the whole army if necessary, and it will be the worse for him."

So the soldiers went, but it was much against their will that they did this errand. And when they saw Achilles sitting outside his tent, they stood in great fear and shame. But Achilles spoke kind words to them, saying, "You need not fear, for it is no fault of yours that you have been sent on such an errand." Then he turned to his friend Patroclus [pah-TRO-klus] and said, "Fetch Briseis and give her to these men. Let them be witnesses to this evil deed, that they may remember it when Agamemnon shall need my help and shall not have it."

So Patroclus brought out the girl and gave her to the heralds. And she went with them, much against her will, and often looking back. And when she was gone, Achilles sat upon the seashore, weeping aloud and stretching out his hands to his mother Thetis [THEE-tiss (*th* as in *think*)], who dwelt in the seas and rivers. And Thetis heard his voice and rose from the sea, as a cloud rises. She came to him where he sat weeping, and she comforted him and stroked his long yellow hair.

"Why do you weep, my son?" she asked.

Then Achilles told her of the wrong that had been done him, and when he finished his story, he said, "Mother, I beg you to go to Olympus and ask mighty Zeus to aid the Trojans in battle so that the Greeks will flee before them and Agamemnon will learn how foolish he has been."

His mother answered him, saying, "Oh, my son, you have been deeply wronged. The Fates have said that your life is to be short, but happy; yet it seems your life is anything but happy. I will go to Zeus as soon as he returns from his twelve-day feast, and I will plead with him. But for now, you must remain away from the battles."

Meanwhile, the girl Chryseis was returned to her father, and very glad he was to see her again. He prayed to Apollo that the plague among the Greeks might cease, and so it happened. The battles with the Trojans resumed, and many warriors from both armies met their end. But Achilles sat in his tent, sulking and fretting, for there was nothing that he liked so much as the taste of battle.

A Few Words More

Here we have seen mighty Achilles acting in a way that is anything but heroic. Because his pride has been wounded, he lets his comrades down and refuses to join them in battle. Today, the phrase "like Achilles sulking in his tent" is often applied to anyone who withdraws from the action just because his feelings have been hurt.

There is another scene in this tale, though, that can help your children understand and acquire dozens of modern words, many based on the Greek word *astron*, meaning "star." When Calchas consulted the stars to understand the reason for the plague, he was engaging in *astrology,* or "a study of the stars." Not only do the modern words *astronomy* ("the arrangement of stars") and *astronaut* ("star sailor") come from this Greek root, but a *disaster* was, literally, the result of having the stars "against" you. There are many other common words that come from *astron* and its Latin counterpart *stella* (as in *constellation),* but the most interesting one to me is the result of adding the Greek suffix *-iskos,* meaning "little," to the end of the root for "star": *asteriskos* meant "little star," and that is why the *asterisk* on the typewriter has the shape that we now associate with that name.

The Gods Take Sides

About the story:

The role of the gods in mythology is a complex one, and children may have many questions about why the gods did or did not alter various events. Primarily, the gods are used to explain the reason for the occurrence of some unexpectedly good or bad human act: a superhuman throw of a spear, for instance.

We have seen the gods, including mighty Zeus, having almost unlimited powers, yet even they cannot alter the ultimate course of events that fate has determined. They can, however, and here they do, allow their passions and sympathies to affect the way in which human destiny is played out.

Approximate reading time: 19 minutes

Vocabulary and pronunciation guide:

Myrmidons [MUR-mid-onz]: the soldiers whom Achilles brought with him to the Trojan War

Stentor [STEN-tore]

Iris [EYE-riss]: goddess of the rainbow; she and Hermes were the messengers of the gods

Briseis [bry-SEE-iss]

bade [BAD]: invited; past tense of *bid*

Thebes [THEEBZ]: an ancient city in Greece

vehement [VEE-uh-ment]: passionate; forceful

When the twelve days of feasting were over, Thetis [THEE-tiss (*th* as in *think*)] rose out of the sea and went to Olympus to plead with the mighty Zeus. "O great Zeus," she said, kneeling before him and laying her hands upon his knees, "I beg thee to give my son Achilles [uh-KILL-eez] the honor that is rightfully his. Agamemnon [agg-uh-MEM-non] has shamed him, taking away the gift that was given him by the Greeks and their chiefs. I beseech thee to make the Trojans prevail for a while in battle, so that the Greeks may find they cannot do without Achilles, and my son shall return to the field in honor."

For a long time Zeus sat saying nothing, for he knew that great trouble would come from granting this request. His wife, Hera [HAIR-uh], and the goddess Athena [uth-EE-nuh] favored the Greek cause, for they still chafed from Paris's choice of Aphrodite [aff-row-DYE-tee] as the fairest of all, and they wanted him and his people punished by the Greeks. At last Zeus decided upon a plan, and he sent a dream down to Agamemnon. He made the dream appear in the form of Nestor, whom the Greeks thought to be the wisest of men, and as Agamemnon slept, he thought he heard wise old Nestor tell him to forget about Achilles and the Myrmidons [MUR-mid-onz] who fought under him, and to take his army into battle and seize the city of Troy. So inspired by this false dream was Agamemnon that he roused all his chiefs with the belief that the long war was about to come to an end.

At daybreak the Greeks charged out onto the plain to meet the Trojan army, which was led by Hector, King Priam's eldest son and the bravest warrior in all of Troy. Though the Greeks were inspired by the urgings of their chiefs, without Achilles to lead them in battle, they were routed by the men of Troy, and Hector slew many of their number and stripped the armor from their bodies. The Greeks were forced back to the shore, to fight on their ships, and several of the ships were set aflame by the Trojans.

When the battle ended at dusk, the Trojans withdrew, but not to the city, for this night they would spend celebrating the day's victory around a thousand campfires out on the plain. The Greeks, meanwhile, extinguished their burning ships and spent the rest of the night digging a trench and building a low wall between their camp and the plain on which the Trojans camped. Agamemnon knew now that his dream had been a false one, and he feared that the end of his army was near.

At the appearance of rosy-fingered dawn, the Greeks huddled behind their wall, waiting for the Trojan attack, and when the armies met, there was much carnage. Hector forded the newly dug ditch and drove his chariot through the low wall of the Greeks. Nor was there a Greek who dared stand up against him, and many of their number perished on Hector's sword that morning. The space between the wall and the ships was crowded with chariots, and no spirit was left in any of the defenders at their ships.

Then Stentor [STEN-tore], the Greek chief who had the voice of fifty men, shouted to his countrymen from the prow of one of their ships. "Shame on you, men of Greece!" he cried. "When Achilles came to battle the Trojans, they feared to come out of the gates of their city, but now they are driving you onto your own ships. Do not let them say they have defeated a land of cowards, but fight to your last breath for the honor of your homeland!" And this cry filled the hearts of the Greeks and inspired them to drive the Trojans back toward the wall. But they could do no harm to Hector, and those who fought around him at the middle of the ships were not pushed back, but boarded the Greek vessels and set them afire.

Queen Hera and the goddess Athena sat high on Olympus and watched the battle that raged on earth. "Shall we not have pity on the Greeks and help them?" said Hera. "Let us do it just this once, for I fear that they will perish altogether by the hand of Hector if we do not. See what harm he has done them already."

Athena answered: "This would not have happened if Zeus had not listened to Thetis and meddled on the side of Troy. But now we shall meddle to make things even for the Greeks. Ready your chariot, and I will put on my armor. Hector will not be so happy to see us coming in battle against him."

So Hera made her chariot ready, and Athena put on her armor and took up her great spear, and she prepared as she would for battle. Then the two mounted the chariot and went through the gates of heaven, down the majestic mountain toward Troy.

But Zeus saw them as they left, and he called to Iris [EYE-riss], who is a messenger of the gods, and said to her: "Go now, Iris, and tell these two that they had better not set themselves against me, for if they do, I will strike their chariot with a thunderbolt and shatter it to pieces, and their injuries will make them suffer for many years."

So Iris made all the haste she could and met the two goddesses on their way, and she gave them the message of Zeus.

Hera and Athena listened well to Iris's message, and they feared Zeus's rage if they continued their journey. So they turned their chariot back to Olympus, and there they sat in their golden chairs, very sad and angry, among the other gods.

Mighty Zeus came to them and spoke, saying: "Do you pity the Greeks for what they have suffered today? Tomorrow you shall see worse things than these, for Hector will not cease from driving the Greeks before him and slaying them till the great Achilles himself shall be moved and shall rise from the place where he sits alone by his ships."

And now the sun sank into the sea, and the night fell. The Trojans were angry that the darkness had come and that they could not see any longer, but the Greeks were glad of the night, for it was as a shelter to them, and gave them time to prepare for the Trojan assault that would come with the dawn.

All the Greek chiefs assembled to devise a battle plan, and at this assembly old Nestor rose up in his place and spoke. "Agamemnon," he said, and all listened to his words, for he had given wise counsel to these chiefs and to their fathers, "the gods have made you lord over many nations, and you are therefore bound to listen to wise words, even though they may not please you. It was an evil day, O King, when you took away the damsel Briseis [bry-SEE-iss] from Achilles. The other chiefs did not consent to your deed, but you followed your own pride, and you shamed the bravest of your followers, taking away from him the prize that he had won with his own hands. Only you can undo this evil deed, and now you must make peace with this man whom you have wronged, and return to him that which is rightfully his."

King Agamemnon stood up, and the chiefs feared his rage, for they thought he had been angered by what had been told to him. But his voice was soft and his manner was calm as he looked at Nestor and said, "You have spoken true words, old sir. Truly I acted as a fool that day; I do not deny it. And now, just as it was I who did Achilles wrong that day, so it is I who will give him many times more than that which I took from him. And when we return to Greece, he shall have whatever treasures and cities he wishes, and he shall be as a son to me, and take any daughter of mine for his bride. All this and more shall I grant him if only he will cease from his anger."

The chiefs rejoiced at these words, for none could fault the gifts that Agamemnon had offered, and all believed that the quarrel would at last come to an end. So Ulysses [you-LISS-eez] led a small party of chiefs to the tent of Achilles in the hope that Agamemnon's offer would shake the heart of this proud and mighty warrior. When they entered, Achilles and his dear friend Patroclus [puh-TRO-klus] both leaped to their feet, a little astonished. And Achilles said: "You are welcome, my friends; though I am angry with the king, you will always be friends to me." And he bade [BAD] them to sit and to share sweet wine and fruits with him and Patroclus.

Ulysses filled his cup and drank a toast to the health of Achilles, and then he said: "Though we are pleased to be here in friendship with you, mighty Achilles, this is not a day to think of feasting, for destruction is close at hand. This very day the Trojans and their allies came near to burning our ships, and we are greatly in doubt whether we can save them tomorrow, for it is plain that Zeus is on their side. What we have come to ask of you is that you will not stand aside any longer from the battle, but will come to help us as of old. The king has sent us to offer you gifts great and many to make up for the wrong that he did to you." And Ulysses listed in order all the treasures that Agamemnon had promised to give, and when he finished the list, he said: "Be content with these gifts, Achilles, which no man can say are not sufficient. And if you have no love for Agamemnon, then think of the many Greeks who will perish because you stand aside from the battle. Take the gifts, and by doing so you will have the wealth and the love and the honor of the Greeks, for you will slay Hector, who thinks there is not a man in all of Greece who can stand against him in battle."

But Achilles was unmoved by this appeal, and he recounted the wrongs that had been done him by Agamemnon, saying how he had been shamed before all men by having Briseis taken from him. "As for the gifts Agamemnon offers," said Achilles, "I scorn them, as I would were they twenty times as great. Not all the wealth of Thebes [THEEBZ] could persuade me to stand by his side in battle. And as for his daughter whom he would give me to be my wife, not if she were as beautiful as Aphrodite or as skillful as Athena would I choose her to share my life. Nay, there is no request he can make of any kind that will stay me from leaving this shore tomorrow and sailing back to my homeland and to the people who still respect and honor me, as Agamemnon does not."

And when Achilles had ended his speech, the chiefs sat silent, so vehement [VEE-uh-ment] was he. Then Ulysses rose and said: "Let us depart at once and carry this message back to those who sent us. What Achilles desires, I know not; I know only that he cherishes his anger and cares nothing for his comrades or his people. We will achieve nothing more here tonight." And the chiefs returned to the assembly and reported what Achilles had said.

Patroclus remained with Achilles in his tent, and it was clear that Ulysses' words had moved him deeply. Well he knew that many brave Greeks would die in battle without Achilles and his two or three thousand Myrmidons to fight against the Trojans. The mere sight of Achilles arrayed in his shining armor would put the Trojans to flight, such fear did Achilles inspire. And knowing this, Patroclus appealed to Achilles, saying: "Be not angry with me, great Achilles, for well I know how you have been wronged and why you remain away from the battle. But thousands, nay, tens of thousands of our friends and countrymen are about to die, and so I must ask what I do in order to save their lives and their honor. Let me put on your armor for the battle tomorrow. The Trojans will think that you have returned to the fight and will fall back in fear, for they know well the sight of your golden armor, and they quake at the power of your sword."

Achilles stood in silence for a while, and then answered his friend: "I said to the chiefs that I would not fight this king's battles, but I see that you, my friend, are bound by honor to fight alongside your countrymen. And so I will grant your request, Patroclus, and you will wear my armor and ride in my chariot and lead my Myrmidons in battle tomorrow. But you will have only my armor, not my skill, and so I command that you be not overbold when you feel the joy of battle in your heart, and that you only drive the Trojans from our camp, not pursue them. Promise this, my friend, for your life is dearest of all to me."

And Patroclus promised not to pursue the enemy, and he put on the shining armor that the gods had fashioned for Achilles, and he called the Myrmidons to prepare for the next day's battle.

At daybreak, as Hector was preparing to lead the men of Troy against the Greek defenders who were massing along the wall, a soothsayer came running up to him with the news that he had seen a bad omen in the sky: A bird had appeared soaring over the left edge of the Trojan army, and this foretold of bad events to come that day. The prophet begged Hector to postpone the battle until the bird could be spotted flying over the army's right flank, which would be a sign of good fortune, but Hector replied that, when one fights for his own country, he needs no omens to help him. Then Hector led the attack, and it seemed that he had been correct about the omen, for the Trojans quickly broke through the Greek line, and once again made their way toward the Greek ships.

Suddenly, from along the shore there came the Myrmidons in close array, helmet to helmet and shield to shield, with Patroclus before them in the chariot of Achilles, and with Achilles' charioteer by his side. And when the Trojans saw the Myrmidons and the warrior in shining armor who was leading them into the heart of the fray, they thought that it was Achilles, who had put aside his anger and had come forth again to the battle. Nor was it long before they turned to flee at this sight, and so the battle rolled back again to the trench, and many Trojan chariots were broken when they tried to cross it in haste. But the horses of Achilles sprang across the trench in stride, and his chariot cleared the edge without incident. So great was the fear of the Trojans that even the great Hector fled back across the plain. But now the heart of Patroclus was set upon slaying Hector, for he had forgotten the command that Achilles had laid upon him—that he should save the ships from fire, but fight no more thereafter.

The Trojans continued to flee, and some even found shelter behind the gates of their city, while Patroclus continued to pursue them, all the way to the walls of Troy. Now that he had driven the enemy to its very gates, Patroclus took it into his mind to take the city itself. Three times he tried to scale the walls, and three times the god Apollo appeared to push him back down to the ground. And when Patroclus climbed for the fourth time, then Apollo cried to him in a dreadful voice: "Go back, Patroclus; it is not destined for you to take this great city of Troy—no, nor even for Achilles, who is a far better warrior than you." Then Patroclus went back from the wall, for he feared the anger of the god.

But Hector had seen what had happened at the wall, and he suspected that it was not Achilles who had put his men to flight. "It must be Patroclus wearing Achilles' armor," he said to his charioteer, "for Achilles would not have failed to climb the wall." Spurred on by this thought, Hector took up his mighty spear and headed his chariot toward that of Patroclus. Now the hour of Patroclus's doom had come, for Apollo gave him a great blow on the head from behind, causing Patroclus's helmet to fall from his head onto the dusty plain. Never before had it touched the ground, from the first day when Achilles wore it. The spear he carried in his hand suddenly broke, his shield fell from his arm, and the breastplate was loosened from his body. Then, as he stood without defense and stunned from the blow to his head, one of the Trojans wounded him in the back. Now Hector bore down upon him and thrust at him with his spear, and hit him just above the hip. The spear went clean through the body of Patroclus, and he fell to the ground, cursing Hector with his dying breath.

And when the Greeks saw this, they sent up a dreadful cry and fled back to their camp. Hector removed the bright armor of Achilles from Patroclus's body, and he claimed it as his prize. But when he laid hold of the body and began to drag it away to the ranks of the Trojans, the mighty Greek chief named Ajax, who was taller and stronger than Hector or any other man, Trojan or Greek, returned and stood over the body, as a lioness stands before its cubs and will not let the hunter take them. The sight of such bravery by Ajax emboldened the hearts of the Greeks, and they returned to protect the body of Patroclus. The battle raged anew, for, though the Greeks could not save the body, neither could the Trojans carry it away.

But mighty Zeus was displeased to see Hector newly arrayed in the armor of Achilles, and he also had pity on the brave Greeks who would not leave Patroclus's body, though such bravery might cost them their own bodies. And Zeus caused the Trojans to fall back so that the Greeks could take the body of Patroclus from where it lay in the dust to the tent of Achilles, who wept uncontrollably over the death of his dearest friend.

This had been a sad day, and to bring it sooner to an end,

Hera commanded the sun to set before its time. So did the Greeks rest from their labors.

A Few Words More

Homer tells us that the Greek herald Stentor had a voice that was "as loud as that of fifty other men together," and it is from this character that we get our word *stentorian* [sten-TORE-ee-an], which means "extremely loud."

We can also see in this tale a strange belief in the "goodness" of things on the right and the "evilness" of things on the left. Recall that even seeing a bird flying on the left was considered a bad omen. This tradition, which spans many centuries and occurs in many cultures, may be due to there being more right-handed people, and so lefties were somewhat "strange" and, therefore, not to be trusted. Whatever the reason, our modern words *dexterity*, meaning "skill in the use of the hands," and *dexterous*, meaning "skillful or handy," are direct descendants of the Latin word *dexter*, which meant "on the right side." Adding the Latin prefix *ambi-*, meaning "both," to *dexter* gives us *ambidextrous*, which might describe someone who has "both right hands." And what of the left side, you ask? Well, the Latin word meaning "on the left" has come into our language with its spelling unchanged: *sinister*.

The Wrath of Achilles

About the story:

*Achilles appears to be a man of excess; his every charac-
teristic is extreme. He is the most handsome, the strongest, the bravest, and so on, of all the Greeks. Yet we have
seen these excesses to be not entirely advantageous, for
it is his excessive pride and his absolute unwillingness
to compromise that have caused the death of many of his
countrymen and especially the death of his dearest
friend, Patroclus. In the following tale, we see the almost limitless rage that his friend's death inspires in
Achilles.*

Approximate reading time: 19 minutes
Vocabulary and pronunciation guide:
  impenetrable [im-PEN-ih-truh-bull]: cannot be pierced
  Myrmidons [MUR-mid-onz]: the soldiers whom Achil-
    les brought with him to the Trojan War
  Aeneas [uh-NEE-us]
  Anchises [an-KYE-seez]
  Poseidon [poe-SYE-dun]: Greek god of the sea (the Ro-
    mans called this god Neptune)
  Priam [PRY-am]
  Andromache [an-DRAH-muh-key]
  Styx [STICKS]: the river that souls must cross to enter
    Hades

W
hen the body of the noble and brave Patroclus [puh-
TRO-klus] was brought back into the camp of the
Greeks, a wailing could be heard from the tent of
Achilles [uh-KILL-eez] that was like unto the sounds from the
lost souls in the Underworld. Such was the sorrow of this bravest warrior of all that the chiefs feared he would kill himself in

his grief, and they took turns in comforting him and watching over his safety.

But his mother heard his cries where she sat in the depths of the sea, and she came to him and laid her hand upon his head, saying: "Why do you weep so, my son? Tell me, and hide nothing from me."

Achilles answered: "All that you asked from Zeus, and that he promised to do, he has done, but what is the good? The man whom I loved above all others is dead, and Hector has my armor, for Patroclus was wearing it. As for me, I do not wish to live at all, except to avenge his death."

Then said Thetis [THEE-tiss (th as in think)]: "My son, do not speak so, for do you not know the prophecy that when Hector dies the hour of your own death will be near?"

"Well I know the prophecy, Mother," Achilles cried in great anger, "but I also well know that I sent my friend to his death, and I, the best in battle of all the Greeks, could not help him. Cursed be the anger that caused me to quarrel with King Agamemnon and so to cause the death of my dearest friend. What does my fate matter now? Let it come when it may, but let me first have my vengeance upon Hector."

Now Thetis knew that she could not keep her son from going into battle, and she answered him, saying: "So be it, but you cannot fight without armor, and Hector has your own. Tonight I will go to see Vulcan at his forge inside Mount Etna, and he will fashion for you a set of armor more than equal to that which you lost." And this she did.

Vulcan was the lame son of Zeus and Hera, but instead of living in luxury on Olympus, he worked at a fiery furnace inside a mountain, where he wrought gold and silver and copper and iron to create whatever metalwork was needed by the gods. After hearing Thetis's request, Vulcan labored all through the night fabricating a most splendid shield adorned with many intricate designs, and a helmet crested with gold, and a breastplate and leg armor of impenetrable [im-PEN-ih-truh-bull] hardness, all perfectly adapted to Achilles' form and of the finest workmanship. By dawn, he had finished all his work, and he gave the shield and other arms to Thetis, who flew, swift as a hawk, to her son's tent near the ships. She found him lying on the ground, holding in his arms the body of

Patroclus, weeping aloud, and the Myrmidons [MUR-mid-onz] were weeping, too.

The goddess stood in their midst and caught her son by the hand and said: "Come now, and put your grieving aside; it was the will of the gods that Patroclus should die. But you must think about other things. Here is the armor that Vulcan has fashioned for you, the like of which has never been seen before."

And as she spoke, she cast down the armor at the feet of Achilles. It rattled loudly as it fell, and it shone so brightly that the eyes of the Myrmidons were dazzled by it. Achilles was glad at heart to see such a gift, and his weeping ceased altogether. "Mother," he said, "these indeed are such arms as could only be made in heaven. Gladly will I put them on for the battle, but first I must make my peace with Agamemnon [agg-uh-MEM-non]."

Achilles strode out along the line of ships, calling all the chiefs to assemble together in council. And when they had gathered, Achilles stood before them and said to Agamemnon: "It was a foolish thing, O King, that we quarreled, for many a Greek is now dead who would still be alive but for this, and the Trojans have profited from our loss. But let bygones be bygones. Here I make an end of my anger."

Then King Agamemnon answered from the place where he sat: "Listen, ye Greeks. You have blamed me for this quarrel, but I say that it was the gods who brought it about. Nevertheless, it is for me to make amends, and this I will do, giving to Achilles all the gifts that Ulysses promised in my name." But Achilles replied: "Give the gifts, O King, if you are pleased to do so, or keep them for yourself. There is one thing only that I care for, and that is to get out to the battle without delay." Whereupon he picked up his shining new shield, and he hefted his great spear, which no man but he could wield, and he called to his Myrmidons and to all the Greeks to join him in avenging the cruel death of Patroclus.

The Greeks swarmed out to engage the Trojans on the wide plain, and the rage of Achilles was such that many brave men of Troy fell by his spear and his sword. None could stand against him, and he slew many men as they fled the approach of his chariot. The Trojans were soon put to rout, and they ran back toward the city gates, though many were struck by Greek arrows and spears in the back as they fled.

Only Aeneas [uh-NEE-us], who was the son that the goddess Aphrodite [aff-row-DYE-tee] bore when she fell in love with a mortal nobleman of Troy named Anchises [an-KYE-seez]—only he of all the Trojans stayed to do battle with the mighty Achilles. And when Achilles' chariot approached him, Aeneas cast his spear, and it struck square into the shield of the Greek, making such a sound as would frighten any man. But the work of Vulcan had been fashioned of five metal plates— two of brass, two of tin, and one of gold. The spear pierced only two thicknesses and was stopped by the third. Now Achilles threw *his* spear, which easily penetrated Aeneas's shield and passed right through, but it touched not his body and caused no wound. Though deadly frightened, Aeneas did not flee. As Achilles drew his sword and rushed at him, the Trojan picked up a large stone from the ground and was about to hurl it at the onrushing figure in gleaming armor, when Zeus looked down and saw that Aeneas would surely be slain. And Zeus commanded the sea god, Poseidon [poe-SYE-dun], to hide Aeneas in a cloud of fog, for it had been decreed that he and his children after him should reign in the time to come over the people of Troy. Achilles approached the cloud, but could not find Aeneas, for he had been lifted away by Poseidon to the rear of the battle, and so Achilles turned his wrath upon whatever Trojan he saw, and many were slain as they fled from him.

Now King Priam [PRY-am] looked down from the city walls and beheld his whole army in flight, and he ordered the gates to be opened so they could have shelter behind the walls. The Trojans flocked into the city through the gates, nor did they stay to ask who was safe and who was dead, so great was their fear and such their haste. Only Hector remained outside to prevent the Greeks from following them into the city. His father, Priam, pleaded with him from atop the wall, saying, "O my son, do not wait to do battle with Achilles, for he is stronger than you and is much loved by the gods. Come within the walls, my dear son, for you are the hope of this city." But he could not move the heart of Hector.

Then Queen Hecuba [HECK-you-bah] cried to him: "O Hector, my son, have pity on me and come inside these walls. If Achilles conquers you, then not only will you die, but the

Greeks will kill all the sons of Troy and carry all its daughters into captivity." But her prayers were in vain, for Hector was determined to await the coming of Achilles, and to stand against him in battle.

Achilles came near, shaking the great spear over his right shoulder, and the flashing of his armor was like to fire or to the sun when it rises. Hector trembled when he saw him, and his heart failed him so that he turned his back and fled, fast as he could toward the city gate. But Achilles pursued him, just as a hawk pursues a dove among the hills, and Hector could not reach the city gate. Turning then, he sped past the watchtower and along the wagon road that ran around the city walls, with Achilles fast upon his heels all the while. In this way they circled the city three times, as the Trojans on the wall and the Greeks upon the plain looked on.

The gods looked down from Olympus and saw brave Hector, who had been the most valiant of warriors, running for his life. And Zeus took pity on him, well knowing that Hector was destined to die by the hand of Achilles, and he ordered Apollo to put strength in Hector's knees so that he might stand and fight Achilles like the brave prince he had always been. Then did Hector stop and cry to Achilles: "Three times have you pursued me round the walls, and I dared not stand against you, but now I fear you no more. Only let us make a covenant that whoever is victorious shall keep the other's armor as his prize, but he shall swear to give the body back to its people. Will you join me in this covenant?"

Achilles frowned at him and said: "Hector, talk not of covenants to me. Men and lions make no oaths to each other, neither is there any agreement between wolves and sheep. I promise only to have vengeance upon you and your body for all my comrades you have slain, and especially for Patroclus, the man whom I loved beyond all others."

Then he threw his great spear, but Hector saw it coming and avoided it, crouching down so that the spear flew over his head and stuck itself in the ground. But Athena [uth-EE-nuh] snatched it up and gave it back to Achilles, although this Hector did not see. Then Hector cast his spear, and his aim was true, though it struck Achilles' gleaming shield and bounded far away. Now Hector drew his great sword and rushed at Achilles, only now to see his adversary armed anew with his

giant spear, its point shining bright as the evening star, and
Hector saw that his own death was near. Achilles aimed his
spear toward a spot unprotected by the armor that Hector had
taken from Patroclus, by the collarbone, where the neck joins
the shoulder. There he drove in the spear, and the point
emerged through the back of Hector, and Hector fell in the
dust. His voice now faint, Hector made his last appeal: "O
Achilles, I beg you, by all that you hold dear, to give my body
to my father and mother that they may bury it, and they will
pay you large sums of gold and silver."

But the wrath of Achilles was boundless, and he replied:
"Speak not to me of ransom, for Priam shall not buy you back,
no, not for your weight in gold. The dogs and vultures shall eat
at your flesh, and noble Patroclus shall know that he has been
avenged." And when Hector had breathed his last, Achilles
fastened thongs of oxhide to the ankles of the body and tied the
other ends to his chariot, and he dragged the body several
times around the dusty plain in full view of Priam and Hecuba
and Hector's wife, Andromache [an-DRAH-mah-key], who
wept uncontrollably at the hideous sight.

Hector's body was dragged back into the camp of the Greeks,
and there it was shamefully treated. Then Zeus sent for Thetis
and said to her: "Go to the camp and bid your son give up the
body of Hector for ransom. It angers me to see him do such
dishonor to the dead." And Thetis brought this message to
Achilles, who agreed to give up the body when Priam came to
ransom it.

It was not long before King Priam appeared at the Greek
camp, with a wagonload of golden basins and cups, silver cal-
drons, and finely woven fabrics; nothing of his treasures was
left behind. He was escorted to the tent of Achilles, and there
he fell to his knees and kissed Achilles' hands, the very hands
that had slain several of his sons. He said: "Have pity on me, O
Achilles, and think of your own father, who is as old as I.
Would you have him beg and grovel at the feet of the man who
slew his son, his only wish being the return of his son's body?"

Then the heart of Achilles was moved with pity and he wept,
thinking now of his old father and now of the dead Patroclus.
At last he stood up from his seat and said: "Surely, old man,
you must have a heart as strong as iron to come here as you
have done. I will accept your gifts of ransom, and when the

body is washed and anointed with oil, it shall be placed in your wagon, and you shall be free to return with it to Troy."

Now Priam thanked Achilles for being so fair, and he offered that there be declared a truce for twelve days so that his son could be buried with proper ceremony. To this Achilles agreed, and Hector's body was taken back within the walls of Troy, where funeral ceremonies and games were held, and the fighting did not resume until the twelfth day.

The Greeks now massed their forces outside the walls of Troy, but no army came from the city to meet them. The Trojan generals knew that they had lost many of their bravest men, including mighty Hector, to the spear and sword of Achilles, and that the rest of their warriors were no match for the Greeks as long as Achilles was there to lead them. Their plan, therefore, was to fight only with arrows from the walls and towers, and to wait for reinforcements to arrive from other kingdoms that were friendly with Troy. And in this way they were able to drive back every Greek attempt to storm the gates or scale the walls.

Now the fiercest archer of all the Trojans was Paris, who had caused the long war by stealing Helen and taking her for his wife. All day he had showered his arrows on the Greeks, so that now his bowstring was frayed. He chose a new bowstring, and fitted it, and strung the bow, and selected the straightest of all the arrows from his quiver, and he dipped its point in a poison and aimed this special arrow at Achilles himself. His aim had to be precise, for there was but one spot on Achilles' body where he could suffer a mortal wound.

When Achilles was born, you see, his mother, Thetis, took him to the Underworld, the Land of the Shades, and dipped him in the river Styx [STICKS] so that every part of his body that was touched by its water would be invulnerable to harm. Thetis stood on the riverbank and held her son by his heel as she lowered his body into the protective waters, and so the boy's heel remained dry. This, then, was the only spot in which he could be wounded, and this was the spot at which Paris aimed his poisoned arrow.

Paris arched his trusted bow as far as it would bend, and he let his arrow fly with a prayer to the gods that it be allowed to find its mark. And so it did. The metal leg armor that Vulcan had fashioned for Achilles ran down to his ankle, but no farther, and here it was that Paris's arrow struck, just above the heel. Achilles wheeled around in surprise and pain; he stumbled and fell, and his shining armor was defiled with dust and blood.

Then Achilles rose again and cried: "What coward has smitten me with a secret arrow from afar? Let him stand forth and meet me with sword and spear!" So speaking, he seized the arrow with his strong hands and tore it out of the wound, and much blood gushed, and darkness came over his eyes. He staggered forward, striking out blindly with his sword and spear, cursing the Trojans, whom he called cowards and vermin. But as he spoke he fell, and all his armor rang around him; yet the Trojans stood apart and watched, as hunters watch a dying lion, not daring to go too near. So the Trojans stood in fear until Achilles drew his last breath. Then from the wall they raised a great cry of joy, for it was Achilles who had slain their noble Hector. And thus the prophecy was fulfilled.

Now the Trojans rushed from the gates to seize the body of Achilles, and a great battle took place before Ulysses could lift the body over his shoulder and carry it to the Greek camp behind the low wall. There was much weeping among the Greeks that night, and for many nights to come. The body of Achilles was placed on a great pile of dry wood, which was set aflame, and in this way was reduced to a handful of white ashes. These they placed in a great golden cup and mingled with them the ashes of Patroclus. And they placed the cup in a tomb they built high above the seashore, so that men for all time might see it as they go sailing by, and would remember Achilles, the greatest warrior who ever lived.

A Few Words More

Vulcan, the Roman name for the god of fire and the blacksmith of the gods, labored at a steaming forge that was hidden deep inside a mountain. It is no wonder, then, that the smoke and fire that spewed forth from some mountaintops were thought by the ancients to be vented from Vulcan's furnace, and these mountains now bear a form of his name: *volcano.*

Just as Achilles had one place on his body that was vulnerable—the heel by which his mother held him when she dipped his body in the protective waters of the Styx—so today, any weak or unguarded spot is figuratively referred to as a person's "Achilles' heel." This myth is also recalled in the name that has been given to the large tendon that runs from the heel bone to the calf: the "Achilles' tendon."

The Wooden Horse

About the story:

> *Perhaps the most famous symbol of the Trojan War, the huge wooden horse that the Greeks used to gain entry into the city of Troy, does not appear in Homer's* **Iliad,** *for that epic is primarily concerned with the quarrel between Achilles and Agamemnon. We learn about the horse from other sources, and we can only guess whether such a device was actually used by the Greeks. It is fitting, though, that the story of Helen of Troy, which began with Paris's treachery in stealing Helen from her homeland, comes to a close with this famous deception that secures her return.*

Approximate reading time: 18 minutes

Vocabulary and pronunciation guide:

> **vehement** [VEE-eh-ment]: passionate; forceful
> **Laocoön** [lay-AHK-uh-wahn]
> **bade** [BAD]: requested or ordered; past tense of *bid*
> **Sinon** [SYE-non]
> **Palamedes** [pal-uh-ME-deez]
> **Calchas** [KAL-cuss]
> **Diomedes** [dye-oh-ME-deez]
> **Iphigenia** [if-ih-jen-EE-uh]
> **citadel** [SIT-uh-dell]: a fortress built within a city
> **Cassandra** [kuh-SAND-ruh]
> **prophesied** [PROFF-uh-sighed]: predicted; foresaw
> **Ilium** [ILL-ee-um]: the Greek name for the city of Troy

*A*fter the death of Achilles [uh-KILL-eez], the battles commenced once again. At times the Trojans would emerge from the gates to fight the Greeks hand-to-hand out on the plain, but these occasions were rare. Most days saw the Greeks gather at the base of the walls of Troy and try to crash the gates or scale the walls, while the Trojans, safe behind their battlements, killed many Greek warriors with their arrows and crushed others with huge stones thrown from the walls above.

After retreating yet again from a day's assault on the high-walled city, the Greeks held a council and asked advice from the prophet Calchas [KAL-cuss]. Now Calchas would oftentimes see omens and portents in the activities of animals and birds, and it happened that on the previous day he had seen a hawk pursuing a dove, which hid in a hole in a rocky cliff. For a long while the hawk tried to find the hole and follow the dove into it, but he could not reach her. So he flew away for a short distance and hid himself; then the dove fluttered out into the sunlight, thinking she was no longer in danger, and the hawk swooped down on her and made his kill. The Greeks, said Calchas, ought to learn a lesson from the hawk and take Troy by cunning, for it was clear that they could not conquer her by force.

The words of Calchas inspired the wise Ulysses [you-LISS-eez], and he rose to describe a trick that would allow their warriors to enter the walled city at last. The Greeks, he said, ought to make an enormous hollow horse of wood, and place the bravest men, armed for battle, inside the horse. Then all the rest of the army should embark in their ships and set sail—not to their homeland—but to a small island that lay but a short distance away. There they could conceal themselves and their ships behind the island, while the Trojans would think they had given up the battle and had sailed for home. The Trojans, he said, would come out of their city, like the dove out of her hole in the rock, and would wander about the Greek camp, and would wonder why the great wooden horse had been made and why it had been left behind. Lest they should set fire to the horse, or smash it open and discover the warriors inside, a cunning Greek, whom the Trojans did not know by sight, should be left in the camp or near it. He would tell the Trojans that the Greeks had given up all hope and had gone home, and he was to say that they feared the anger of Athena [uth-EE-nuh], who protected the city from harm. To soothe the goddess and to prevent her from sending violent storms to sink their ships, the Greeks (so the man was to say) had built this wooden horse as an offering to her. The Trojans, believing this story, would surely drag the horse inside the city walls. In the dark of night, then, the army would return from the nearby island, and the horse's belly would quietly issue forth the hidden warriors, who would open the city gates for their waiting comrades. Troy would be theirs at last!

The prophet was much pleased with the plan, and so on the next day, half the army was sent, axes in hand, to cut down trees and to hew thousands of planks that would shape the giant figure. In three days, the horse was finished, and Ulysses asked for brave warriors to hide inside, and for the bravest volunteer of all to stay behind and be captured by the Trojans. Then a young man called Sinon [SYE-non] stood up and said that he would risk himself and take the chance that the Trojans might slay him outright or not believe him and burn him alive. Certainly none of the Greeks, throughout the ten years of war, had done anything more courageous, yet Sinon had never been considered a brave man. He had not fought in the front ranks, nor had he distinguished himself in any individual battles, yet there were many brave fighters among the Greeks who would not have dared to do what Sinon undertook.

The ten or twelve warriors—including the wise Ulysses and Menelaus [men-uh-LAY-us], the husband of Helen—who climbed into the horse, first embraced their fellows as if for the last time, and then they wrapped themselves and their armor in soft silks so that no sounds would give their presence away. The rest of the army then burned all the huts along the shore and launched their ships, every man hoping that the Trojans would be so foolish as to drag the image into their town and so invite their own destruction.

From the walls the Trojans saw the black smoke go up thick into the sky and the whole fleet of the Greeks sailing out to sea. Never were men so glad, and they armed themselves for fear of an ambush and went cautiously, sending forth scouts in front of them, down to the seashore. Here they found the huts burned down and the camp deserted, and some of the scouts also caught Sinon, who had hidden himself in a place where he was likely to be found. They rushed on him with fierce cries, and bound his hands with a rope, and kicked and dragged him along to the place where Priam [PRY-am] and the Trojan generals were staring in wonder at the great wooden horse that had been so mysteriously left along the shore.

One of the leaders said, "It is a very curious thing. Let us drag it into the city that it may be a monument of all that we have suffered for the last ten years." But others said, "Not so; we had better burn it, or drag it out into the sea that the water may cover it, or cut it open to see whether there is anything inside."

Of these, no one was more vehement [VEE-eh-ment] than Laocoön [lay-AHK-uh-wahn], one of Priam's sons and the priest of Apollo's temple at Troy. "Take heed what you do, men of Troy," he cried. "Who knows whether the Greeks have really gone away? It may be that there are armed men inside this wooden horse; it may be that it has been made so big so that warriors hidden from our sight may use it to scale our walls. No matter what its purpose may be, I fear the Greeks, even though they bear gifts." And as he spoke, he threw the spear that he had in his hand at the horse of wood, and struck it on the side. A great rattling sound was heard, and the Trojans, if they had not been so blind and foolish, might have known that there was something wrong.

While the dispute was going on, the scouts arrived with Sinon in tow, and they announced that they had found the Greek hiding not far away. Perhaps he could tell them the meaning of the giant horse of wood. The Trojans crowded around him and began to mock at him, but he cried out in a very piteous voice, "What shall I do? Where shall I go? The Greeks will not let me live, and the Trojans cry out for vengeance upon me." Then they began to pity him, and they bade [BAD] him say who he was and what he had to tell.

Then the man turned to King Priam and said, "I will speak the truth, whatever may happen to me. My name is Sinon, and I will not deny that I am a Greek. Perhaps you have heard of my cousin, Palamedes [pal-uh-ME-deez], whom the Greeks called a traitor but whose only fault was that he wanted to have peace. Yes, they put him to death, and now that he is gone, they are sorry, but there is nothing they can do to bring him back. It was, in fact, because of the lies that Ulysses told against my cousin that Palamedes was accused and punished, and I swore that someday I would have revenge upon all those who wronged him. So Ulysses was always eager to do me harm, and at last, with the help of the prophet Calchas—but why do I tell you of these things? Doubtless you hold one Greek as bad as another. Kill me, if you will, only remember that my death is the very thing that Ulysses himself would give much money to secure."

Then the Trojans said, "Tell us more."

And he went on. "Many times would the Greeks have gone home, for they were very tired of the war, but the sea was so stormy that they dared not go. Then they made this great horse of wood that you see, but the storms grew worse and worse. Then they prayed to Apollo to guide them in their actions, and Apollo said, 'Men of Greece, when you came here, you first had to sacrifice the beautiful Iphigenia [if-ih-jen-EE-uh], daughter of Agamemnon [agg-uh-MEM-non], and so appease the winds with blood. You must appease them with blood as you leave or you will never see your homeland again.' All of us trembled at this message, for everyone feared that it might be his blood that would be sacrificed to the winds. After a while, Ulysses brought the prophet Calchas into the assembly and said, 'Tell us now who it is that the gods will have for a victim?' All the Greeks had long respected the prophecies of Calchas, and so no one guessed that he and Ulysses had secretly plotted together to seal my fate. 'Sinon is the man,' said Calchas, and all in the assembly agreed, for now Sinon's doom meant each of them was out of danger. So they fixed a day on which I was to be sacrificed, and everything was made ready. But before that day came, I broke my bonds and escaped, hiding myself in the reeds of a pond, until at last they sailed away. And now I shall never see my own country again—no, nor my wife and children—and doubtless these cruel Greeks will take vengeance on them because I escaped. And now I beseech you, O King, to have pity on me, for I have suffered much, though, indeed, I have not done harm to any man."

Then King Priam had pity on him and bade the Trojans unbind his hands, saying, "Forget your own people; from today you are one of us. But tell us now, why did the Greeks make this great horse of wood that we see?"

Then Sinon lifted up his hands to the sky and said, "O sun and moon and stars, I call you to witness that I have a good right to tell the secrets of my countrymen. Listen, O King. From the beginning, when the Greeks first came to this place, their hope resided in the help of the gods, but after ten long years of battle, they saw that they were no closer to capturing your city and returning fair Helen than they were when they first sailed to your shores. And so Agamemnon called a council of all the chiefs, and there he asked the prophet Calchas to consult the stars and omens and to reveal the will of the gods. And Calchas said to them: 'The gods have allowed us to kill many Trojan princes and to make the people cower behind their city walls, but to capture the city itself, we must go home to Greece before returning here to begin this war anew. Furthermore, we must make a horse of wood to be a peace offering to the goddess Athena. We must build it so large that the Trojans cannot take it within their walls, for if they do, Athena will never allow us to conquer the city. Nay, once the gift is within their walls, it has been foretold, the Trojans will soon lay siege to our own cities and kill our wives and children. This the gods have ordained, and also that whoever harms the horse in any way shall perish.' And my countrymen did as Calchas advised; they have gone back to Greece, but they will soon return."

This was the tale that Sinon told, and the Trojans believed it. Nor is this to be wondered at, for even the gods took part in deceiving them. And this is what they did.

While Laocoön, the priest who had thrown his spear at the great horse, was praying that his people would not bring the image into the city, the gods sent two great serpents across the sea from a nearby island. All the Trojans saw them come, with their heads raised high above the water, as is the way of certain snakes when they swim. And when they reached the land, they came on straight to where the Trojans were gathered. Their eyes were red as blood, and blazed like fire, and they made a dreadful hissing with their tongues. The Trojans grew pale with fear, and fled. But the serpents did not turn this way or that, but came straight to the altar at which Laocoön stood, with his two sons by his side. And one serpent laid hold on one of the boys, and the other on the other, and they began to devour them. Then the father picked up a sword, but before he could lash out, the serpents caught hold of him and wound themselves, two times, around his body and his neck, their heads standing in triumph high above his. And still he tried as hard as he could to tear them away with his hands, but to no avail.

And when the serpents had done their work, and both the priest and his sons were dead, then they glided to the hill on which stood the temple of Athena and hid themselves under the feet of her image. And when the Trojans saw this, they said to themselves,"Now Laocoön has suffered the due reward of his deeds, for he threw his spear at the holy thing that belongs to the goddess, and now he is dead and his sons with him."

Then they all cried out together that the horse of wood should be drawn into the citadel [SIT-uh-dell]. So they opened the great gate of the city, pulling down part of the wall so that there might be more room, and they put rollers under the feet of the horse, and they fastened ropes to it. Then they drew it into the city, boys and girls laying hold of the ropes, and singing songs with great joy. And everyone thought it a great thing if he could pull on any one of the ropes.

The rejoicing was so complete that no one gave heed to the ample signs of evil to come. Four times did the horse halt as they dragged it, before it passed through the gate, and each time there might have been heard a great clashing of metal sounds within. Also, Cassandra [kuh-SAND-ruh] spoke out and prophesied [PROFF-uh-sighed] that the horse would bring on the destruction of Troy. But ever since Apollo had punished her by decreeing that no one would believe her predictions again, the people refused to give any heed to her warnings. So the Trojans drew the horse of wood into the city, and that night they held a great and joyous feast to the gods, not knowing that the end of their city was now close at hand.

All through the wild festivities that night, the giant wooden horse stood in the courtyard at the very center of the city. The people of Troy danced and drank and sang songs of celebration, and even the guards who had been posted at the gates to the city joined in the revelry and drank wine until they were quite useless as sentinels. All the while, the Greek ships silently made their way from behind the island to the banks of their former camp.

Sometime after midnight, when the celebrants had either fallen asleep from drink or had gone to their homes to enjoy the first night of peace in ten years, Sinon—who had been accepted as a citizen of Troy—carefully opened the secret latch in the belly of the horse, and the Greek warriors let themselves down softly to the ground. Some rushed to the gate, killing the sleeping guards and letting in the army of the Greeks. Others sped with torches to burn the houses of the Trojan princes and to slay those who had killed their friends and brothers during the war. Terrible was the slaughter of men, unarmed and half awake, and loud were the cries of women. All through the city were the sounds of fighting and slaying and dying.

When dawn came, Troy lay in ashes, and the women were being driven with spear shafts to the ships, and the men were left unburied, their once-noble bodies now food for wild dogs and birds. All the gold and silver, and the rich embroideries, and the ivory and amber, and the horses and chariots were divided among the army. Agamemnon was given the beautiful Cassandra, daughter of King Priam, as a prize, and lovely Helen, whose capture had begun this war ten long years ago—whose face had "launched a thousand ships and burnt the top-less towers of Ilium [ILL-ee-um]"—was led in honor to the ship of Menelaus, and eventually back to Sparta, where she and her husband ruled as queen and king.

A Few Words More

Although the great wooden horse was built by the Greeks, it has always been referred to as the "Trojan Horse." This name and a paraphrase of Laocoön's advice, "Beware of Greeks bearing gifts," have come into our language as a symbol and a warning of impending treachery or infiltration.

Another phrase from this myth, a description of Helen as having "the face that launched a thousand ships," is actually the creation of Christopher Marlowe, a sixteenth-century English dramatist. Today the phrase, as well as any mention of the beautiful Helen of Troy, has come to signify a beauty so rare that it, by itself, could cause men to go off to war.

The Return of Ulysses

The following group of tales all concern the voyage of one of the greatest heroes of ancient Greece, Ulysses, and the adventures he had as he made his way back to Ithaca after the end of the Trojan War. The name Ulysses was the one the Romans used to refer to this character. The Greeks called him Odysseus [oh-DISS-ee-us], and his story was told in the great epic poem titled the *Odyssey* [ODD-ess-ee], which meant "the tale of Odysseus." Our modern word *odyssey*, meaning a long or adventurous journey, comes directly from the title of this epic poem.

Homer—the poet whose other great epic, the *Iliad*, tells the story of the Trojan War itself—relies not so much on historical fact as on folklore in telling of Ulysses' travels and exploits following the war. Here we encounter more monsters and witches and magic spells than we found in the tale of Helen of Troy, and the places that Ulysses visits are not identifiable on any map. Still, it is the human struggles that are the real focus in this epic, just as they were in the *Iliad*. Ulysses pits his wisdom and his courage against not only the supernatural dangers that are set in his path, but against the very natural enemies that all humans face, such as fear, ignorance, and the evil hearts of some fellow humans.

The pronunciation guide that follows includes words and names that occur frequently throughout the stories of Ulysses. It is best to become familiar with these pronunciations before beginning this saga; other troublesome words will be identified and explained at the beginning of each story.

Pronunciation guide (names that recur frequently in the story):
>   **Ulysses** [you-LISS-eez]
>   **Ithaca** [IH-thick-uh]
>   **Athena** [uth-EE-nuh]
>   **Zeus** [ZOOSE]
>   **Agamemnon** [agg-uh-MEM-non]
>   **Poseidon** [po-SYE-dun]
>   **Penelope** [pen-EL-oh-pee]
>   **Telemachus** [tell-EM-uh-cuss]

The Greeks Set Sail

About the story:

Although the **Odyssey** *actually begins "in the middle of things," as was the custom for epic poetry, the story of Ulysses' return is told here in the order that his adventures occurred. In this opening tale, we see the Greeks setting sail for their homeland after ten long years of war with Troy, and we see the gods once again taking an active part in the affairs of mortals.*

The most famous of Ulysses' adventures, his capture by a Cyclops, is mentioned only briefly here. A complete treatment of this story can be found in **Classics to Read Aloud to Your Children.**

Approximate reading time: 10 minutes

Vocabulary and pronunciation guide:

hubris [HYOO-briss]: arrogance and overbearing pride, as when mortals assume that their own deeds, rather than those of the gods, determine the events of the world

Mycenae [my-SEE-nee]: a city in ancient Greece; the kingdom of Agamemnon

Cyclopes [sye-KLOPE-eez]: a race of one-eyed giants; plural of Cyclops [SYE-clopps]

Polyphemus [pol-ee-FEE-mus]: a Cyclops; son of Poseidon

ogres [OH-gurz]: monsters

lotus [LOW-tuss]

Aeolus [ee-OH-lus]: god of the winds

*B*y deceiving the Trojans into taking their huge wooden horse into the city, the Greeks who were hidden inside were able to slip out of the horse at night and open the gates of Troy to their comrades. Once inside the city, the Greek army took its vengeance on the sleeping Trojans, and ten long years of war came to a most violent end in one terrifying night of murder and mayhem.

The Greeks left Troy a mass of smoldering ashes; they slew King Priam [PRY-am] and his sons, they abused and murdered many of the Trojan women and children, and they set fire to every house and temple. The madness and fury of their victory celebration that first night inside the city walls knew no bounds. The chiefs were powerless to control the ten years of rage that had built up within their men; indeed, some of the leaders were the cruelest of all who took vengeance on the defeated people of Troy.

But in these excesses lay the seeds of their own destruction, for the Greeks forgot that it was not by their hands that the city had fallen, but by the will and the acts of the gods. And so, in their pride, they paid no attention to the honor and praise that was due the gods, and especially to Athena [uth-EE-nuh] and Poseidon [po-SYE-dun], who had been their allies and without whose aid they would surely have been defeated. No ceremonies were held nor any sacrifices made in the name of these divine benefactors, and such hubris [HYOO-briss] did not go unnoticed by those who looked down on the days and nights of savagery from high above the clouds.

Athena and Poseidon pleaded that the Greeks must be punished for their pride, and mighty Zeus nodded his head in concurrence. And so, from the time the Greeks set sail back to their homes, they encountered troubles that were as black as any they had brought down upon the Trojans. Poseidon caused the seas to swamp their boats, and the winds to drive them far off course, and vicious monsters to claw out at them from the deep. Countless men were drowned or left battered on isolated ocean reefs, and those who survived—like King Menelaus and the fair Helen, his newly rescued queen—were driven by the winds to Egypt and other far-off lands before they could manage to find their way back home to Sparta. King Agamemnon [agg-uh-MEM-non], who had led the Greeks in battle and who had been given much of the treasure of Troy, was murdered by his wife and her lover as he entered the gates of his own city of Mycenae [my-SEE-nee].

None of the chiefs, though, had a longer or a more perilous journey home than did wise Ulysses [you-LISS-eez], who left the shores of Troy with twelve ships, each with fifty men, but who arrived in his kingdom of Ithaca [IH-thick-uh], ten years later, all alone. It was the god Poseidon who was the cause of Ulysses' troubles, and this is how Ulysses brought down upon himself the wrath of the god of the sea.

A great storm had carried Ulysses' ships far off their course and beached them on the coast of a land inhabited by one-eyed giants who lived in caves. This was the land of the Cyclopes [sye-KLOPE-eez], a race of hideous monsters, each a giant with one huge eye in the middle of his forehead and an eyebrow beneath. The Cyclopes tended their flocks and worked in their vineyards and led lives of ease, for they were the ill-formed sons of the god Poseidon. But woe be it to any stranger who came upon these creatures, for the Cyclopes obeyed no laws and thought nothing of hospitality. Indeed, they saw humans merely as morsels of food that were put in their grasp as gifts from the gods.

Ulysses and a party of his men became trapped in the cave of one of these giants, a Cyclops [SYE-clopps] named Polyphemus [pol-ee-FEE-mus], who ate two men from the group each day for his dinner. But crafty Ulysses devised a trick by which they could escape. After the giant fell asleep from drinking too much wine, Ulysses drove a burning stake through the middle of his one eye, blinding Polyphemus and causing him terrible pain. Now the giant could not see Ulysses and his men clinging to the wool of the sheep that Polyphemus let out of the cave to graze, and so the Greeks escaped to their ships and sailed away. Polyphemus prayed to his father, Poseidon, for vengeance against Ulysses, and the sea god vowed that this Greek would suffer long for his sins, and that none of his men would ever see their homes again.

Poseidon began immediately to punish Ulysses and his men. Over several days the currents and winds had pushed their boats to a rocky harbor in which all of the ships except that of Ulysses moored in a row. Ulysses tied his own vessel to a large rock outside the harbor, and he climbed up to a point from which he could see out across the land. This was a wise thing for Ulysses to do, for the people turned out to be cannibals, and they flocked down in crowds to crush the ships under a shower of rocks and spears, killing the poor sailors like fishes. Ulysses and his shipmates cut their cable and rowed for their very lives out to sea, amid a splash of rocks that were pelted at them from the cliffs above the harbor. And they managed to escape these cruel ogres [OH-gurz], but they wept a long while for their comrades who had not been so lucky.

Now Ulysses had but a single ship and a small company of men to guide back to Ithaca, but it would not be soon that they would see their homeland and their families again.

For ten days they sailed, until a fearsome storm tattered their sails and drove their ship onto a sandy beach in an unknown land. Ulysses took three men ashore and, while he searched the area for a source of fresh water, he sent the three inland as scouts to learn about what type of people inhabited this land. And the scouts did discover a quiet and friendly people, who fed them from a fruit that was strange to the sailors. This was the fruit of the lotus [LOW-tuss], for little did they know that they had arrived in the land of the lotus-eaters. Whoever tastes of that fruit has no longer any desire to return home, or to do anything at all but to sit and dream happy dreams and forget the troubles of the world, and even forget his home and family. The three men ate of the lotus, and sat down in a daze to dream, but Ulysses went after them, and drove them to the ship, much against their will, and he bound their hands and feet, and tied them to their benches. Then quickly did Ulysses order the oars to strike the water, for well he knew the powers of the lotus, and much did he fear the dreamy idleness that this flowery food might offer him and his men as a balm for all their troubles and sorrows.

The ship sailed on, in what direction and for how long no one is sure, but in time a lookout spied a far-off island that appeared to be floating above the sea. As they came nearer, they found that the island had a steep cliff of bronze, with a palace on the top. Here lived Aeolus [ee-OH-lus], the King of the Winds, with his six sons and six daughters. Aeolus treated Ulysses kindly and encouraged him to tell of his deeds in the war with Troy and of his adventures on the journey home. Ulysses told his tales, which were fascinating to Aeolus and his children, but there were so many stories to tell that Ulysses remained on the floating island for a month.

But now Ulysses was of a mind to continue his voyage home, and Aeolus thanked his guest and made him a gift of a leather bag tied with a silver cord, in which he had bound up all the winds but one: the kind and gentle west wind. Ulysses' ship sailed away on a smooth sea, wafted by the fair wind of the west alone, for the harsher winds were still imprisoned in the leather bag. They sailed on in this way for nine days, and they came so close to Ithaca that they could see the beacon fires that had been set along its shores to guide them in their journey home. All this time Ulysses had remained at the helm and steered his ship, but on the tenth day he fell asleep. Then it was that his men said to each other, "What treasure is it that Ulysses keeps in the leather bag as his present from King Aeolus? No doubt the bag is full of gold and silver, and it is only right that some should belong to us." So they opened the bag and out rushed all the winds, and carried the ship past the coast of Ithaca and into unknown seas. When Ulysses awoke, he was sick at heart to learn what his foolish men had done. He had been so close to his home but was now so far away, and in his misery he thought about drowning himself in the sea. But he was of an enduring heart, and so he returned to the helm and awaited the adventure that lay ahead.

A Few Words More

The fact that islands play such a prominent part in the wanderings of Ulysses can provide children and adults with a focus for some interesting word histories. The Latin word for "island" was *insula,* from which we get not only our adjective *insular,* meaning "like an island," but also the several forms of the word *insulate,* which means "to surround or separate (with a material that does not conduct heat, for example)." Rather like an island, don't you think? Even the drug *insulin* derives its name from the fact that, in the human body, this hormone is secreted by the *islands* of Langerhans in the pancreas.

Now, if we add the Latin prefix for "almost," which

has come down to us in the form *pene-*, to their word for "island," we get a land mass that is "almost an island": a *peninsula*. This same prefix appears in the word *pen-ultimate*, which means "the next to the last" (literally, "almost the last").

Circe's Palace

About the story:

The tale of Ulysses' stay in Circe's palace is an enduring one because it touches on a theme that is common in the literature of all ages and cultures. Even though Ulysses and his men are granted their every wish and enjoy living in the lap of luxury, in time they grow homesick for the simple pleasures, and even the pains, that were part of their lives in Ithaca. There is, after all, no place like home.

Approximate reading time: 10 minutes
Vocabulary and pronunciation guide:

Circe [SIR-see]

Eurylochus [you-RILL-oh-kus]

ogre [OH-gur]: monster

bade [BAD]: commanded; invited; past tense of *bid*

Hermes [HER-meez]: Greek name for the messenger of the gods; also served as the god of cunning and invention. The Romans called him Mercury.

*U*lysses [you-LISS-eez] and his men sailed on until they came to an island, and so tired were they from their journey that on coming to shore they lay for two days without being able to stir. On the third day Ulysses took his spear and sword and climbed up a hill that was near, to see what kind of a place they had come to. From the top of the hill he saw a great forest, with smoke rising out of the midst of it, showing that there was a house there. But as he went back toward the shore to report what he had seen, he saw a large deer coming down to drink at a nearby spring, passing closely in front of him. He threw his spear at the beast and killed it; then he tied its feet together and put it on his back, though it was a heavy load indeed for a man to bear. When he arrived back at the ship, he threw down the stag on the shore, and the men were glad to see the great beast, for they had had no meat in many days. So they feasted on the deer, and Ulysses told them of the smoke he had seen from the top of the hill.

In the morning they began their search of the island, though having lost so many of their group in the voyage up to this point, they were now prudent enough to divide themselves into two companies: one under the command of Ulysses and the other headed by his lieutenant Eurylochus [you-RILL-oh-kus]. Lots were cast to see which party would be the first to set off in exploration, and when Eurylochus's stone was pulled from the helmet first, he went off with about twenty men, each fearing that he would soon be in the hands of some evil ogre [OH-gur], while their comrades on the shore lamented as if they would never see their mates again.

When the party reached the middle of the wood, where the smoke had guided them, they found an open space, and within that open space was a fine palace, guarded all around by wandering wolves and lions. The men were very much afraid of the beasts, but they were astonished when the animals came right up to them, wagging their tails and rubbing their noses against the sailors like dogs giving their master a friendly greeting. Then they heard the voice of someone inside the palace singing in a very sweet voice as she worked at her loom. And one of the men said: "Let us call to this singer and see whether she is a woman or a goddess." And they called out to her. From the palace came a beauty who called herself Circe [SIR-see] and who bid them to come in and refresh themselves, which they did—all but Eurylochus, who hid himself outside in cautious suspicion.

And well it was that he did so, for when the rest of the party drank from the cup of honeyed wine that Circe gave them, they found that it contained a strange drug that turned them all into pigs! They had snouts and bristles and they grunted and squealed as they ran to join the lions and wolves, who also used to be men but who had been transformed by another one of Circe's spells. Eurylochus looked on as Circe locked all the pigs in pens and scattered acorns and beechnuts on the floor for them to eat; then he ran back to the ship and told Ulysses what had happened.

When Ulysses heard Eurylochus's report, he slung his sword

belt around his shoulders, seized his bow, and bade [BAD] Eurylochus to come back with him to Circe's palace. But Eurylochus was afraid of being turned into a pig, and he refused to
go. "Stay here then, if you will," chided Ulysses, "and eat and
drink in comfort while your brothers are penned in cages. But I
must go to their rescue, for I am their chief."

So off he went, alone, and when he came near the clearing in
the woods, he met a most beautiful young man, who carried a
golden staff. The youth took Ulysses by the hand and said,
"Ulysses, have you come to rescue your comrades? If so, you
will never overcome this wicked enchantress by your powers
alone, and you will surely perish in the attempt." Then the
young man pulled up a plant from the ground—one with a
flower as white as milk but with coal-black roots—and he said,
"Take this herb of grace, which will render Circe's drugs powerless. Put it in the cup of wine that she will offer you to drink,
and the drugs therein will have no power over you. Then draw
thy sword, and rush at her, and make her swear to free your
men and never again attempt to harm you with her magic." So
saying, the young man departed, but Ulysses knew from his
actions that he was no mortal at all, but rather the cunning god
Hermes [HER-meez], the messenger of Zeus.

So Ulysses took the herb and made his way to the palace in
the woods, where he called out to Circe. She opened her door
and, in a friendly voice, invited him to come inside. A great
chair of carved oak was brought for him, and he was offered a
golden cup of wine to drink, which, of course, had already
been drugged. But Ulysses made sure to put the herb that
Hermes had given him in the cup before drinking from it, and
when he had quaffed it all, Circe struck him with her wand and
cried, "Now go to the sty of pigs and lie with your fellows!" But
to her amazement, Ulysses did not change into a pig, but instead he unsheathed his mighty sword and rushed at her, as
though he were about to run her through. Terrified, she fell to
her knees and cried out, "Who are you on whom my spells
have no power? Surely you must be Ulysses of Ithaca [IH-thick-
uh], for the gods have foretold that one day he would come to
this island on his return from Troy. If this be who you truly are,
then sheathe your sword and let us now be friends."

But Ulysses, still holding the point of his sword against her
chest, replied, "How can we be friends when you have turned

my companions into swine? And now I fear that you will try to drug me again if I allow you to live. Swear to me then, by all the gods, that you will do me no harm." And this the enchantress did swear.

Then her maidens, who were lovely fairy damsels of the streams and woods, prepared a feast for Ulysses. They threw silk covers over the chairs and brought in silver tables and golden bowls, and they bathed Ulysses in fragrant water and clothed him in the finest of gowns. But when the luscious foods were set before him, Ulysses would neither eat nor drink.

"Did I not swear a great oath?" asked Circe. "And do you still think I mean to bring you harm?"

Ulysses replied: "How can I eat and drink when my companions have been changed into brute beasts?"

Then Circe arose from her chair and took her wand in hand, and she went to the sties where she had put the sailors who had been turned into swine. She opened the doors of the sties, and as each beast came out she touched it with her wand. Instantly, the bristles fell from their bodies, and they became men again. And when they saw their chief, they hugged him about his neck and legs, weeping for joy.

After this they all went into the palace and had a bounteous feast. And when they had finished, Circe said to Ulysses: "Go now to your ship and store all that is on it in the caves that lie along the coast. And fetch the rest of your crew and return, for you shall all live here in splendor and happiness, and shall have no wants for as long as you wish to remain."

So they went back to their ship, and their friends were very glad to see them for they feared the worst had befallen them all at the hands of Circe. Ulysses then reported how Circe had given them a great feast and had treated them as her royal guests, and that she had invited the entire crew to live in the splendor of her palace. But some of the crew were hesitant, especially when Eurylochus said that Circe's offer was only a trick to get them all together so that she could change them into wolves and lions. This angered Ulysses greatly, and he drew his sword and threatened Eurylochus, calling him a coward and a traitor. But the others came between them and suggested that Eurylochus be left behind to guard the ship. So Ulysses left him, but Eurylochus didn't have courage enough to be left alone, and so he slunk behind them as they made their way to Circe's palace.

When they arrived, Circe welcomed them all and prepared for them a feast, and made them comfortable in her palace. Her maidens attended their every wish, and so here they rested and feasted in peace and idleness for a full year.

But during that year, they grew less and less attracted to their life of leisure, and more and more homesick for their wives and families. The pain of longing for their homeland grew so strong that Ulysses finally made an appeal to Circe that she allow them to resume their voyage home. He feared that she would think him ungrateful and punish them all with some of her magic, but instead she gave him guidance and advice about how to set his course and how best to avoid the terrible dangers that lay between him and his home. He listened, and remembered all that she said, and then they said good-bye forever. Circe wandered away alone and sad into the woods, and Ulysses led his men back to their ship and off into unknown seas.

A Few Words More

Ulysses and his men had not seen their homeland for almost twenty years, and they were lonely for the sights and sounds that had been so familiar to them before they set off for war. They were suffering from *nostalgia*, which is made up of two Greek words: *nostos*, meaning "a return home," and *algos*, meaning "pain." (English words that contain the root *algia* usually have something to do with pain, such as *neuralgia*, which is the pain that comes from inflamed nerves; an *analgesic* [ann-al-JEE-zick] is a drug that relieves pain.) Originally, you see, people thought of *nostalgia* as a type of disease, because the pain of melancholy was very real. Even today we speak of being "homesick," which suggests a kind of physical illness. But *nostalgia* has taken on a happier aura in modern times, and has lost this sense of acute pain. Now it conveys a more pleasant mood, but still one of longing or affection for the things of the past.

The Perilous Voyage Homeward

About the story:

Of all the examples of wisdom that Ulysses demonstrates during his many adventures, one stands out as, perhaps, the most useful to children—especially to older children. In this tale we see that Ulysses understands that, mighty as he is, even he is powerless to resist the Sirens' temptation all by himself. He also comes to the understanding that humans cannot attain all things, which is a lesson that Achilles never learned.

Approximate reading time: 14 minutes
Vocabulary and pronunciation guide:

Circee [SIR-see]

Charybdis [chah-RIB-diss]

Scylla [SILL-uh]

Hyperion [high-PEER-ee-on]: one of the original Titans; Hyperion and his son, Helios, were both called "the sun god"

bade [BAD]: ordered; commanded; past tense of *bid*

Eurylochus [you-RILL-oh-kus]

shrouds: the rope ladders that help support the mast

abated [uh-BAIT-ed]: subsided; lessened

nymph [NIMMF]: a beautiful nature spirit

Calypso [kuh-LIP-so]

The favoring wind that took them from Circe's [SIR-sees] island and out onto the high seas fell at midday, and a deep calm forced the men to return to their benches and take to their oars. Presently, they saw in the distance a most beautiful island, covered all over with flowers, and from it they could hear the faintest sound of beautiful singing. Now Ulysses [you-LISS-eez] knew who these singers were, for Circe had warned him about the Sirens: beautiful mermaids who lured sailors to their island by singing sweet songs that promised each man just the things he most wanted in the world. And when any sailor who was drawn by the songs would near the island, the Sirens would snatch out and snare him, and tear him to pieces, and then feed on his flesh. The beautiful flowers that covered the island also covered the bones of many men who had listened to that strange music, for no one who heard it could resist its call.

Ulysses now took a great cake of beeswax, which Circe had given him, and he cut it up into small pieces. These he gave to each of his men, telling them to soften the wax and place it firmly in their ears, so that they would not be able to hear the Sirens' songs. But he himself was always desirous of knowledge and experience, and he wanted to hear the sweet singing without falling under its spell. So Ulysses told his men to bind him tightly to the mast with heavy ropes, and they must not unbind him however much he might implore them to set him free. When all this was done, the men sat down on their benches and struck the gray sea with their oars, and the ship rushed along through the clear still water as it tried to skirt the island in its path.

The Sirens saw the ship, and they directed their songs toward it, and especially toward Ulysses, who they could see was bound to the mast. Their songs offered him all the world's knowledge and all its wisdom, for they knew that these he loved more than life itself. To other men, no doubt, they would have offered other pleasures. Ulysses heard these songs, and they thrilled his heart; he struggled to free himself from his bonds, but he could not escape. His men rowed on, hearing neither the captivating music of the Sirens nor the cries of Ulysses. When two of the crew saw his frantic attempts to free himself, they rose from their benches, and Ulysses was glad to see that they had understood his desires. But they did not free him; they rose only to tie him tighter to the mast with stronger ropes than before.

The crew pulled hard at their oars, and the ship was driven far past the island. Although they could see its outline in the distance, they knew that the enchanting songs coming from the island were now too far away to be heard. Only now did the crew remove the wax plugs from their ears and remove the ropes that bound Ulysses to the mast. For once, the Sirens had sung their songs in vain.

But this danger had hardly passed before another loomed in front of them. They had drifted to a place where the sea narrowed between two high black rocks, and where the sea roared as it dashed great waves and clouds of spray against the rocks on either side. Under the rock on the left was a boiling whirlpool called Charybdis [chah-RIB-diss], which sucked all that came near into its powerful gulf and in which no ship could survive. The opposite rock appeared to pose no danger, but Ulysses had been warned by Circe that here, too, lay great peril, for within this rock there was a cave, and in that cave dwelt a terrible monster, Scylla [SILL-uh] by name. Scylla was a repulsive creature who yelped in a shrill voice and who had six hideous heads. Each head hung down from a long, thin, scaly neck, and in each mouth were three rows of greedy teeth; on each head were two long feelers, with claws at the ends of them, which would drop down and snatch at any sailor who passed within the monster's reach.

All this Ulysses knew, for Circe had warned him. But he also knew that on the other side of the strait, where the sea spray flew even higher above the rock, was Charybdis, which would swallow up his whole ship if it came within its current. "It will be better," Circe had advised him, "to go near Scylla than to go near Charybdis; one or the other you must do, for there is no room in the middle. It is true that Scylla will pounce down upon your ship when it comes within her reach, and each of her six heads will devour one of your men, but if you go too near Charybdis, then will your whole ship be swallowed up. It is better to lose six men than that all should be drowned."

For this reason he bade [BAD] the helmsman to steer close to the rock of Scylla, and he did not tell the sailors about the danger that lurked there, which was hidden within a deep cave. Though they came as near as they could to that side of the strait, still they were on the very edge of the whirlpool, and it was a wondrous sight, for in its middle they could see the seabed itself, and above them the water seemed to boil almost to the top of the cliffs. So they all stood and watched the whirlpool, and did not see the six heads of Scylla spring out from the hole in the cliff and snatch away six of the bravest men in the crew. Ulysses heard them cry out for help as they were swept up into the cave, but he was powerless to come to their aid. And this, he would say afterward, was the very saddest thing that happened to him in all his many adventures and voyages.

The ship swept through the roaring narrows between the rock of Scylla and the whirlpool of Charybdis, into the open sea, and the men, weary and heavy of heart, bent over their oars and longed for rest.

Now a place of rest seemed near at hand, for in front of the ship lay a beautiful island, and the men could hear the bleating of sheep and the lowing of cows that were being herded into their stalls. But Ulysses remembered what Circe had told him about this island—that it was a sacred place and that the cattle there were those of Hyperion [high-PEER-ee-on], the god of the sun. He warned his men that if they killed and ate from these herds Hyperion would visit upon them a great punishment. "Listen to me!" he cried. "It is better that we sail by this island and arrive home safe than to risk any anger to the gods. Think, now, how many of our companions have been lost, and that only we remain."

But Eurylochus [you-RILL-oh-kus], who had shown himself to be a coward in the adventure on Circe's island, now spoke up and said, "Truly, Ulysses, you seem to be made of iron, for you are never tired, and now you would have us pass by this beautiful island without landing, though we have been working for days and nights without rest. And besides, it is not safe to sail at night. Let us stay and sleep on land, and tomorrow we will set sail again for our home." And all the others agreed with what Eurylochus had said.

Then Ulysses knew that a terrible thing would befall them all, but he agreed to put into shore if the men would swear an oath not to lay hands on any of the sheep or cattle, no matter how hungry they might be. So they all swore the oath, and they moored the ship, and they ate their meal that night along the shore. They mourned for their companions whom Scylla had carried off, and with tears of grief still in their eyes, they fell fast asleep.

The next morning they tried to put out to sea, but a strong wind blew up from the south, and the waves crashed against the shore, and they could not row their ship against such wind and waves. So they spent another day and night on the island, and Ulysses told them again that they must not touch the sheep or cattle, but must be content with the food that they had.

The storm that blew from the south lasted a whole month, day after day, and so Ulysses and his men could not put out to sea for thirty days. As long as the food that Circe had given them remained, they were content, but when this was all eaten, they were forced to wander about the island, searching for food. They snared birds and caught some fish, but never enough to satisfy their hunger, which before long became very hard to bear.

Then did Ulysses go out alone to find an isolated place on the island in which to pray to the gods, and while he was gone, Eurylochus spoke to his companions, saying: "Listen to me, my friends, for our plight is a dire one indeed. Death is a dreadful thing, but nothing is so dreadful as to die of hunger, and this we are likely to do. Let us take some of these oxen for our dinner, but let us sacrifice some as well to the gods and pray that they send us a fair wind. If Hyperion is angry and drowns us because we have eaten his cattle, let it be so; it is better to be drowned than to die of hunger."

To this they all agreed, and Eurylochus drove some of the fattest oxen down to the shore, and the men sacrificed some to appease the gods, but the others they feasted upon, and heartily. This was the scene that Ulysses came upon when he returned from his pilgrimage, and sad he was to see that his men had broken their oath.

When the sun god arose on the next morning and found that his sacred herds had been violated, he called upon the council of gods to punish Ulysses and his men for their cruel acts. "I will not shine anymore upon the earth," he vowed, "unless they pay with their lives for the evil they have done." And mighty Zeus replied, "Shine on, O Sun, just as is your custom, for I will put these sailors back to sea and break their ship apart with one of my thunderbolts."

Ulysses was very angry with his companions, and he rebuked them for breaking their oath. But he could not undo what had been done, for the oxen were dead and were roasting on the spits. The crew continued gorging themselves on the sacred meat for six days, and on the seventh day, a fair wind began to blow offshore and they raised their sails and put out into the open sea.

For a time all seemed to go well, for the wind blew as they desired. But as soon as they were out of sight of land, all the sky became covered with a dark cloud, and a great wind came down on the ship and snapped the shrouds on either side of the mast. Then the mast fell backward and broke the skull of the man who held the rudder and steered the ship, so that he fell into the sea. Next there came down a great thunderbolt from the sky, which rocked the very timbers of the ship and filled it with fire and smoke from one end to the other. All the men were knocked overboard, some on one side and some on the other.

Only Ulysses was left on board, but his ship was breaking into pieces all around him. He stayed on the deck until even that was torn apart into the planks from which it had been made, and now he found himself in the water, the wreckage of his ship strewn all about him. He bound together the remains of the mast and the keel and whatever other large pieces he could find, and in this way he built a raft, on which he floated, paddling with his hands. He paddled throughout the remainder of the storm, his weary arms keeping the tiny raft from being swamped by the gigantic waves that tossed him to and fro. At last the storm abated [uh-BAIT-ed] and Ulysses lay on the raft and slept for a whole day and night.

Ulysses remained on his raft and was carried by the waves for the next eight days, and on the ninth day he came to a pleasant island where there dwelt a sea nymph [NIMMF] named Calypso [kuh-LIP-so], who welcomed her visitor with kindness and love. Beautiful Calypso comforted Ulysses as he rested from his weary wanderings, and his days on the island soon became months and then years, and he lived as if in a dream.

After seven years, though, he longed to see his own homeland again and to see the faces of his wife and son. But Calypso's island was so far away that no ship ever came near to it, and without a ship to sail, Ulysses would never see the smoke rising from the chimneys of Ithaca [IH-thick-uh]. And so it was that many days he would sit by the shore alone and gaze wistfully out over the waves, hoping to spy a ship that would carry him home, but none did he see this day, nor the next, nor the next. . . .

A Few Words More

It is difficult to see much similarity between the shriek-ing sounds of the sirens that are so common on emer-gency vehicles today and the beautiful music produced by the Sirens in this tale; yet, this is precisely the origin of the name. A closer tie, however, does occur between the figurative use of the term "Siren song" and the ir-resistible allure (the "call of fame and fortune," for ex-ample) that draws some people to their doom.

The twin dangers of Scylla and Charybdis have come into our modern vocabulary as representing something similar to the alternatives in the phrase "out of the fry-ing pan and into the fire," or, perhaps, "between a rock and a hard place." Being "between Scylla and Charyb-dis" is facing two dangers, where one cannot be avoided without incurring equal peril from the other. This, by the way, is a classic example of a *dilemma*, which, in strict usage, describes a situation involving two (and only two) unacceptable or distasteful alter-natives. The word is often carelessly or casually used to describe a *problem* or *difficulty*, but careful speakers and writers will reserve its use for a situation more similar to that faced by Ulysses in this tale.

What Had Happened in Ithaca

About the story:

> *This is the point at which the* **Odyssey** *of Homer actually begins, the previous stories being presented as flashbacks. Here we see Ulysses' kingdom in a state of anarchy, mainly due to the Trojan War's having taken away all the strong leaders from the island. The youths of Ithaca have, therefore, grown up without any respect for the law or even for the royal family of their land.*

Approximate reading time: 13 minutes

Vocabulary and pronunciation guide:

> **Laertes** [lay-AIR-teez]
> **shroud:** a cloth used to wrap a body for burial
> **Calypso** [kuh-LIP-so]
> **Menelaus** [men-uh-LAY-us]
> **Laconia** [luh-CONE-ee-uh]: a province in ancient Greece; Sparta was its capital city
> **Agamemnon** [agg-uh-MEM-non]
> **Hermes** [HER-meez]
> **bade** [BAD]: ordered; commanded; past tense of *bid*

Ulysses [you-LISS-eez] left his kingdom of Ithaca [IH-thick-uh] and went off to fight in the Trojan War when his son, Telemachus [tell-EM-uh-cuss], was still only a baby, and so the boy was put in the care of a wise man named Mentor, who was a teacher, not a warrior. Ulysses had instructed Mentor to guide Telemachus in his growth toward manhood, and to help the boy understand how to behave like a king, which he would someday be.

But now almost twenty years had passed since Ulysses had sailed for Troy, and that span had been a very unhappy one for both Ulysses' wife, Penelope [pen-EL-oh-pee], and for Telemachus in Ithaca. Ulysses had not come home after the war, as had many of the chiefs from other kingdoms in Greece, and as nothing was heard from him, it was supposed that he must be dead. By this time Telemachus was yet only twelve years old and, though he had learned much from Mentor, he was still only a boy. Ulysses' father, Laertes [lay-AIR-teez], was a very old man, and he had gone to live on his farm in the country. There was, therefore, no king in Ithaca. The boys who had been young when Ulysses went off to war were now grown up, and, because their fathers had all gone off to the war too, they did just as they pleased. No one could tell them what to do, for there was no ruler, except for the boy Telemachus, and so they broke whatever laws they wished and had the run of the kingdom for years.

At least twelve of these rude youths saw themselves as suitors for the hand of Penelope, each believing that he was a fitting replacement for her presumably dead husband, Ulysses. These suitors, with about a hundred others as wild as themselves, virtually moved into the house of Ulysses to court the queen's favor and to badger her into choosing one of them as successor to the throne of Ithaca. They ate all the food that was in the house, and they drank all the wine; they killed the cattle, and they amused themselves with Penelope's handmaidens and servant girls. Nobody could stop them, and they would never go away, they said, until Penelope had chosen one of them to be her husband and king of the island, even though Telemachus was the rightful prince and was now growing into manhood.

Now Penelope believed in her heart that her husband was alive, and that he would come back one day, but she knew that hardly anyone else in the kingdom believed it. The people of Ithaca thought that she ought to marry again, for they were badly governed while there was no king. Even if the man whom she chose was not very good as a king, this would be better than to have a whole crowd of ruffians coming day after day to the palace, eating and drinking and gambling, and wasting the king's goods. So she tried to gain time, thinking to herself, "If I can put off these suitors for a while, perhaps Ulysses will come back before too long and set things right again." So she came into the courtyard of the palace one day and announced to them: "You know that my husband's father is an old man, and that it would be a great disgrace to me if he were to die and there were no proper grave clothes in which to bury him. He has, after all, been a king, and he should be buried with honor. Let me weave a shroud for him, and when this is finished, then I will choose one from among you to be my husband and the new king of this island."

The suitors were glad to hear this, and they said to themselves: "This weaving cannot take a very long time, and when it is finished, then one of us, at least, will get what he wants." So they waited, but somehow the weaving went far more slowly than anyone thought it would. The truth was that Penelope undid every night what she had woven during the day. How long this would have gone on no one knows, for at last one of the queen's handmaidens told the secret to a friend of hers among the suitors. So the queen could not put the suitors off any longer in this way; the shroud was finished, and she did not know how to stall them any longer.

Now there was one among the gods and goddesses who more than all the others cared for Ulysses, and this was Athena [uth-EE-nuh], the goddess of wisdom, and she loved Ulysses because he was so wise. It happened that Athena went to the council of gods as they sat high on Olympus, and she told them how good, wise, and brave Ulysses was, and how he was kept on the island of Calypso [kuh-LIP-so] while men ruined his wealth and wooed his wife. She said that she would go to Ithaca in the guise of Mentor, and she would tell young Telemachus that he could no longer sit and do nothing, just because he was outnumbered; he must set about searching for news of his father, and he must see to it that his mother was protected while he was away.

And this the goddess did; arraying herself in Mentor's clothes, she walked through the streets with Telemachus, whispering encouragements and advice in his ear. And the boy responded, for on the very next day, he called an assembly of all the people in the kingdom and announced that on the following morning he would take a ship and twenty oarsmen, and he would journey to Sparta, the land of King Menelaus [men-uh-LAY-us] and Queen Helen of the fair hands, to learn what there was to know about his father's whereabouts. The suitors, who were in the crowd, mocked him and jeered at his newfound boldness. But Telemachus continued: "If I should hear that Ulysses is still alive," he announced in a strong voice, "I will tolerate the presence of you suitors for one year more, for surely my father will return in that time. But if Ulysses is indeed dead, then I will insist that my mother make her choice of one among you, and this upon my return to Ithaca."

This arrangement seemed to please most of those who heard it, and so Telemachus was allowed to fit out a ship with twenty men and provisions of food and wine, and with him on his journey went Mentor—not the disguised Athena, but the mortal adviser himself.

For several days they sailed until they came to the land of Laconia [luh-CONE-ee-uh] and the city of Sparta, and here they were greeted by King Menelaus and his beautiful queen Helen, who recognized Telemachus at once because he had so much the appearance of his father. They feasted together and talked of the chiefs who had fought at Troy. And they wept for all the many who had died on the field of battle or who had been shipwrecked on their way home.

Then Menelaus told the boy about what he had learned while he was in Egypt, on his own wandering way back from the war. Menelaus had captured a wise old man of the sea and had, by force, wrung out of him the news of what had happened to many of the Greek chiefs. It was in this way that he learned how his own brother, Agamemnon [agg-uh-MEM-non], had arrived safely enough, only to be murdered in his own home by his wife and her lover. He also learned that Ulysses of Ithaca was still alive, though unhappy, for he was being kept on the island of Calypso, and he now had lost all his companions and had no ship on which to sail home.

This, of course, came as wonderful and happy news to Telemachus and Mentor, and they made haste to begin their return to Ithaca on the next tide.

Meanwhile, Athena again spoke to the council of the gods and said, "It seems to me that a good king is not in the least better off than a bad one. Look at Ulysses; he was like a father to his people, and see how he is kept like a prisoner for seven years now on Calypso's island."

Then Zeus said to Hermes [HER-meez], who was the messenger of the gods: "Go now to Calypso on her island, and tell her that it is my will that Ulysses should go back to his own country."

So Hermes tied his golden sandals on his feet, and he flew from Olympus to Calypso's island, and to the cave in which she dwelt. There Calypso greeted him, for she knew well who he was, and she asked him why he had come to this lonely isle. "I have come," replied Hermes, "because Zeus bade [BAD] me come, and we must all do what Zeus tells us. And so must you, Calypso, do as Zeus directs. You have a man on your island here—yes, and have had him for seven years, and he is very unhappy because he wishes to go home. He fought against Troy for ten years before he set out for his homeland. But many misfortunes happened to him, and he lost all his companions, and somehow he was brought to this island. Now send him back to his home as quickly as you can, for this is his fate: that he should live the rest of his life among his friends."

Calypso became exceedingly angry at hearing this order, and she said: "Did I not save this man's life when Zeus broke his ship apart with a thunderbolt? And now you say that Zeus has resumed his affection for the man, but that I am the one who must suffer by his loss? Well, Zeus may do as he wishes, but I have no ship here, and so I cannot send the man away."

Then Hermes replied: "Nevertheless, send him you must, or Zeus will be very angry with you. If you want to remain un-punished, you must find a way to send Ulysses home again." And with this he spread the wings on his shoulders and those on his sandals, and off he flew.

Now Calypso was very ill-pleased by this order, but she knew that she could not just disregard it. Yet, when she sought out Ulysses to tell him that his wish had been granted, she still wanted in her heart for him to stay. Calypso found Ulysses down at the seashore, looking out at the waves, longing to go over them that he might see his own dear country again. And she stood by him and said: "Weep no more, Ulysses, for you may have your wish, if you still desire it. But if I have come into your heart, as you have captured a place in mine, then you need not face all the perils of a voyage to Ithaca. Stay here with me, and I, Calypso, who loves you more than any human can, and who is far more beautiful than she who waits for you in Ithaca, will share with you my immortality. We will live in peace and happiness for ever and ever, if only you will choose to do so."

Now when Ulysses heard that he was free to continue his journey, he at first thought that it must be some kind of trick, for it seemed too good to be true. But Calypso swore that the offer was genuine—that he could stay with her or build a boat and sail to Ithaca; it was all up to him. Oh, it wrung her heart to hear him say, "Lovely Calypso, it is true that you are more beautiful by far than Penelope, who waits for my return. But it is she that I love, and so I must choose to set my course for home."

Much as her heart was against his leaving, Calypso did what she could to help him prepare for his voyage. "Take this ax," she told him, "and cut down trees to make a raft, and tie the beams together with these ropes. I will weave a sail for you and will give you food and wine for your journey—yes, and clothes, too—for the gods have said that it is time for you to go."

For the next three days, Ulysses felled twenty trees on the island, and he hewed them into the shapes of beams and planks. He made, as well, a mast and a rudder by which to steer his raft. On the fourth day he assembled his craft, and Calypso brought him the sail she had woven, as well as the provisions and the clothes she had promised him. Early the next morning, Ulysses pushed his raft out into the sea and set his sail, while Calypso, who had powers much like a goddess, sent a fair wind blowing behind him. At long last, Ulysses was on his way home once again.

A Few Words More

Ulysses feared that he would be away from his home for quite a while fighting the war with Troy, and he knew that his son would need someone to give him the sage advice that his father was not there to provide. So Ulysses appointed Mentor to be his son's counselor, and it is he whom we see whispering advice in the boy's ear. Today, the modern English word *mentor* means "a trusted guide or counselor." Other common words that are based on Mentor's name are *monitor*, which is "someone or something that cautions or reminds," and the verb *admonish*, which means "to warn or counsel against something."

Ulysses Returns to Ithaca

About the story:

The concluding tale shows Ulysses at his crafty best, disguising himself so that he can surprise his enemies. But it also shows how truly evil these enemies were, and what the ancients thought were the most sinful acts that humans could commit. Not only do the suitors hound Penelope and show her no respect whatsoever, but they mistreat an innocent and helpless old beggar, and it is this cruelty that brings down upon them the wrath of the gods and retribution at the hands of Ulysses.

Approximate reading time: 24 minutes
Vocabulary and pronunciation guide:
>   **Eumaeus** [you-ME-us]
>   **swineherd:** a keeper of pigs
>   **alms:** a gift or gifts for the poor
>   **bade** [BAD]: ordered; commanded; past tense of *bid*

*F*or seventeen days and nights Ulysses [you-LISS-eez] sailed his raft toward Ithaca [IH-thick-uh], always being sure to keep the Dog Star on his left, just as Calypso [kuh-LIP-so] had told him. And so keen was he to see that nothing would prevent this voyage from taking him home that he did not sleep for all those seventeen days and nights, but kept his hand on the tiller and steered a true course.

On the eighteenth day he spied the coast of Ithaca, and he put his raft into a cove on a deserted part of the island. At last he was home! Twenty years had passed since he had left these shores, but now his feet were walking on the ground of his homeland once again, and he lay down and kissed the land. So weary was he from his sleepless journey that he did not arise for many hours, but remained on the shore in the deepest and most peaceful sleep he had ever known.

When at last he awoke, he looked about him in wonder and confusion, for Athena [uth-EE-nuh] had spread a great mist over all the land, and Ulysses did not know where he was. He feared that his happiness at coming home at last had all been a dream, and that Poseidon [po-SYE-dun] was punishing him once more by carrying him off to another foreign land. "Where am I?" he cried out loud. "What shall ever become of me now, for all my hope is lost and my dreams dashed upon this shore." While he walked to and fro, lamenting his fate, Athena appeared before him in the form of a tall and beautiful woman. She said to him, "I am Athena, the goddess of wisdom, who has stood by you because you are the wisest and the most cunning of men. So I will stand by you now that you have arrived in your homeland, but you must tell no one who you are, for there are many here who would do you harm."

Ulysses answered, "O Goddess, you have always been good to me, and you protected me throughout the battles at Troy, but tell me now and truly: What is this place? You say that it is Ithaca, but it seems a strange country to me."

Then Athena blew the mist out to sea so that Ulysses could see the land as it really was, and he knew it to be Ithaca, and again he fell to the ground and kissed the land, for he was very thankful in his heart to be home at last. Then Athena told him of the crowd of princes who had come hoping to marry Penelope [pen-EL-oh-pee], and how they sat day after day in his palace and wasted his possessions. "And how," the goddess asked, "will you gain back your palace, for you are but one man, and they are so many?" But Ulysses answered: "If you will stand by me, I will fight against a hundred, or even a thousand, and know that I will not fail."

Then Athena devised a plan to disguise Ulysses so that his return would not be known to those who wished him evil. "I will so change you," she said, "that no man shall know you. I will make the skin of your face and hands withered and cold, and take the color out of your hair, and make your eyes dull. The suitors will think nothing of you, and even your wife and your son will not know you." And when she touched him with her staff, his skin withered, like the skin of an old man, and his hair turned white, and his eyes grew dim. The clothes on his body became torn and dirty, and over his shoulder was slung a battered pouch, such as beggars use to carry scraps of food.

Then Athena told him: "Go now, Ulysses, to the house of Eumaeus [you-ME-us], who looks after your swine, for he has been faithful to you, lo, these twenty years; but do not reveal yourself to him. I will fly to Sparta and guide your son Telemachus [tell-EM-uh-cuss] safely back, and I will tell him to go first to the swineherd's cottage upon his return." So saying, the goddess disappeared, and Ulysses made his way along a familiar path to the cottage of his swineherd.

When he arrived at the edge of the property, four dogs ran at him, barking fiercely, and they would have done him great harm if Eumaeus had not hurried out of the cottage and driven the dogs away with stones. "Old man," he said to Ulysses, "these dogs nearly killed you, and that would have grieved me deeply. Already I have more than my share of grief, for my lord has been away these twenty years, and no one knows where he is. Do, I pray, come into my house and share my food, old man, for happy am I that no harm has come to you."

Now Ulysses knew that Eumaeus had been fooled by the disguise Athena had given him, and so he sat at the swineherd's table and spoke with him at length. "Tell me, friend," Ulysses said, "who was this master of yours, who you say has been absent from his home so long? Perhaps I may have seen him or heard of him, for I have wandered over many lands and have seen and known many men."

And Eumaeus replied: "This is what all the travelers say, for they know that the queen has ordered to see every vagabond who comes to this land, so that she might question him about the whereabouts of her husband, Ulysses, King of Ithaca. And if he tells a good tale and can make the people think that their king will return soon, he is rewarded with food and drink and a place in the streets of the city to beg without harm. So save your story for the queen, old man, for it breaks my heart to hear such false tales of my dear master."

But Ulysses persisted, saying, "I hate such liars, too, and this I promise to you, kind Eumaeus: that your master will return to you before the moon is full again, and things will be as they were in this kingdom once more."

The swineherd wept at the mention of his master, and he

spoke to the beggar in a sobbing voice: "Say no more, I beseech you, old man. Though you tell a good story, there is more woe here than you can imagine, for even now my master's palace is overrun by young nobles who seek the hand of his wife in marriage, and even now his son searches for news of his father, while the suitors plot to fall upon him and kill him when he returns. But these are woes that no mere story can soothe, and so let us talk no more of idle tales, but let us dine together, for it is only right that a stranger be nourished when he comes to another's home."

And the two sat and feasted on one of the fatted pigs, and when the night grew late, Eumaeus led the beggar to a small room, and he covered him with a cloak, for the night was cold and the wind blew out of the north. "Sleep well, my friend," said the swineherd to his guest, "for in the morning you must put on your old rags again and beg in the streets of the city."

The next day, while Eumaeus was making breakfast ready, Ulysses heard someone approaching on the path, yet the dogs did not bark. "Here comes some friend to see you," Ulysses called out, surmising that the dogs would surely have barked at any stranger. It was Telemachus; Athena had guided his journey home, and he had come to the swineherd's cottage to avoid the suitors who lay in wait for him on the road to the city. Eumaeus dropped the bowl that he was holding, and he ran to the boy and kissed his head and his hands and his eyes, just as a father kisses an only son who comes back to him after being away for many years. Ulysses almost rushed to embrace him too, but he remembered Athena's warning not to reveal his true identity until the proper time.

Telemachus turned to the beggar and asked Eumaeus who it was that shared his cottage this day. The swineherd replied, "He is but a stranger who has asked for help. But now I put him in your care, for you are the master and I the servant."

"Not so," said the boy, "for who can be called 'master' who is not master in his own house? Do not the suitors still overrun the palace and devour all that is within it? No, I will give this stranger food and clothes and take him to the city, but I will not take him into my house, for the suitors will only make trouble for him there."

Then Telemachus said to the swineherd: "Go to my mother, the queen, and tell her that I have come back safe from my voyage. But see that no one hears you, for it will be better for all of us if they think I am still at sea. Hurry now; I will stay here with the beggar until you return."

When he turned to speak again with the stranger, he could not believe his eyes, for Athena had changed Ulysses back into his manly appearance and had instructed him that the time had come to make his true identity known to his son. Standing in front of the boy now was a taller, far more handsome man than had been there just a moment before. This stranger was wearing a bright new tunic instead of old rags, and his hair and beard had grown dark. "Stranger," the boy implored, "you are not the same that you were but a few moments ago. Can it be that you are a god and not a man?"

"I am no god," said Ulysses. "I am your father, the father for whom you have been looking and waiting for these twenty years. Athena has changed my appearance, but my name remains Ulysses, King of Ithaca, husband of Penelope, and father of Telemachus, whom I love more than life itself."

Then the boy threw his arms around his father's neck, and they both shed many tears. After a while, Ulysses explained to Telemachus how he happened to come to the swineherd's cottage, and how he planned to deal with the suitors who had taken over his palace. He said to the boy, "Tomorrow you must go to the palace and take your usual place there, and I will come in the appearance of a shabby beggar. If the suitors should treat me badly, you must endure it without complaint, for they will soon be punished as they deserve. When the time is right, I will give you a sign, and you will take away all the swords and spears and other weapons that hang in the great hall and hide them in your chamber. If any man asks why you do this, say that the smoke from the fireplace has soiled them, and they must be cleaned. But keep two swords and two spears close at hand, for these will be for you and me. Mind that you tell no one of this plan—not the servants, nor the swineherd, nor Penelope herself."

While they were still talking, Eumaeus returned from the city, but before he came into the cottage, Athena changed Ulysses back again into the image of the old beggar. Telemachus then instructed the swineherd to allow the beggar to sleep another night in the cottage, and to accompany him into the city on the following morning. He then bid them both good day, and set off for the palace, for there was much to prepare if Ulysses' plan had any chance of success.

On the following morning, Eumaeus and the beggar made their way to the city, and when some of the rowdies of the town saw the swineherd's companion, they said: "Why do you bring beggars to the city? We have more than enough beggars already." And one of them kicked Ulysses in the thigh, thinking the blow would easily knock the old man over. But Ulysses stood firm. He wished he could give this lout a good bashing, but he kept true to his disguise, knowing that he had more important work to do.

Then the swineherd and the beggar went to the palace and into the great hall, where the suitors sat eating the king's food, prepared by the king's servants. Telemachus took plates of food to the two as they entered, and he told the withered old stranger that he was free to beg among the suitors for money. Ulysses then went among the suitors, stretching out his hand and asking for alms, as beggars do, but most rebuked him, saying, "Get away, old man, and do your begging in the streets with the other dogs!" One even struck him an angry blow with a footstool, but Ulysses stood firm as a rock and said nothing; his heart, though, was angered anew, and he seethed with rage as he sat by himself near the door to the hall.

Telemachus was furious to see his father treated this way, but he kept it to himself; he did not shed a tear nor speak a word of protest. But he longed for the day when these suitors should be made to suffer for all their wrongdoing. When the queen heard of how the beggar had been treated, she thought that the gods would surely punish the entire kingdom, for it was a great sin to treat a stranger and a guest without kindness. "Bring this stranger to me," she commanded. "I should like to talk with him. Perhaps he has heard something of Ulysses, for I understand that he has traveled far."

Ulysses was soon escorted into the queen's chamber, and a chair and a cushion were brought for him, and then Penelope said: "Stranger, tell me who you are and what was your father's name and from what country do you come?" Ulysses replied: "Lady, ask me what you will, but not my name or country, for thinking of these brings tears to my eyes. You can see that hard times have befallen me, and I weep when I think of what I used to be."

Then the queen said: "I, too, have many sorrows and have shed many tears since the day when my husband left me, going with the Greeks to fight against the men of Troy. I know not how to escape the rude princes who have for years sat in my husband's house and wasted his goods. And tomorrow I must make my choice among them. I have promised that whoever shall best bend the great bow that belonged to Ulysses, and whoever shall best shoot the arrow as Ulysses used to do, he shall be my husband and the king of this island. But I should not burden you, a stranger, with my troubles. Rest, kind sir, and let my nurse wash the dirt from your feet."

And Penelope called for her nurse, who was very weak with age. She had cared for Ulysses ever since he was born, and she wept to see how alike this stranger was to the image of her master. As she bathed his feet in the warm and fragrant waters, she stopped suddenly and her mouth fell open. For there on the stranger's leg was the very same scar that was on her master's leg! The mark of the wild boar that had gored Ulysses during a hunting trip when he was still a boy. This nurse, herself, had bandaged the wound and had cared for the lad until it healed. No two men could sustain such a wound and live, and so this beggar must be Ulysses, returned at last!

But Ulysses laid his hand upon her mouth before she could cry out, and he said in a whisper: "Kind lady, do not be my death. I am come back after these twenty years, but no one must know until I have made ready my plan. Keep your silence, and all will be set right in due time."

Ulysses bid the queen good-night, and he returned to the great hall, where the suitors were asleep from the wine and the lateness of the hour. He whispered to Telemachus: "Now is the time for us to take away the swords and spears from the hall." And this they did, and Telemachus made certain that all the maids were locked up in their rooms. When their work was done for the night, both father and son lay down to sleep in front of the embers that still glowed in the great hall, but their rest was not easy, for they thought many times about what they must do on the morrow.

When the sun had risen on the next day, Penelope awoke and took down the great bow of Ulysses from the peg on which it hung, and she laid it across her knees and wept over it. Then, after a while, she rose and carried it to the hall, where the suitors sat feasting once again. She brought with her a full quiver of arrows, too, and, standing on the balcony above the great hall, she threw down the bow and the quiver, saying: "You, who come here day after day and ravage the stores of this house, pretending that you wish to marry me, listen to me. With this bow and these arrows I will test you, for they belong to the great Ulysses. Whoso among you that shall most easily bend this bow with his hands and shall shoot straightest at a target, him will I take for my husband. Let the winner alone come to me in my chamber, for there I will stay until only one of you remains within this house."

Then the first of the suitors, the strongest among them, took up the bow and tried to string it, bending the bow with all his might. But it would not bend, and the effort only made his hands sore and caused the others to jeer out loud at his failure. Then one of the suitors brought into the hall some fat from the kitchen, and they all took turns rubbing it on the bow and the string, trying to soften them with the fat. But they still could not bend the bow, and now the last of them was making his try.

Ulysses slipped from the hall and called the swineherd to him, saying, "If you do truly wish for Ulysses to come back and rescue his kingdom, then be glad in your heart to see me, for I am your master. Now I make only one request of you—that you close these doors to the great hall and bind them shut with a heavy rope from the outside. For none of the suitors shall leave this place alive." And the swineherd did as he was commanded, so that once Ulysses left him, there would be no escape from the hall.

Now Ulysses, still in the guise of a helpless beggar, said to the suitors: "Let me have a try at the bow. I should like to see whether I still have the strength that I had when I was young."

The suitors were angry that such a man should make this request, but Telemachus spoke up and told everyone that it was his bow, and he had decided that the stranger should have his chance to bend it, just as the others had had theirs. Then Ulysses took the bow in his hand, and he felt it to see whether it had suffered any harm, and the suitors laughed to see him behave like a strong man. And when he found that it was as it should be, he bent it in one motion and strung the bowstring so tight that it gave off a shrill *twang* with the slightest pluck.

The group was now struck dumb, and they fell back as he selected an arrow from the quiver and laid the notch upon the string, and drew the bow back to its full bend. "Come stand by me," he called to Telemachus, "for there is much hunting to be done before the sun goes down."

The first arrow he aimed straight at the suitor who had hit him with the footstool and had treated him so cruelly. The head of the arrow passed through the neck of the surprised suitor, and blood ran from his body as he fell backward, over-turning the table that was near him. For a moment, the room of suitors doubted whether the stranger had killed their friend by chance or on purpose, but as they leaped for their weapons and found that none remained in the great hall, they knew that they were in grave danger from this stranger, and that their plight was no accident.

"I am Ulysses!" the stranger shouted at them. "You dogs thought I'd never return, so you lived off my wealth and courted my wife, and had no fear of any god or man. But now you shall pay for your acts with your own destruction." *Twang!* The bowstring sent another arrow speeding toward the heart of one of the suitors, and the rest crashed against the great doors, but found them fastened shut. *Twang!* Another shot, and an-other suitor fell forward, dead in the place where he stood.

Now all the suitors could do was wait until Ulysses used his last arrow, and hope that it would not be aimed at them. Soon enough, Ulysses had launched all the arrows in the quiver, and the suitors then rushed toward him and tried to overpower him with their numbers. But Telemachus handed his father one of the swords and spears he had brought from the armory, and he armed himself with the others. The two stood side by side and repelled the onrushing suitors, killing many and gravely wounding many more. The others fled around the hall in great haste, but Ulysses and Telemachus followed them in a fury, and slew them all, every one of them.

At last the doors were opened, and Ulysses bade [BAD] the hall and the tables be washed with water and smoked with sulfur. When this was done, he bathed himself quickly and hurried up the winding staircase to the chamber of Penelope. Here he met the old nurse who had recognized him from the scar on his leg, and it was she who carried the news to a sleep-ing Penelope.

"Awake, dear child," the nurse cried excitedly to the queen, "for the face you have longed to see for so many years has returned. Ulysses has come back, disguised as the old beggar you spoke with last night, and he has slain all the wicked men who troubled you."

But Penelope answered: "Surely, dear nurse, the gods have taken away your senses. That beggar could not have been Ulysses. Why do you mock me with such a tale as this?"

But the old nurse insisted, "It is indeed Ulysses, my queen. Your son knew it, but he kept the matter secret so that the suitors should be taken unawares."

Then Penelope was glad, and she kissed the old nurse and held her tightly. The queen quickly put on her robe and went out into the hall, where Ulysses stood waiting.

"Forgive me, my lord," she sobbed, "for being so slow to know you. So many times have I been deceived into thinking that you were near, but now I know that in truth you are Ulysses and no one else."

So they wept over each other, and they kissed each other, and they were happy once again. Thus did Ulysses come home at last after twenty years.

A Few Words More

The star that Calypso told Ulysses to steer his course by was the Dog Star, a common aid in navigation even today because Sirius [SEE-ree-us], the Dog Star, is the brightest star in the sky. It is known as the Dog Star because it is the most prominent star in the constellation Canis [KAY-niss] Major, which means the "Great Dog." This constellation does not appear (to viewers in the United States) until the end of summer, and so the hot days of late August are frequently referred to as "dog days."

Canis, the Latin word for "dog," is at the root of our modern word canine, which means "characteristic of dogs (and wolves and foxes, too)" and is also used to describe the pointed teeth we have in our upper jaw. Curiously enough, this Roman word for "dog" is also the basis for the English name of another household pet. When the Romans first set foot on one of the group of islands off the northwest coast of Africa, they were met by packs of wild dogs, and so they named this island *Canaria Insula*, meaning "Island of the Dogs." Later explorers, who now called the islands the Canary Islands, got past the dogs and discovered that a small, yellow singing finch dwelt on these islands, and the species became named for its habitat: the canary. The islands, you see, were not named for birds; the birds were named for dogs. Got that?

The Wanderings of Aeneas

The Roman Empire commanded the known world during the time of the Caesars, and it was thought fitting that such a powerful state should have an epic poem glorifying its history and extolling the virtues of its founders. What was needed, then, was a truly Roman epic that would be the equal in scope and in artistry of Homer's *Iliad* and *Odyssey*. A Roman poet, who today is known as Virgil, was commissioned to write such an epic, and the task took him eleven years. He never completed the project to his satisfaction, and when he died in 19 B.C., he asked in his will that the unfinished manuscript be destroyed. Augustus Caesar, however, recognized the merit and the importance of the work, and he had it prepared for publication anyway.

The world is fortunate, indeed, that Virgil's wish was not met, because his great epic, titled the *Aeneid* [uh-NEE-id], became one of the most important works in all of western civilization. Although it was modeled on Homer's epics and, therefore, follows all the conventions that were considered appropriate for epic poetry, the *Aeneid* tells a vastly different tale from that in the Greek epics. Instead of focusing on and praising the individual strengths of heroes such as Odysseus (Ulysses) and Achilles, as Homer's works did, the qualities that Virgil praises in his hero, Aeneas [uh-NEE-us], are his sense of duty and his concern for order—attributes that were considered noble in the Roman view of the world. Aeneas is brave, to be sure, but he does not achieve his victories through deceit or cunning, like Odysseus, nor does he place individual glories above the welfare of his people, like Achilles.

Pronunciation guide (names that recur frequently in the story):
    Aeneas [uh-NEE-us]
    Anchises [an-KYE-seez]
    Ascanius [ass-CAN-ee-us]
    Juno [JEW-no]
    Sicily [SIS-uh-lee]

Aeneas's Escape from Troy

About the story:

Although the **Aeneid** *opens in medias res ("in the middle of things"), as was the custom in epic poetry, Aeneas's wanderings actually began with the destruction of Troy by the Greeks. Virgil's account of the terror and bloodshed that took place once the Trojan Horse was brought into the city serves to show not only the savagery of the Greeks, but the concern that Aeneas had for his family and his people as well. The Romans traced their lineage to the people of Troy, and both Julius Caesar and Augustus Caesar (from whom we get the names for July and August) claimed they were descended from Aeneas himself. It was important, then, that the hero of this tale should embody qualities that conferred honor upon the empire and upon the Caesars.*

Approximate reading time: 14 minutes
Vocabulary and pronunciation guide:

> **Sinon** [SYE-non]
> **Ulysses** [you-LISS-eez]
> **Cassandra** [kuh-SAND-ruh]
> **King Priam** [PRY-am]
> **Queen Hecuba** [HECK-you-bah]
> **Pyrrhus** [PEER-us]
> **agèd** [AA-jid]: advanced in years, old
> **Creusa** [kree-YOU-suh]
> **Jove:** another name for Jupiter, the Roman king of the gods; the Greeks called this god Zeus
> **aghast** [uh-GAST]: terrified
> **Tiber** [TYE-bur]: a river in central Italy that flows past the city of Rome
> **Janus** [JAY-nus]: Roman god of beginnings and endings

T he wooden horse had fooled the men of Troy, who had taken it into their city as a captured prize from their ten-year war with the Greeks. While the Trojans slept after their wild celebrations that night, however, Sinon [SYE-non] unlatched a secret door in the belly of the beast, and out came an armed band of Greek chiefs, led by Ulysses [you-LISS-eez], who opened the city's gates to the rest of their army, and the sack of Troy began with a vengeance. Soon the Greeks were setting fire to every home and temple in the city, and they were slaughtering the sleeping and unsuspecting citizens. The city became filled with cries of horror, and the streets flowed with a crimson tide of blood.

All this while, Aeneas [uh-NEE-us]—a handsome Trojan prince whose mother was the goddess Venus—lay sleeping in his house, for it was in a less populated part of Troy, enclosed by a dense row of trees. It was not long, though, before the din of the slaughter reached his ears and awakened him from his sleep. Springing up from his bed, he quickly ascended to the roof of his house to see what was causing such commotion. He stood there, almost in shock, for he could see the flames rising from hundreds of buildings, and he could hear the shouts of men and the call of trumpets.

Seizing his armor, he rushed out into the streets, shouting to his neighbors who were still asleep to arm themselves and fol-low him. He was soon joined by a frenzied band of comrades, and together they rushed toward the place where the din of combat was loudest. Aeneas assumed that the hated Greeks had somehow gained entrance to the city, and he was deter-mined to make them pay a dear price for their treachery. Around him burst the flames of burning buildings, while the shrieks of the dying pierced the very skies.

No words can describe the scenes of terror and confusion or the strife and carnage of that fateful night. Not just the Trojans, but many Greek heroes as well perished in the bloody conflict. In the midst of the fighting, Aeneas and his companions heard a shriek, and looking up saw Cassandra [kuh-SAND-ruh], the young daughter of King Priam [PRY-am], being torn away from the temple where she had sought refuge. With her eyes raised to heaven, she was dragged through the streets by cords that bound her tender hands.

Now Aeneas's thoughts turned to old King Priam himself, and to Queen Hecuba [HECK-you-bah], for surely the Greeks would be at their palace by now. He hurried to the palace gate, which had already been broken down, and on to the king's bedchamber. But the Greeks had been there, too, especially young Pyrrhus [PEER-us], the son of Achilles [uh-KILL-eez], who was bent on avenging the death of his father. Aeneas found the bodies of Priam, Hecuba, and one of their sons there on the floor, and he was overcome with grief. He staggered to the balcony, tears streaming from his eyes, and he looked down on his burning city with darkest despair in his heart.

It was hopeless to think that Troy could be saved now, and so Aeneas turned his thoughts to saving himself and his family. His mind raced with anxiety about the fate of his agèd [AA-jid] father, Anchises [an-KYE-seez], and his wife, Creusa [kree-YOU-suh], who had been left at home with his little son, Ascanius [ass-CAN-ee-us]. Had the Greeks already slain them, too, and flung their bodies into the flames? He hurried back toward that part of the city where he had left them only a few hours ago, and hope of escape revived in his breast when he found that the area was not in flames.

As he crept through the streets, not wanting to attract the attention of any Greeks, he spied a female figure lurking in the shadow of an altar near which he had to pass. Coming nearer, he saw that it was Helen, the woman who had been the cause of all the strife and woes of his country, and who now hid in fear that the Trojans would take vengeance upon her. The flame of hatred rose within him, and he said to himself, "Is it right that this woman should be carried back to Sparta as a queen, and be waited upon by captured Trojan slaves? No, and though there is no honor in killing a woman, yet the sons of Troy must be avenged!" And drawing his sword, he was about to rush upon her when, all of a sudden, in his path stood his mother, the goddess Venus, arrayed in glorious and heavenly splendor. "Why, my son, are you so filled with rage?" she said, taking him by the hand. "Think of your agèd father, and your loving wife, and your little son, and fly to them before the Greeks can slay them or carry them away into captivity. As for Helen, it is not she, nor Paris, that is to blame for the destruction of Troy, for the immortal gods had decreed that the city must fall. Therefore, my son, make haste to those who are dear

to you, and fear not, for I will stand by you in every danger."
So saying, she vanished into the shadows of the night.

Then Aeneas, heeding his mother's advice, ran through the
crowded streets toward his home. When he arrived, he gave
thanks to Venus that his family was still alive, and he announced to them all that there was no hope of saving Troy, and
that their only chance was to flee up into the mountains. But
Anchises, who was broken-hearted at the loss of his homeland
and the destruction of his city, refused to flee, saying, "You
who are in the flower of your days may run if you choose, but I
am old and will not attempt to save the little remnant of life that
remains to me. If the gods had wished me to live any longer,
they would have spared this city, which has been my only
home. No, here will I stay, and here will I die by my own hand
before I allow my life to be taken by any Greek."

At these words, both Aeneas and Creusa burst forth into
tears, and they pleaded with Anchises to flee with them, but
their appeals were in vain. Seeing that his father's mind was
made up, Aeneas said to him, "Can you, my father, expect that
I would ever leave you behind? If you are determined to stay,
then so shall we all, and we shall all perish here together as a
family."

Then Anchises, who wished no harm to come to anyone on
his account, raised his eyes to heaven and, stretching out his
arms, uttered a prayer to Jove. He asked the god of gods to
send down some sign to show him what to do. No sooner had
he spoken than the roar of thunder was heard and a star was
seen to fall from its place in heaven and shoot through the
darkness like a shaft, as though marking the pathway for their
flight. Now Anchises, seeing that it was the will of the gods
that he should leave the city, gave his consent, saying, "Delay
no more; whither you goest, I shall follow, for the gods must
not be disobeyed."

Meanwhile, the noise and uproar in the city was drawing
nearer and nearer, and the light of burning buildings breaking
out at new points showed that no time was to be lost. Anchises
was too old to run, so Aeneas carried him upon his shoulders,
and he held the hand of little Ascanius, and Creusa, his wife,
followed close behind, so that she would not lose the others in
the darkness. He instructed his servants and the comrades he

met to leave the city in different directions, so that one blocked gate would not prevent their escape, and to meet him at an old, deserted temple that stood in the mountains, not far from Troy.

Through the gloomy streets of the city, illuminated occasionally by flashes of light from the flames of burning houses, Aeneas and his family moved steadily toward the city gates. For a time they seemed to escape all danger, but just as they neared the gates and began to think they were safe at last, a sound of rushing feet fell upon their ears and filled them with alarm. "Fly, fly, my son!" yelled Anchises. "They are upon you, for I see their gleaming weapons as they rush to destroy us!"

Aeneas was terrified by the shouts and the uproar around him, and he became confused and hardly knew which way to proceed. But, pressing forward, still with his father on his shoulders and his son in tow, he began to run, first this way, now that, wherever there seemed to be a chance of escape. Finally, he saw a small opening in the frantic mob of Trojans, with the Greeks behind them, and through it he could see the open city gates. Gripping his son's hand hard, he dashed headlong through this gap, and he soon found himself outside the city, heading up into the mountains. Nor did he stop to look back, either, until he reached the meeting place he had designated—the old, deserted temple. Then, lifting his father from his shoulders, he placed him on the ground and turned to embrace his wife. But she was nowhere to be seen! Whether she had gotten separated in the confusion at the gate, or whether she had become weary along the way and had stopped to rest, no one could say.

Almost frantic with grief at the loss of his wife, Aeneas hid his father and son away in a small cave near the temple, and, buckling on his armor, he hastened back to the city to search for his beloved Creusa. He found the gate through which he had just passed, and, re-entering the city, he began to retrace, as well as he could with only the light of the flames to guide him, the path of his escape. On every side a scene of horror met his eyes, and at times a sudden silence sent a chill into his heart. He tried to think of what Creusa would do when she found herself separated from him, and he decided that she would probably go back to their house and wait there for

Aeneas to return. But when Aeneas did return, he found the house already enveloped in flames, its treasures strewn around the grounds. Nearby he saw a long line of boys and women who had been taken captive and would from now on be Greek slaves, and he so feared that this fate had befallen his wife that he cried out "Creusa! Creusa!" many times, even though these cries turned the heads of the Greek soldiers who guarded the slaves.

Just then a miraculous thing happened, for an image of Creusa suddenly appeared, standing right in front of him. Aeneas knew it was not her mortal self, for the image was vast in size and had shadowy features, though its expression was calm and full of affection. He stood aghast [uh-GAST], his hair almost on end, as this image of his wife said to him in a gentle voice, "My dearest husband, do not grieve or blame yourself for losing me. It was not the will of the gods that I should accompany you in your flight. You are destined to wander for many years, over the land and the sea, and you will meet with many dangers and difficulties. But at last you will reach a peaceful and happy home, where the River Tiber [TYE-bur] flows softly through a fertile land, and there you will build a kingdom. Even now a princess is waiting for you and will become your bride. Weep not, then, for Creusa, but rejoice that I was not captured and carried away as a slave. I am now at peace, and so you must not lament my fate. Farewell, dear Aeneas, and always love our son Ascanius as you loved me."

With these words the vision began to fade away and vanish into the air. Three times did Aeneas try to throw his arms around her neck, and three times did he grasp only vapor. With a heavy heart he turned and slowly made his way toward the gates of the city.

Having made a second escape from Troy, he soon came to the cave where he had left Anchises and his son. Now, however, he found gathered there a large number of companions— men, women, and children—who had come to join Aeneas and were glad to follow him wherever he might lead.

They could see the flames of their city below them in the distance, and the morning star, the herald of the dawn, rising overhead. Aeneas uttered a prayer to Janus [JAY-nus], the god of beginnings and endings, and all in the group understood that, although the world of Troy had come to an end, they themselves were embarking upon a new beginning. And Aeneas led them deeper into the mountains, where they could no longer see the flames of Troy, and here they camped and prepared for their journey.

A Few Words More

It was appropriate for Aeneas to ask the favor of the god Janus as his journey began, for Janus watched over the beginnings and the endings of events. This god is usually portrayed with two faces: one looking forward and the other backward. It is for this reason that the expression *Janus-faced* means "two-faced, hypocritical." It is also because Janus watched over the beginnings of things that the month beginning each year is called *January*.

Janus had one other important role, however, and that was as the god of portals and doorways: this is in keeping with the idea that events begin and end with entrances and exits. Today the people who maintain these doorways, and the buildings in which the doorways exist, derive their name from this Roman god. They are called *janitors*.

Aeneas Searches for a Home

About the story:

In his wanderings, Aeneas encounters many of the same dangers and creatures that Ulysses faced in the preceding saga. He is also subject to the wrath of the gods, in this case the continuing hatred of Juno, who still despises the people of Troy for Paris's failure to select her as most beautiful of all the goddesses. Aeneas, however, has Olympian allies, too, especially his mother, Venus, and Neptune, god of the sea.

Approximate reading time: 14 minutes

Vocabulary and pronunciation guide:

Delos [DEE-lus]

Anius [AN-ee-us]: king of the island of Delos

Crete [KREET]: a large island south of Greece

Jove: another name for Jupiter, king of the gods

agèd [AA-jid]: advanced in years; old

Hesperia [hess-PEER-ee-uh]: the ancient Greek name for Italy

hallowed: holy; sacred

odious [OH-dee-us]: offensive; obnoxious

Charybdis [chah-RIB-diss]: a giant whirlpool

Polyphemus [pol-ee-FEE-mus]

Cyclops [SYE-clops]: a monstrous, one-eyed giant

Scylla [SILL-uh]

Ithacans [IH-thick-anz]: people of Ithaca, Ulysses' home in Greece

Aeolus [ee-OH-lus]: king of the winds

nymphs [NIMMFS]: beautiful female nature spirits who served as attendants to the great gods

*A*s soon as the Greeks had completed the destruction of Troy and had set sail for their home, Aeneas [uh-NEE-us] and his companions came out from their hiding place in the mountains and began building a number of small ships—each fitted with both sails and oars, as was the custom in those days. Small parties of Trojans who had also fled the burning city came in day by day from their own hiding places to join Aeneas's band, ready to follow him wherever he might lead.

When at last the fleet was ready and well furnished with provisions, they all went on board, the sails were hoisted, and they started on their voyage in search of a new home. As the vessels slowly moved away, the people gazed mournfully upon the receding shores of their native land, which they would never see again. Aeneas stood in tears upon the deck, not just from seeing embers where his high-walled city used to stand, but from being so uncertain as to where fate would have him go or where he would finally settle.

With peaceful seas and favoring winds they sailed for many days, and the first land they sighted was the isle of Delos [DEE-lus], which used to be a floating island until Apollo anchored it with chains to the sea floor. Into this port they sailed, and here they tied their ships. The king of the island, Anius [AN-ee-us], who was also the priest at Apollo's temple on the island, came to meet them, and he recognized Anchises [an-KYE-seez] as a friend of former years. Anius treated the voyagers with great hospitality, and they stayed in his palace until they were well rested and ready to sail once again.

Before leaving, Aeneas took his companions to the temple of Apollo, which was on a nearby mountain. And there he prayed, saying, "O great god of light and truth, give to us, we beseech thee, a home where we may dwell, since ours has been taken from us by Achilles [uh-KILL-eez] and the Greeks. Grant us some sign that we may know thy will."

Scarcely had he spoken, when suddenly the walls of the temple and the sacred laurel tree and even the very mountain seemed to tremble and rock to and fro. Falling to the ground in reverence, they heard a voice saying, "Brave Trojans, the land that bore you first from your ancestral stock will take you back into its warm heart. Search out, therefore, your ancient motherland, for it is there that the race of Aeneas shall find a home in which to dwell forever."

At these words, loud murmurs of delight arose, though all were curious about where this land might be, for they knew not the origins of their own people. Then Anchises, calling to mind the records of ancient heroes, said, "In the middle of the ocean lies a certain island named Crete [KREET], the land of mighty Jove himself. On this island are mountains and fertile fields, and already many great cities have been built there. This is, if I remember correctly, the cradle of our race, and it must be there that Apollo intends for us to build our empire." Then they offered sacrifices on the altars of the temple, and they returned to their ships with joyful hearts.

Their vessels skimmed over glassy waters for several days before they landed on the island of Crete. Straightaway they went to work and laid out a city, building high walls around it, building houses within, and establishing laws by which they should live. But after a while there came a great sickness over the people, and a blight also on the trees and harvests, filling the land with death and lasting throughout the year. In sore distress, agèd [AA-jid] Anchises advised that they send a messenger back to the oracle at Delos to inquire whether they had rightly understood the earlier command, and if they had not, to learn what exactly was the will of the gods.

That night, as Aeneas lay sleeping in his chamber, a voice came to him in a dream, saying, "This island of Crete is not the place the gods mean for you to settle, Aeneas. There is a land far away that the Greeks call Hesperia [hess-PEER-ee-uh], an ancient land of valiant people, a lush land of vineyards and wheat. There is your proper home—the land of Hesperia, which men also call Italy."

Astonished by this vision, Aeneas lay for a while in great fear, with a cold sweat upon him. Then he rose and poured out hallowed offerings to the gods for revealing his destiny. He sought out his father, Anchises, to tell him of his vision, and Anchises listened and recalled that Cassandra [kuh-SAND-ruh], the prophetess of Troy, had spoken of Hesperia, and had also predicted that in that land lay the destiny of the Trojan race, though no one listened to her prophecies at the time.

So Aeneas and Anchises called together all the people, and

they revealed the message that had come to Aeneas. Then the people all agreed to take to the sea once again, for they were weary of the plague that had befallen them. They gathered their possessions and fitted out their ships; then they raised the sails and departed once again on an uncertain voyage to an unknown land, where they hoped to build yet another city and to begin their lives anew.

It was not long after they departed that a great storm arose; the sky turned black with clouds, the lightning flashed and the thunder sounded all about them, while angry waves threatened to swamp their vessels. So dark was it that the helmsman could not maintain his course, and so for three days they were driven, tossed upon the deep, beneath starless skies, not knowing where they were. On the fourth day, the clouds lifted, and they could see some land rising in the distance. Now the men took to their oars in earnest, and before long the ships were safe upon the shores of this unknown land.

As soon as Aeneas and his companions began to investigate the island, they saw several herds of oxen and goats feeding on the plain, with no one tending them. So, being in need of food, they killed some of the cattle and prepared their tables for a welcome feast. But what the voyagers did not know was that they had been blown onto an island that was inhabited by monstrous creatures called Harpies. The Harpies were huge birds with faces like women, but pale with hunger, and with long, pointed claws that could carry a grown man away or rip his flesh to pieces.

Now, suddenly, a great clamor was heard in the air and a flock of these odious [OH-dee-us] Harpies came swooping down, flapping their wings with a deafening roar, seizing in their talons the meat from the platters, and defiling everything on the tables with their foul waste. When the men of Troy sought out another place in which they could eat their food in peace, the screeching Harpies came again and stole their food and fouled the area as they had before.

Then Aeneas summoned his men to draw their swords and slay the birds, but the Harpies took to the air, leaving behind them a horrid smell and traces of their filth. The leader of the Harpies sat perched high above Aeneas on a neighboring cliff, and screamed out a prophecy to him, saying, "You Trojans have stolen our cattle and have slaughtered them in our presence, and now you would slaughter us, too? Hear then, my words, men of Troy, for I tell you that you shall arrive in Italy after all, but not until you have suffered a famine so great that you shall be compelled to eat your own tables for food." All the Harpies then soared away, but this prophecy caused the blood of the men below to run cold with fear. They made haste to their vessels, and they bent their backs to the oars, and they rowed out to sea, where a favoring breeze filled their sails, taking them away from the land of the Harpies. But they greatly feared, now, what lay ahead.

All day long they sailed, until by evening they could see the shores of the island called Sicily [SIS-uh-lee], which they knew lay along the course to Italy. In the distance, though, they could also hear the loud roar of the ocean and the crash of breakers on the coast. Suddenly their vessels began to toss upon a ruffled sea, and Anchises cried out, "Oh, no! We are in the pull of Charybdis [chah-RIB-diss]! To your oars, comrades, and pull with all your strength!"

So the men quickly sprang to their oars, for they, too, had heard tales of this monstrous whirlpool. But no matter where the helmsmen turned their prows, the ships still were lifted up toward the heavens and then flung back down almost to the Lower World itself. Three times did the waves crash upon them from overhead, with such fury that the stars seemed drenched with the spray. But at last, with sturdy rowing, they made their escape from the arms of Charybdis, and they drifted aimlessly for the rest of the night.

By morning they found that they had been tossed far off their course and now had little idea where they were or in which direction they should proceed. In this confusion, which lasted for many days, they came upon many strange lands and they braved many dangers. They were almost captured by Polyphemus [pol-ee-FEE-mus], the same hideous Cyclops [SYE-clops] who had eaten several of Ulysses' men and whom Ulysses had blinded with a burning shaft. They narrowly escaped the clutches of the six-headed monster Scylla [SILL-uh], the same creature who had snatched up and devoured six brave Ithacans [IH-thick-anz] from Ulysses' ship. And they had many other adventures as well before they again spied the coast of Sicily and knew that Italy lay ahead.

But scarcely had they gotten on course once again, when Juno [JEW-no] looked down upon them, and her old grudge against the Trojans was revived. She still had not forgotten the humiliation she had suffered when Paris awarded the golden apple for beauty to Venus. She said to herself, "Am I, the wife of mighty Jupiter, to go unavenged and allow these men of Troy to reach Italy? Who will worship me hereafter if they do?"

With a chafing in her heart, she hastened to the mountain cave of Aeolus [ee-OH-lus], who keeps the angry storms and raging tempests all confined in prison walls underneath his throne. Deep down within the mountain's heart they rave and roar, while Aeolus, with his scepter in hand, holds them back and curbs their rage. To him, Queen Juno came and said, "O Aeolus, whom Jupiter has made king of the winds, I pray thee to loose now thy winds against the ships of Aeneas. Do this for me, and I will give you twelve of the fairest nymphs [NIMMFS] who wait upon me, and much treasure besides."

Aeolus was much tempted by this offer, and he struck the hollow mountainside with his scepter, allowing the winds of every kind to rush forth. From east and west they came, plowing the deep and raising the waves, which crashed upon the shore. The sky grew black with clouds, the thunder rolled, the lightning flashed. The oars of the Trojan ships snapped like twigs, and the masts were about to do likewise. A roaring blast from out of the north struck three of the ships broadside and tossed them upon some hidden rocks where they splintered into many pieces. A mighty south wind drove three others upon some shoals and quickly buried them in the sand. Mountainous waves crashed over the decks of the remaining craft, spilling many of their crew overboard and turning some of the vessels completely upside down. The sea was by now covered with floating men and oars and shattered planks, while other bodies and wreckage sank beneath the waves.

Meanwhile, Neptune, the god of the ocean, hearing the raging of the waves and knowing that he had given no orders for a storm, raised his head above the water and saw the fleet of Aeneas scattered by the gale. Neptune guessed that Juno's wrath was responsible for the storm, and so he called the winds to him, and he chided them like children for leaving home without his consent. "Return to Aeolus," he commanded, "and tell your king that *I* am ruler of the sea!" Then he stilled the waves and cleared the clouds so that the ships of Aeneas that had remained afloat, now only seven, might find a safe harbor nearby.

And so the seven ships and their weary crews found themselves on the coast of Africa, in a pleasant cove protected by high granite cliffs. And here they lay their brine-soaked bodies on the beach and rested, for they had wandered far and wide and had lost many of their company along the way. Their journey was not over, but they had found a place without monsters or storms, and that was enough for now.

A Few Words More

Here we have seen how Aeneas and his party have had to wander from place to place seeking a home. There were at least two Latin words that meant "to wander," and each has spawned several words that are common today. The Latin word *vagari* can be seen in the English words *vagrant* and *vagabond* (both having to do with "a wanderer") as well as in *vague* ("wandering away from the specific") and *extravagant* (literally, "wandering outside the limits"). Another Latin word for "wander," *errare*, gives us the sense of "wandering or deviating from the standard" that we find in *error, erratic, erroneous*, and *aberration*.

The Greeks, too, had a word for "a wanderer," and its root still thrives in English. When the ancient Greeks looked up into the night sky, they saw that, while the position of most of the stars remained relatively fixed, there were a few that seemed to "wander" around the sky. The Greek word for "a wanderer" was *planetes*, and these "wandering" stars are known today as *planets*.

Aeneas and Queen Dido

About the story:

The tragic romance of Dido and Aeneas is among the most well known in all of literature. It is here we see how strongly Aeneas is ruled by his sense of duty, for he subjugates his desires and will not allow his love for the beautiful and capable Dido to sway him from his mission.

It is appropriate that here, too, we find mention of Romulus and his brother Remus, who were fabled to have founded the city of Rome. Rome was named for Romulus, and Romanus came to describe the informal or colloquial style of Latin that was used for such non-official writings as stories of love and adventure in lands that had fallen under the influence of Rome. Later the description came to identify the tales themselves, and that is why we call the story of Dido and Aeneas a romance.

Approximate reading time: 17 minutes

Vocabulary and pronunciation guide:

Dido [DYE-doe]
Romulus [RAHM-you-luss]
Remus [RAY-muss]
Ilia [ILL-ee-uh]
Achates [uh-KAY-teez]
Carthaginians [car-thuh-JINN-ee-anz]: the people of Carthage
Ilioneus [ill-eye-OH-nee-us]
Cupid: god of love; son of Venus
Jove: another name for Jupiter, king of the gods
wingèd [WING-id]: this two-syllable pronunciation is common in poetry and mythology
pyre [PIRE]: a heap of combustible materials

Now, the goddess Venus, who was the mother of Aeneas [uh-NEE-us], looked down upon his troubles from high on Olympus, and with a mournful heart she sought out mighty Jupiter and said, "O great father, who rulest over all the affairs of gods and men, I beg thee to say what offense Aeneas and the Trojans have given thee that they should be made to suffer so. Did thou not decree that from them would come the race that would rule over both the land and the sea? Then what, dear father, have they done that thou should alter their destiny?"

Then Jupiter smiled upon his daughter, and, kissing her gently, replied, "Do not be afraid, dear Venus, for the fate of thy people remains unchanged." Then he waved his arm, and visions of what would be appeared before them, quickly vanishing as Jupiter described each to Venus and revealed to her the future that had been planned for these men of Troy. "Aeneas," he said, "shall come to Italy and wage a mighty war, and he shall subdue the people there and give them laws and manners, and there he shall build a high-walled city. His son, Ascanius [ass-CAN-ee-us], shall reign after him, and the Trojan line shall rule there for three hundred years. Then, it is decreed that a royal priestess named Ilia [ILL-ee-uh] shall bear twin sons fathered by Mars, the god of war. They shall be called Romulus [RAHM-you-luss] and Remus [RAY-muss], and they shall be suckled and raised by a she-wolf. But Romulus shall one day build a city and a nation and name it after himself, and it shall be called Rome, and its rule over the world shall have no end."

Then Jupiter summoned his messenger, Mercury, to travel to the kingdom of Carthage on the northern coast of Africa, near where Aeneas's ships were tied, and move the hearts of the Carthaginians [car-thuh-JINN-ee-anz] so that they would open their city to the Trojans in friendly welcome. And so Mercury descended to earth, and he put kind thoughts into the heart of Queen Dido [DYE-doe], who ruled over Carthage, so that she might welcome Aeneas and his people.

Meanwhile Aeneas and his faithful friend Achates [uh-KAY-teez] investigated the land to which their ships had been driven. When they saw the great city of Carthage in the distance, they were filled with wonder, for its towers and gates and strong walls recalled in them memories of their own fabulous city of Troy. They feared to go into the city itself, not knowing whether the people there would do them harm, but Venus shrouded them in a cloud of mist, so that they could not be seen. Thus protected, they entered the city gates and wandered about in awe at the spectacles before them, especially the temple that had been built in honor of Juno [JEW-no], for along its walls were painted heroic scenes from the Trojans' war with the Greeks. Aeneas and Achates wept aloud at these sights, recalling all their noble comrades who had perished so valiantly, and their sobs almost gave their presence away.

But just then Queen Dido came into the temple, followed by a long train of attendants. Aeneas gazed upon her in silence, for her beauty was so radiant that it shone throughout the hall. She seated herself upon a lofty throne, and there she decreed new laws for her people, and she sat in judgment over the affairs of those who petitioned her. Her competence was every bit the equal of her beauty, and Aeneas became thoroughly enraptured with this queen of the Carthaginians.

Suddenly, into the great temple came a group of ragged sailors, and Aeneas and Achates recognized them at once as their companions whose ships had been lost during the storm at sea. So full of joy were these two at seeing their comrades again, and so eager were they to embrace the friends they thought had perished, that they almost burst through the misty veil that had hidden them from view. But Aeneas wisely thought it best to see how these Trojans would be treated at the hands of the Carthaginians before renewing old acquaintances. And so he kept silent as one of his trusted captains, Ilioneus [ill-eye-OH-nee-us], approached Queen Dido and told her how they had come from Troy, seeking a land called Italy, and how they had endured many hardships, including a great storm that had separated them from the rest of their people and had tossed their ships on the coast of this land that was strange to them. "We had a leader, Aeneas," he said, "and no man was more dutiful to the gods or braver in battle than he. If he were still alive, we would not be so desperate, but he has no doubt perished in the storm. We ask now only that you have pity on us and allow us to bring our boats upon the land for repair, so that we may set out again to find our home upon the Latin shore."

Then Dido replied: "Do not fear, ye men of Troy, for your valiant deeds in battle are not unknown to us. You and your people are welcome to stay, and the city I am building shall be yours if you decide to settle here. Bring up your boats for repair, as you wish, but if you choose to remain instead of seeking another home, I shall make no difference between the people of Troy and those of Carthage. I only wish that your great prince, Aeneas, had been driven here, too, and I shall forthwith send out troops to search the coasts for him."

When Aeneas and Achates heard these words, they were glad of heart, and they knew that they need not conceal themselves any longer. The cloud that had encircled them vanished, and Aeneas stood before Queen Dido looking like a god himself, for his mother, Venus, had given him the golden locks and lustrous eyes and all the charms and bearing of a man who was more than mortal. He addressed the queen, saying: "I am he whom you seek, Aeneas of Troy, son of Anchises [an-KYE-seez]. You alone, great Queen, have shown pity upon the sons of Troy, and no act of ours can ever repay you for your kindness. While rivers run into the sea and stars glitter in the sky, so long with me your name shall live in gratitude and honor." Then with both hands outstretched he greeted Ilioneus and the others, and all wept to embrace their leader and friend, whom they had thought they would never see again.

Queen Dido, hearing these words, stood silent for a while, astonished to see this hero, about whom she had heard so many tales of glory. At last she said: "Are you truly Aeneas, whom fair Venus bore Anchises on the plains of Troy? For many years I have known your fame. The fate of Troy and that of all the Grecian kings are much discussed in my palace. Come, then, with your companions, and rest beneath my roof. I, too, have wandered far and suffered much, and I have thus learned to comfort those who are in need."

So saying, she led Aeneas to her palace, and she sent much food and wine to his companions who remained at the shore with his ships. Within the palace she had a large banquet table prepared, and all the wondrous luxuries of Carthage were heaped upon the visitors from Troy. With a father's pride, Aeneas sent word to the ships that his young son, Ascanius, should be sent to join him at the feast. Ascanius was to bring with him fabrics and treasures rescued from Troy as presents for Queen Dido.

Meanwhile, Venus still feared that Juno might somehow turn the queen and her people against the Trojans, and so she devised a plan by which Cupid would cause Queen Dido to fall in love with Aeneas, thereby ensuring that the queen would not be used for any of Juno's treacherous plots. Venus called for her son, Cupid, and instructed him to take on the appearance of

Ascanius, who would be lulled into a deep sleep on his way to the palace. Once in this guise, Cupid could draw near enough to the queen to touch her heart with one of his golden darts, and the flame of love would burn within her from that time on.

And so it happened that young Ascanius did, indeed, become drowsy on his way to the palace, and he laid himself down in the woods along the road and fell fast asleep. And Cupid, as Venus had requested, took off his wings and assumed the form of Ascanius, and before long he appeared at the banquet bearing the presents Aeneas had ordered for the queen. Dido was so moved by the gifts and by the charms of this child that she took him up in her arms and hugged him on her lap, not guessing, of course, that it was the god of love she was holding. While she encouraged Aeneas to tell her all the tales of Troy and especially all his adventures during the war with the Greeks, Cupid skillfully touched her heart with his magic potion. And though she was deeply moved by Aeneas's stories of suffering, it was Cupid's power that had affected her more deeply still, for she fell madly in love with Aeneas, and she determined to keep him and his companions in Carthage at all cost.

When the banquet was over, Queen Dido returned to her chamber, but she could not sleep. Thoughts of the godlike stranger, who had all the virtues of a hero and all the charm of a prince, recurred and dwelt in her mind. When morning finally came, she called her sister, Anna, to her side and said to her, "O my sister, I have been troubled this night with dreams that offered my heart no peace. This stranger, Aeneas, who has come to our shores—is he not the noblest of men you have ever seen? How handsome he is, how patient in his sufferings, and the words of his stories are as poetry to my ears. I confess that since the day when my husband died, this man alone has moved my heart to love, and had I not made a vow never to wed again, this is the man to whom I might yield my heart."

Then Anna, seeing the tears fall from her sister's eyes as she spoke, replied: "Why should you waste your youth in sorrow, with neither children nor husband to provide you joy and comfort? No one among the men of Carthage is pleasing to you, and is it right that this great land should have no king? Surely it was by the will of the gods that the ships of the Trojans came to our coast, and so the gods must just as surely have decreed this alliance of love between the leaders of Troy and Carthage. Let us, then, pray to the gods and offer sacrifices so that we may devise good reasons why these strangers should tarry here a while."

Anna's words comforted Dido and fed the flame of love in her heart for the Trojan prince. The sisters then offered sacrifices to the gods, and especially to Juno, for she watched over and cared for those who would be joined in marriage.

From that day on, Dido felt no pleasure in her former joys of providing laws for her people, building the great city, and negotiating treaties with other heads of state. Day after day, she walked about the land with Aeneas by her side, showing him the treasures of her land. And when the evening came, she would dine with him and beg him to tell, again and again, the tales of Troy, and she would hang upon every word that fell from his lips. Thus enslaved by her passion, she soon began to neglect the duties of a queen, and she became unmindful of her people, and the walls of the city soon ceased to be built.

Before long mighty Jove turned his eyes toward Carthage and saw the discontent of the people, and he heard them blame Dido's desire for Aeneas as the cause of the troubles in the city. And so he called Mercury to him, and he sent his wingèd [WING-id] messenger to earth to warn Aeneas not to linger in Carthage, but to depart at once upon his voyage to Italy. "Say to him that this is not the land assigned to him by the decrees of fate, nor was it for this that he was spared death at the hand of the Greeks," Jove ordered. "His fate is to found a nation in Italy that will one day bring the whole world under its power. Tell him to think of the glory of this deed, and of the future glories of his son, Ascanius, and to depart at once."

Mercury then, binding up his wingèd sandals, did as he was commanded, and finding Aeneas asleep in the palace, whispered Jupiter's message in his ear. Aeneas began to burn with desires of old, and he called his captains to him and ordered them to secretly prepare their ships to sail. He did not know how to tell the queen his purpose, and he knew that she would not give her consent, for her love had grown to madness. Nor did he mean to deceive her, but still he prepared to leave, for his duty was clear, even if the way to accomplish it was not.

The queen was not deceived, for she had learned of the Trojans' secret preparations, and she fairly flew through the streets of the city and came upon Aeneas in a frenzy. "Why do you run off from me in the dark?" she raged. "Are you so false that you would steal away from my coasts unseen after all I have done for you, without a word of explanation or a care for the torture you bring to my soul?"

At last Aeneas spoke briefly. "I do not deny, O Queen, the many favors you have done for me, nor will I ever forget you for as long as I live. But never did I promise that I would abide here forever, and now the gods command that I go to Italy. It is not by choice, dear Queen, but for duty that I must leave you."

But Dido would not be moved. "I was a fool to take this ship-wrecked beggar into my heart and home, for now he tells me that it is the gods who call him away! Go then, and leave me here with the memory of one who has been false to me throughout. Go seek your Italy across the sea, but if there be any vengeance in heaven, may it fall upon you for treating me this way. May you be wrecked upon some rocks in the sea and vainly call upon Dido for help, for Dido will never again be moved." Then she turned to leave, but her strength failed her, and she fell to the ground in a swoon. Her maidens raised her up and bore her to the palace and cared for her until her faint-ing had come to an end.

Aeneas was deeply hurt by Dido's curses, but his duty was clear, and so he and his people pressed ahead with the outfit-ting of their ships. And just as soon as they had finished, the ships were launched all along the shore. Dido saw their un-furled sails from her chamber window, and she became over-whelmed with grief. To her it now seemed clear that the end to her suffering could come only with death, and so she resolved a plan to take her own life.

She called upon her sister, Anna, to gather up everything that Aeneas had left behind, that it might be burned on a sacri-ficial pyre [PIRE] that would burn away the image of this Trojan from her heart and put an end to her miseries. The pile was prepared, and on it were placed some clothes Aeneas had worn, mementos from times he had spent with Dido, and even one of his swords. Soon it was made ready for burning, but just as the torches were setting it ablaze, Dido climbed to the top and drew Aeneas's sword out of its scabbard. "Let the cruel Trojan out in the bay feed his eyes upon these flames and take with him the knowledge that he has brought about my death," she cried. And so saying, she fell upon the sword, and the blood flowed from her body as the flames engulfed the pyre in a rising fireball.

Aeneas and his companions looked back upon the city, and they saw a great fire leaping toward the sky. They did not know its cause, but many feared some form of evil, for they knew the rage that was in Dido's heart. Soon the ships were far out to sea, and the light disappeared from the night sky. The waves began to roll, and there were signs of a rising storm. The Trojans were once again at the mercy of the elements, and their perilous journey to find a homeland commenced once again.

A Few Words More

In this tale we saw Dido and Anna offer sacrifices to Juno, who was the goddess of marriage, in the hope that the queen of the gods would somehow bring about the wedding of Dido and Aeneas. There was one month in the year that was sacred to Juno and was, therefore, commonly believed to be favorable for weddings. The sixth month of the year, *June*, is named for this goddess, and it is still the traditional month for weddings.

Juno's husband, Jupiter, was frequently referred to as Jove, and it is from this name, although indirectly, that we get our modern adjective *jovial*. Ancient astrology claimed that various planets and other celestial bodies caused specific character traits in people who were "born under their influence." Because the planet Mercury, for example, appears to move faster than the other lights in the heavens, those born under its influence were destined to be *mercurial*, that is, "quick-witted, swift, volatile." Because those who had the planet Jupiter prominent in their horoscope were thought to be happy people, *jovial* took on the meaning "happy, joyous, convivial."

Aeneas Visits the Lower World

About the story:

Although the story in the Aeneid *goes on to tell of Aeneas's eventual conquering of the tribes that inhabited Italy, the following tale of his journey to Hades provides a colorful and imaginative point of departure. Virgil's vision of how earthly lives are punished or rewarded after death was intended to encourage his readers toward moral behavior. Whether it had that result is unknown, but the images that he created in this vision have been re-created by other writers for centuries, and are the basis for many references and allusions today.*

Approximate reading time: 15 minutes

Vocabulary and pronunciation guide:

Hades [HAY-deez]: the Lower World, the Underworld; the land of the dead

agèd [AA-jid]: advanced in years; old

myrtle [MUR-tul]: an evergreen shrub native to the Mediterranean

Jove: another name for Jupiter, king of the gods

Pluto: king of Hades; brother of Jupiter and Neptune

Elysium [ih-LEEZ-ee-um]: a peaceful land in Hades where the blessed live after death

Sibyl [SIBB-uhl]

Cumae [KOO-me]

Proserpine [PRAH-sir-pine]

gnashing [NASH-ing]: grinding or snapping the teeth together

Charon [CARE-on]

River Styx [STICKS]

Cerberus [SIR-burr-us]

Morpheus [MORE-fee-us]: the god of dreams; "wrapped in the arms of Morpheus" describes someone who is in a deep and peaceful sleep

Tartarus [TAR-tah-rus]

Sisyphus [SIS-uh-fuss]
Tantalus [TAN-tuh-lus]
River Lethe [LEETH-ee]: the river of forgetfulness
Romulus [RAHM-you-luss]
Tiber [TYE-bur]: a river in central Italy that flows past
the city of Rome

The storm that Aeneas [uh-NEE-us] and the Trojans encountered after leaving Carthage raged for several
days, buffeting the ships about and washing huge
waves across the decks. In the darkest hours of the tempest,
Aeneas's agèd [AA-jid] father, Anchises [an-KYE-seez], died in
his sleep, and Aeneas, overcome with grief, embraced his father's lifeless body and wept uncontrollably for many hours.

When, at last, the storm abated, Aeneas ordered the ships to
depart from their original course and to put in at the nearby
island of Sicily [SIS-uh-lee], so that Anchises could be given a
proper burial. Once on the shore, Aeneas called his people together and said, "This is a day that I shall always keep in sorrow and in reverence, and it is fitting that we celebrate it with
proper rites." And so they built a tomb for Anchises and then
proceeded to honor him in the manner that befitted great men
of the time: They all crowned their heads with myrtle [MUR-
tul] wreaths and held a great feast, and then they joined in
athletic contests featuring ship races and tests of running, boxing, and archery skill. Swords and garments and jewels were
given as prizes to the winners, and these funeral games went
on for nine days.

On the last night of the celebration, as Aeneas slept soundly
in his tent, he was visited by the ghost of his father in a dream.
Aeneas heard his father say to him: "My son, the great Jove
wishes me to tell you many things about your journey to Italy,
but first you must visit me where I dwell—in Pluto's dark do-
mains. Fear not that I am tortured with the evildoers, for I am at
peace in Elysium [ih-LEEZ-ee-um] in the company of the
blessed. The Sibyl [SIBB-uhl] will show you how to find me,
and then you shall learn of your glorious future and of the city
you are to build. Till then, my son, farewell." The vision in the

dream vanished like smoke into the air, and Aeneas awoke with a start.

He called to him his friends and captains, and he told them about what Jove had commanded him to do. Straightaway they set sail for the land of Cumae [KOO-me], where the Sibyl, who had the power to disclose the future, lived in a dark and hidden cave near the temple of Apollo. And when their boats were anchored at last along the shore, several of the Trojans went into the forest to cut firewood and to find fresh water; others hunted for whatever game the countryside might provide; Aeneas, though, went alone to find the cave of the Sibyl.

He located Apollo's temple easily enough, and as he stared at it wondering which direction to go next, he heard a strange voice, or voices perhaps, nearby, and he walked on to see from what source they were coming. All of a sudden he was at the mouth of a cave that was cut out of solid rock, and as he stepped just inside, he could see that it was very deep and spacious, with a hundred doors, out of which rushed the many voices of the Sibyl. Though his knees trembled and cold shudders ran through his bones, Aeneas offered a prayer to the prophetess, saying, "O great Sibyl, grant me the power to descend to the Lower Regions and to hear the message that is intended for my ears, and my people will honor thee forever."

The hundred doors flew open with a blast, and a voice from each bellowed a reply: "Son of Anchises, it is easy to go down to the Land of the Shades, but to retrace one's steps and reach the upper air again—this is not so light a task. Only few have done it, but if you are still of a mind to try, listen to my words. There lies hidden in the forest a bough of gold which is sacred to Proserpine [PRAH-sir-pine], the queen of the dead. No one can go upon this journey unless he brings with him this bough as a gift for the queen." All the doors suddenly slammed shut, and an eerie silence was all that filled the deep, dark cave.

Aeneas searched the forest high and low but could find nothing like a bough of gold. Then a pair of doves swooped down from the sky and settled on some grassy turf near where Aeneas was walking. Almost in despair he called to them, "If only you could be my guides, for with your lofty view you must know where this golden bough is hidden." Then the birds rose into the air and circled Aeneas's head several times before flying, very slowly, ahead of him. He followed their lead and within minutes they alighted upon the tree that bore the golden bough. Aeneas gave thanks to the gods for sending these guiding doves, then he quickly broke off the glittering branch and returned to the Sibyl's cave, glad of heart that he now had the means to gain the favor of the queen of the dead.

When Aeneas arrived back at the Sibyl's abode, she appeared to him in her own womanly form, and she asked again whether he was certain that he wanted to go on. Aeneas replied that he was duty-bound to hear his father's message, and so the Sibyl led him into the deepest reaches of the cave, past a gloomy lake from which deadly vapors arose. They continued on deeper and deeper into the cave and into the earth. The path was steep and rocky and the footing uncertain. All about them there was gloom and silence. In the dim light of the single torch the Sibyl carried, shadows looked like contorted faces, and the rocks protruding from the walls of the passageway seemed like arms jutting out to snatch at Aeneas as he passed.

After a great while, they came to the gates of Hades, where the figures of Grief and Remorse lay sleeping on their beds. There also Aeneas could see the shapes of Fear and Hunger— forms so horrible that he had to turn his eyes away. Gorgons and Harpies and all manner of monsters roamed about the entrance, breathing fire and screeching and gnashing [NASH-ing] their teeth. Aeneas drew his sword and would have rushed at them had the Sibyl not assured him that they were but airy apparitions, ferocious but without substance.

Passing through the gates, they reached a wide stream where a ferryman, Charon [CARE-on] by name, stood on the deck of his rusty boat, leaning on a pole. Upon the bank were throngs of souls—wives and mothers, men of war, boys and girls—as thick as leaves that fall to the earth at the first frost of autumn, and all stood stretching out their hands and calling to the ferryman to take them across to the other side.

Aeneas was moved by this sight, and he turned to the Sibyl, saying, "O lady, tell me who are these spirits and what do they seek?" And the Sibyl replied, "This is the River Styx [STICKS], and those you see are souls whose bodies have been left unburied on earth. It is not permitted for spirits to be delivered to their rightful place in the Underworld until their bones have been laid to rest, and so they wander to and fro along the shores for a hundred years before they are allowed to cross."

Aeneas's heart was touched with pity at their sad fortune as he and the Sibyl pressed on through the crowd toward the ferryboat. When Charon saw them coming, he roared out in an angry voice, "Stay back, whoever you are, for this is the abode of ghosts, and no living soul can cross in my boat." But the Sibyl held up the golden bough for the ferryman to see, and he was amazed to behold this marvelous gift, and he laid his anger aside. Without a word more he brought his boat near the bank, and driving out the ghosts that sat in crowds upon its benches, he took on board Aeneas and the Sibyl. The boat, accustomed only to the light freight of bodiless spirits, groaned under the weight of these living souls, but soon it reached the opposite shore.

Here Aeneas beheld another gate, and stretching in front of it lay three-headed Cerberus [SIR-burr-us], the watchdog of Hades [HAY-deez]. The air resounded with the fierce barking from his triple throats, and the Sibyl, to quiet him, flung him a cake of honey and poppy seeds, which would drug him into a sound sleep. Mad with hunger, Cerberus tore at the morsel with his three mouths, and soon his limbs relaxed, and he stretched himself out before the gate, wrapped in the arms of Morpheus [MORE-fee-us], the god of dreams. Aeneas bounded from the ferryboat out upon the shore, from which no one could hope to return.

As he pressed on through the gate, he could hear the crying of the ghosts of young children, who had died before their lives had scarcely begun. Here, too, were the souls of those who, being tired of life, had sought death by their own hands, and now were wishing they might return to earth again. Nearby, amid groves of myrtle, were the souls of those who had died of love, and among these was Dido, whom Aeneas could see faintly through the shadows. Tears came rushing to his eyes, and he called to her, "Dido, can it be you, O beautiful queen? And can it be, then, that it was I who sent you here? As the gods are my witness, I beg you to believe that I did not wish to leave you, but my duty gave me no other course." But she, standing for a moment with her eyes cast to the ground, set her heart against him and abruptly walked away.

The Sibyl took him by the hand and led him to a place where the path parted into two roads. "The one on the right," she said, "leads to Pluto's palace and to the Elysian [ee-LEEZ-ee-an] Fields, but on the left lies the path to Tartarus [TAR-tah-rus], where the wicked of the world are punished for their crimes." Aeneas peered down the road on the left and saw in the distance a high wall, with a river of flames licking at it from below. He could hear a din of deep groans and cracking whips and dragging chains coming from behind the wall, and he asked the Sibyl to tell him their meaning. She answered him, saying, "The feet of the righteous may not pass down that road, but Proserpine has told me of the terrors that are contained within those walls." And the prophetess described to Aeneas the many torments that there afflict those who had done the deepest wrongs to their fellowmen on earth. Among the tortures was that of Sisyphus [SIS-uh-fuss], the cruel king of Corinth, whose task was to roll a huge stone up a hill, but when the top was nearly reached, the rock would rush headlong down to the plain again, and so he toiled and toiled, while the sweat bathed his weary limbs, but all to no effect. There, too, was Tantalus [TAN-tuh-lus], another wicked king, who was condemned for all time to stand in a pool, his chin level with the water, yet he was parched with thirst, for when he bowed his head to drink, the water receded. Tall trees laden with luscious fruit stooped their branches to him, but just when he reached for their treasures, a sudden wind would raise the branch just above his grasp.

There were other torments, too, even harsher, but all had in common that they would endure for ever and ever without pause, nor was there any hope for those who suffered.

The Sibyl then advised Aeneas that it was time for him to turn his attention toward the abodes of the blessed, and she led him down the path on the right until they reached the fields of Elysium. Here the air is pure, the skies are bright, and the green of springtime abounds. Some of the happy souls could be seen exercising on the grassy lawn, while others joined in dance and song. Here Aeneas could see kings of old, who had died for their country, and priests, and those who had improved the world with their inventions, and those whose worthy deeds had lessened the suffering on earth.

Across a shining plain, he beheld Anchises, who stretched his arms out toward his son, tears of joy streaming down his cheeks. Aeneas wrapped his own arms around his father in a loving embrace, but found that he was embracing a phantom—

there was no substance within his encircling grasp. Anchises then, with a knowing look, comforted his son and assured him that his happiness was not diminished just because his mortal body had been left on earth. They walked along together, and Aeneas asked Anchises to identify the souls they met and to explain why so many were gathered on the bank of the peaceful river that flowed gently across the plain. "These souls," Anchises answered, "all seek to live again in a mortal body. They drink from the River Lethe [LEETH-ee], whose waters bring about forgetfulness, and thus they lose all memory of the past and may return to the world above in another human form."

Anchises then went on to tell Aeneas and the Sibyl all the events that the future held for his son and the race that would be founded by the people of Troy. He showed them visions of how Aeneas would land in Italy and conquer the tribes who dwelt there, and give them laws and order. The great nation Aeneas would found there would have many heroes and in time would rule the world with imperial sway. He told them of Romulus [RAHM-you-luss], the founder of the city on the seven hills; of Brutus, the avenger of his country's wrongs; and of the line of Caesars, who would plant the Roman way in every foreign land. "All this, my son, will come to your children's children. Other civilizations may create great works of art, and some may devote themselves to science," he said, "but the work of the nation you shall found is to conquer the world, to set the rule of peace, to spare the humble, and to subdue the proud."

And so it came to pass, just as Anchises had said. Aeneas conquered the tribes of Italy and brought them under the rule of law. Ascanius ruled the land after him, and his children after him. And Romulus founded the greatest city of all on the banks of the Tiber [TYE-bur], and its armies conquered the world and brought about a peace that would know no end. Thus did the seeds of Troy take root and flower in the Roman Empire.

A Few Words More

The realms of the Lower World are rich with imagery, and the ancients' visions of hell provide the basis for many common words that no longer pertain to the Infernal Regions at all. Even in this abbreviated tale of

Aeneas's subterranean journey, we learn about the waters of forgetfulness that come from the River Lethe, a name that is at the root of the words *lethargy* and *lethargic*, which now convey the feeling of "apathy or listlessness." We see Tantalus being punished not by just eternal hunger and thirst, but by having food and drink remain nearby, but just outside his grasp. There is little wonder, then, how the modern verb *tantalize* came to mean "teasing or tormenting one with hopes that remain out of reach." We are led to the peaceful paradise called the Elysian Fields, and we understand why the magnificent avenue in Paris bears the French form of this name: Champs Elysées [shahn zay-lee-ZAY].

Still another word source that appears in this tale, as well as elsewhere in Roman mythology, is the name of the god of dreams: Morpheus. It was because of the hypnotic effect that a newly discovered chemical had on patients that a German chemist in 1803 named the drug *morphine*. Even the word *hypnotic* itself comes to us from the Greek name for the god of sleep: Hypnos, which is also the root of *hypnosis*.

Index to
"A Few Words More"

The numbers below indicate the pages on which the origins or the roots of the following words and phrases are discussed.

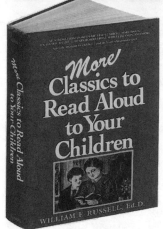